International financial integration

T0381871

In the past two decades, national financial markets in the major industrial countries have undergone a revolutionary change. Market pricing has replaced price-setting by government regulation or market conventions, and the removal of capital controls has opened national markets to international competition. Along with changes in markets has come improved understanding of how interest rates across different currencies are related. This study examines the progress in integrating the financial markets of the Group of Five (G-5) industrial countries: Britain, France, Germany, Japan, and the United States. Professor Marston shows that deregulation and liberalization have succeeded to such an extent that interest rates in any single currency are nearly the same regardless of whether they are offered in national or Eurocurrency markets. Currency denomination remains a barrier to full financial integration, however, since both nominal and real returns on financial instruments vary widely by currency, even between currencies tied together by the European Monetary System. This study examines relative returns in the money and bond markets of these countries, investigating whether there are systematic variations in relative returns across currencies.

Professor Marston's study won the inaugural Sanwa Monograph Prize, awarded by an international selection committee at The Center for Japan-U.S. Business and Economic Studies, The Stern School of Business, New York University.

International financial integration

A study of interest differentials between the major industrial countries

RICHARD C. MARSTON
Wharton School, U. of Pennsylvania

CAMBRIDGE
UNIVERSITY PRESS

CAMBRIDGE
UNIVERSITY PRESS

32 Avenue of the Americas, New York NY 10013-2473, USA

Cambridge University Press is part of the University of Cambridge.

It furthers the University's mission by disseminating knowledge in the pursuit of education, learning and research at the highest international levels of excellence.

www.cambridge.org
Information on this title: www.cambridge.org/9780521599375

First published 1995
First paperback edition 1997

A catalogue record for this publication is available from the British Library

ISBN 978-0-521-47100-8 Hardback
ISBN 978-0-521-59937-5 Paperback

Cambridge University Press has no responsibility for the persistence or accuracy of URLs for external or third-party internet websites referred to in this publication, and does not guarantee that any content on such websites is, or will remain, accurate or appropriate.

To Jerrilyn

Contents

Foreword

KENJI KAWAKATSU
Senior Advisor, Sanwa Bank Limited

The deregulation of international financial markets in the eighties generated an impulse effect that created short-run turmoil in the market, as well as a less visible but lasting change that had a profound impact in the long run. The difficulties faced in the integration of the European economies and the formation of new free trade in North America show that further institutional changes are to be expected.

In the late eighties, the Center for Japan-U.S. Business and Economic Studies and the Sanwa Bank sponsored three conferences to analyze and evaluate the changes that were taking place in the financial markets. The papers that were developed in these conferences were published in a volume, *Japan, Europe and International Financial Markets: Analytical and Empirical Perspectives,* edited by Ryuzo Sato, Richard M. Levich, and Rama V. Ramachandran (Cambridge University Press, 1994).

On the successful completion of these conferences, the Sanwa Bank established The Sanwa Research Endowment Fund on International Financial Markets at the Leonard N. Stern School of Business of New York University to provide continuing support for research on international financial markets. One of the activities supported by the endowment is an annual financial award to write a monograph based on original research in financial markets.

The first award was given to Professor Richard C. Marston, James R. F. Guy Professor of Finance and Economics at the Wharton School of the University of Pennsylvania, in the spring of 1992. According to the terms of award, he had to complete the monograph by the fall of 1993. I am now very pleased to read his study of international financial integration. He shows a deep understanding of the working of American, European, and Japanese markets, and I am sure that both academics and practitioners will find this an instructive volume.

I would like to express my gratitude to the Selection Committee of the Sanwa Monographs on International Financial Markets for their careful deliberation, Dean George Daly of the Stern School for the support in furthering this project and Professor Ryuzo Sato, The C.V. Starr Professor of Economics and Director of The Center, for his effort in making the monograph series such a success.

Preface

World financial markets have evolved substantially since I first studied them in my dissertation at MIT 20 years ago. At that time national markets were riddled with capital controls and regulations. The Eurocurrency and Eurobond markets were free of controls, but these markets were small relative to the major national markets. Exchange rates were still not freely floating, although the Bretton Woods system of fixed exchange rates had already broken down. In the last 20 years, the national financial markets have undergone a revolutionary change. Market pricing has replaced cartel-like arrangements in several major countries, and interest differentials due to distortions have largely disappeared. Along with changes in markets has come improved understanding of how interest rates in different currencies are related. The advent of floating exchange rates induced economists to reexamine the pricing of foreign exchange, incorporating many of the insights of financial economics. Along with the advance in international finance has come improved econometric techniques to take into account the distributional behavior of exchange rates. This book attempts to incorporate many of these advances in a reexamination of linkages across the major financial markets.

Although I had planned this book for several years, it might still not be written if not for the generous support of the Sanwa Bank through its Sanwa Monograph Program. I would particularly like to thank Mr. Kenji Kawakatsu, Chairman of Sanwa Bank Limited, for his commitment to this program and Professor Ryuzo Sato of the Center for Japan-U.S. Business and Economics Studies at New York University for originating it. I would also like to thank Professors Sato and Rama Ramachandran for their encouragement at all phases of my project.

While writing this book, I had the privilege of spending three months as a Visiting Scholar at the Institute for Monetary and Economic Studies of the Bank of Japan. I would like to thank the staff of the Institute, and particularly Mr. Hiroo Taguchi, the head of Division I, for helping to make this visit a productive one.

Most of this book was written while in residence at the Wharton School of the University of Pennsylvania, which has provided me with an unrivaled research environment over the past 20 years. A special acknowledgment is due the George Weiss Center for International Financial Research for support in obtaining the data used in the study.

Several of my colleagues at the Wharton School and other institutions offered comments and advice on various parts of the book. I would particularly like to thank Gordon Bodnar, Richard Herring, and Karen Lewis of Wharton, Robert Cumby of New York University, Bernard Dumas of HEC School of Management, Paul De Grauwe of Katholieke Universiteit Leuven, James Lothian of Fordham University, and Lars Svensson of Stockholm University.

Finally, I would like to thank my wife, Jerrilyn, and my daughters, Heather and Hilary, for their continuing encouragement while I completed this book.

Philadelphia, Pennsylvania

CHAPTER 1

Determinants of interest differentials: an introduction

The industrial countries emerged from World War II with controls on virtually all types of international transactions. Many currencies were not even convertible. In such cases, all currency transactions, including those involving international trade, had to be settled through special clearing facilities. In the two decades following the war, the industrial countries began to ease restrictions on the convertibility of currencies and to liberalize international trade in goods. It was only in the 1970s, however, that the liberalization of international capital flows became a major goal. Even then, many industrial countries continued to maintain controls on capital flows. In fact, some countries actually strengthened their controls in the 1980s. At various times in the last two decades, firms found themselves paying widely differing rates for national and international loans even when the loans were in the same currency.

This study examines the progress made in integrating the financial markets of the Group of Five (or G-5) industrial countries: Britain, France, Germany, Japan, and the United States. Integration involves two interrelated elements: the deregulation of national markets and the liberalization of controls on international capital flows. When financial markets are deregulated and when restrictions on capital flows are lifted, interest rates in national and international markets in the same currency may be equalized. Yet even then, interest rates need not be equalized across national markets because national financial instruments are denominated in different currencies. So this study also examines the extent to which interest returns, both nominal and real, have been equalized across currencies.[1]

Since 1970, capital flows have grown at phenomenal rates. Table 1.1 provides estimates of cross-border transactions in bonds and equities over three decades. Cross-border transactions between U.S. residents and others, for example, have risen from 2.8 percent of GDP in 1970 to 92.5 percent of GDP in 1990. In the case of Japan, the growth in cross-border flows is even more dramatic. Despite rapid increases in the size of capital

---

1. Financial integration need not be measured solely in terms of interest returns. For alternative measures, see Kenen (1976).

Table 1.1. *Cross-border transactions in bonds and equities (as percentage of GDP).*

Country	1970	1980	1990
United States	2.8	9.3	92.5
Britain	n.a.	n.a.	690.1[a]
France	n.a.	8.4[b]	53.3
Germany	3.3	7.5	57.5
Japan	1.5[c]	7.0	118.6

[a] The estimate for Britain reflects the role of London as an international financial center.
[b] The first French figure is for 1982.
[c] The first Japanese figure is for 1975.

Source: Bank for International Settlements, *62nd Annual Report,* 15th June 1992, p. 193.

flows, however, the *stock* of cross-border holdings remains a small fraction of total assets outstanding. This is the conclusion of two recent studies of international diversification by French and Poterba (1991) and Tesar and Werner (1992).[2] Investors in each national market have a "home bias," which in most cases limits their investment in foreign markets to less than 10 percent of their assets. This is true even of institutional investors with long-term horizons such as life insurance companies and pension funds.[3] Despite the growth in cross-border transactions, international diversification appears to be limited. So it remains to be seen how well integrated financial markets have become.

2. As Tesar and Werner point out, however, estimates of portfolio holdings are unlikely to be accurate because they are based on benchmark surveys that in the case of the United States are over 40 years old.
3. See the evidence in Tesar and Werner (1992, Table 15). Note that we do not have reliable evidence on cross-border holdings of the specific short- and long-term assets studied below.

I.   Patterns of deregulation and liberalization

In the 1960s and earlier, official regulations together with nonofficial market conventions limited the degree of competition in most national financial markets. Interest rates on many bank loans and deposits, for example, bore little relationship to competitively determined interest rates in the national money markets. Since that time, many of these markets have been deregulated. In some countries deregulation was initiated by explicit government programs, while in others deregulation was spurred on by competition from new financial instruments like commercial paper.

The liberalization of international capital flows also played a role in the deregulation of national markets. Liberalization opened the national markets to the intense competitive pressures of the Eurocurrency markets and other international markets.[4] Firms denied competitive pricing for loans at home could easily turn to Eurocurrency loans or to medium-term international bonds. Similarly, investors who were denied market rates of return at home could seek them in Eurocurrency deposits or other international instruments.

By the end of the 1980s, interest rates on many short-term national instruments were indistinguishable from those on Eurocurrency deposits and loans in the same currency. But deregulation and liberalization did not happen overnight. In the 1970s and 1980s, interest rates in some key national markets remained regulated and shielded from international competition. It is important to realize how different markets today are from those of just a few years ago. Too many studies of national financing costs have implicitly assumed that the degree of international integration has remained constant over time. In fact, the deregulation and liberalization of national markets have left markets today much more integrated than they were in earlier decades. As a result, evidence on relative financing costs based on experience in the 1970s and 1980s may tell us little about costs in the 1990s.

In an integrated financial market, there should be no significant gap between national interest rates and Eurocurrency interest rates in the same currency. So it is possible to speak of the dollar financial market or the yen financial market as a unified whole without specifying whether financial instruments are national or international in origin. In such a world, relative financing costs are governed primarily by currency factors rather than by the peculiar characteristics of each national market.

---

4. The Eurodollar market developed in the late 1950s when banks in London began accepting dollar deposits and extending dollar loans. Eurocurrency markets in other currencies were established soon after. The international bond (Eurobond) market developed in the 1960s.

Even after deregulation and liberalization have occurred, however, there can be differentials between interest rates in different currencies. The study will investigate interest differentials measured in both nominal and real terms. Although nominal interest differentials can persist as long as exchange rates are flexible, whether there are differentials in nominal *returns* expressed in a single currency, where these returns consist of interest plus capital gains on currencies, depends on how assets are priced. Later chapters examine the effects of risk premia and market inefficiencies on ex post returns. Differentials between real or inflation-adjusted interest rates are also consistent with well-functioning financial markets. Real differentials can arise because of differentials in nominal returns or because of changes in real exchange rates. Later chapters will analyze real differentials in national markets as well as those in the competitive Eurocurrency markets.

II.   Determinants of relative financing costs

One way to assess how national markets are related is to compare the real costs of financing faced by firms from different countries. This section examines the principal determinants of such real interest differentials.

The cost of financing in any country can be unambiguously defined if we examine a firm financing itself in its own market and selling products in that market. Consider the case of real interest comparisons between Japanese and American firms. Suppose that a Japanese firm's primary source of funding is from bank loans with a (continuously compounded) interest rate of i_{JLt} and that the expected inflation rate in Japan is π_{Jt}. Throughout this volume, all interest rates will be expressed in continuously compounded form and all percentage changes will be expressed as changes in the logs of the variables.[5] So i_{JLt} and π_{Jt} are defined as follows:

$$i_{JLt} = \ln(1 + I_{JLt})$$
$$\pi_{Jt} = E_t[\ln(P_{Jt+1}/P_{Jt})]$$

where

I_{JLt} = the (simple) Japanese loan rate
P_{Jt} = the price level in Japan[6]

Then the real cost of borrowing for the Japanese firm can be defined as

$$i_{JLt} - \pi_{Jt}$$

---

5. Using continuously compounded interest rates makes it easier to express returns in foreign currency and in real terms.
6. The notation E_t is used to denote the expected value formed at period t.

Similarly, if American firms face an interest rate on bank loans of i_{ALt} and an inflation rate of π_{At}, then the real cost of borrowing is

$$i_{ALt} - \pi_{At}$$

Under certain special conditions, these two real borrowing costs are the same:

$$(i_{JLt} - \pi_{Jt}) = (i_{ALt} - \pi_{At}) \tag{1.1}$$

In that case, then "real interest parity" is said to hold.[7]

Some observers believe that real interest parity should hold as long as financial markets are free of any controls or distortions. But real interest parity involves comparing borrowing costs for two or more distinct sets of firms who measure nominal interest costs in different currencies and real costs by deflating by different inflation rates. As will be made clear, if real interest rates favor one set of firms over another, no simple arbitrage operation will eliminate the real interest differential.

Four distinct factors affect relative borrowing costs between firms in different countries. Two of these factors are associated with government regulations and market conventions, which are likely to be of far less importance in the current era of deregulated markets than they were in past decades. But two other factors are characteristic of completely deregulated markets and therefore may persist in the future. I will describe each of these factors as they affected real borrowing costs in the last two decades.

A.   Domestic distortions

In many of the national markets, there were often large differentials between bank loan rates charged to firms and money market rates offered for large-scale, short-term investments (which I denote i_{JMt}, i_{AMt}). These differentials could be due to official controls on bank interest rates or to market conventions maintained within each banking system.[8] The resulting differential

$$U_{1t} = (i_{JLt} - i_{JMt}) - (i_{ALt} - i_{AMt}) \tag{1.2}$$

is a measure of the impact of these distortions on real interest rates. In the next chapter, the specific nature of these distortions will be discussed in detail. That chapter analyzes the process of deregulation of bank loan and deposit rates in the G-5 countries.

7. Studies of real interest parity include Cumby and Obstfeld (1984), Frankel and MacArthur (1988), and Mishkin (1984). Other references are given in the following chapters.
8. Studies of national banking systems include Hodgman (1974), Mullineaux (1987), and Swary and Topf (1992).

B.   *National capital controls*

There were also capital controls separating the national markets from the Eurocurrency markets abroad, although by the end of 1973 the United States and Germany had lifted most of their controls. Considering the example of the dollar and yen again, the impact of the controls can be measured by comparing Japanese with Euroyen interest rates and American with Eurodollar interest rates. The resulting differential

$$U_{2t} = (i_{JMt} - i_{\yen t}) - (i_{AMt} - i_{\$t}) \tag{1.3}$$

can be positive or negative depending upon how the controls were designed. Chapter 3 will examine the effects of capital controls on interest differentials and will assess how far the liberalization of financial markets has progressed.[9]

C.   *Two illustrations of the effects of regulations and controls*

It is useful to illustrate the importance of the distortions introduced by national banking regulations and controls on international capital flows by examining interest rate behavior in two of the markets, the French and Japanese. Figure 1.1 compares the Eurofranc deposit rate and the French rate for bank loans over the 1973–91 period. Because the Eurocurrency market is so competitive, the Eurofranc loan rate should be only slightly above the Eurofranc deposit rate for prime customers. (See the evidence in Chapter 2.) The figure shows that the French and Eurofranc rates follow very different paths for most of the period. At times the differential between the two rates is over 10 percent. For part of the period, that differential favors a French firm borrowing within the national market (behind the capital control) over a foreign firm borrowing in the Eurofranc market. But at other times the relative positions of the two firms are reversed. Figure 1.2 shows a similar pattern in the yen markets. The Japanese loan rate is at times below the Euroyen rate in London and at other times above it. The differentials are sometimes 3 or 4 percent in absolute value.[10]

Notice how *sluggish* the national loan series are in both countries. The rates appear to be fixed for months at a time. In contrast, the Eurocurrency rates are very volatile, being free to reflect current market conditions.

9. Previous studies of capital controls include Aliber (1973), Dooley and Isard (1980), and Ito (1986).
10. The first two years, 1973–74, were omitted from the graph because the Euroyen rate rose to a peak of 40 percent, thus making it hard to see interest differentials later in the period. The differential between the Euroyen rate and the Japanese loan rate reached a peak of over 30 percent during that two-year period. See the discussion of the Euroyen market in Chapter 3.

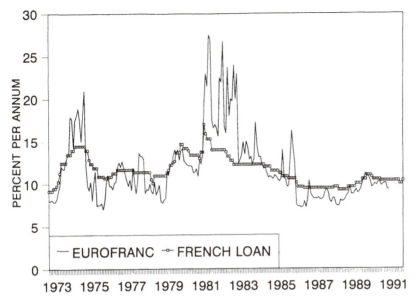

Figure 1.1. French loan and Eurofranc interest rates.

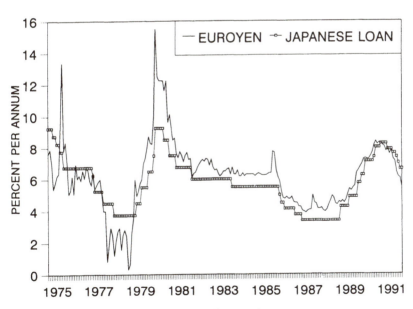

Figure 1.2. Japanese loan and Euroyen interest rates.

This characteristic of loan rates will be discussed in the next chapter. It is important to remember that most firms borrow in national markets, especially when capital controls are in effect, and for those firms it is this sluggish loan series that determines the real interest costs of borrowing.

D.   Deviations from uncovered interest parity

The third source of differentials in real borrowing costs is the differential in the expected nominal cost of financing in different Eurocurrencies,

$$U_{3t} = i_{¥t} - (i_{\$t} + \Delta X_{¥t}) \tag{1.4}$$

where $\Delta x_{¥t} = E_t[\ln(S_{¥t+1}/S_{¥t})]$ is the expected depreciation of the yen and where $S_{¥t}$ is the yen price of the dollar. This differential compares the cost of financing in the Euroyen market with the cost of financing in the Euro-dollar market, but with both costs being measured in a *common currency.* If there is no differential between these costs, then, as discussed in Chapter 4, "uncovered interest parity" is said to hold.[11] That chapter reviews the literature on foreign exchange risk premiums and market efficiency, then examines evidence on whether uncovered interest parity holds for the G-5 currencies. Chapter 5 then studies nominal interest differentials in Europe's fixed exchange rate system, the European Monetary System.

Equation (1.4), describing deviations from uncovered interest parity, can also be written in real terms as follows:

$$U_{3t} = (i_{¥t} - \pi_{Jt}) - (i_{\$t} + \Delta X_{¥t} - \pi_{Jt}) \tag{1.4'}$$

This differential compares the real borrowing costs of a Japanese firm in the Eurodollar market with the real borrowing costs of that same firm in the Euroyen market.[12] It is this real interest differential, rather than one involving both countries' inflation rates, that can be eliminated by market forces as firms shift financing to the cheaper source.

E.   Expected deviations from purchasing power parity

The final factor causing relative interest differentials between the two countries is the expected deviation of inflation rates from purchasing power parity (PPP):

$$U_{4t} = \pi_{Jt} - (\pi_{At} + \Delta x_{¥t}) \tag{1.5}$$

Notice that what matters is the expected inflation rate and expected rate of depreciation of the yen over the upcoming period, not the level of prices

---

11. Hodrick (1987), Levich (1985), and Obstfeld (1986) survey the extensive literature on uncovered interest parity and a related topic, the expectations theory of the forward rate.
12. Expression (1.4) could also be written in real terms using American inflation rates, in which case the comparison would be from the American firm's perspective.

and exchange rates this period. Chapter 6 investigates this "expectational" form of PPP, and presents estimates of real interest differentials between national interest rates as well as between Eurocurrency rates.[13]

The four factors together account for the gap between real lending rates in any two countries, since

$$(i_{JLt} - \pi_{Jt}) - (i_{ALt} - \pi_{At}) = U_{1t} + U_{2t} + U_{3t} - U_{4t} \qquad (1.6)$$

The first two factors together correspond to the domestic/Eurocurrency differential studied by Frankel and MacArthur (1988), among others.[14] It is useful to decompose this differential so that the deregulation of national markets and liberalization of capital flows can be treated separately. The last two factors together correspond to the real interest differential between Eurocurrency rates studied by Cumby and Obstfeld (1984) and Frankel and MacArthur (1988), among others.

In most industrial countries, *indirect* financing by bank loans is more important than *direct* financing using the securities market. Therefore much of this volume will focus on bank loan rates in the national markets and their counterparts in the short-term Eurocurrency markets. But in Chapter 2 I will also discuss the deregulation of national bond markets and show how the introduction of new financial instruments and competition from abroad has helped to open these markets. Then in Chapter 6 I will examine real interest rates in the bond markets of the G-5 countries. Chapter 7 will summarize the evidence on real and nominal interest rate behavior and draw some conclusions about the future of international financial integration.

13. The expectational form of PPP is analyzed in Roll (1979) and Adler and Lehmann (1983).
14. As discussed in the following, the first two factors can also be written as a covered interest differential between national loan rates as long as the Eurocurrency differential is equal to the forward premium.

CHAPTER 2

The deregulation of national markets

National financial markets in the 1990s bear little resemblance to the markets of the 1960s and earlier. Deregulation in the major industrial countries has provided investors and borrowers alike with rates that are much more competitive than in earlier decades. Instead of having bank deposit and loan rates tied by official regulation or by market conventions, these rates are in many cases closely related to interbank rates available to the banks themselves. This chapter examines how far this process of deregulation has proceeded in the financial markets of the G-5 countries.

I.   Patterns of deregulation

Deregulation has proceeded furthest for those instruments accessible to large firms and institutional investors. This chapter will focus on such "wholesale" instruments even though the deregulation of instruments available to the retail customer (small firms and individuals) may be of interest for other reasons. As will be evident, the pressures for deregulation are greatest in the wholesale end of the market.

Domestic financial markets offer a wide variety of instruments, some of which are peculiar to one national market. Rather than try to delineate all of them, I will focus on four short-term instruments in my analysis of the deregulation process:

1. *Interbank loans:* Usually unsecured and in large amounts.
2. *Bank loans:* Loans to the most highly rated corporations, usually termed "prime" loans.
3. *Bank deposits:* Large deposits, the exact scale of which varies from market to market.
4. *Commercial paper:* Unsecured notes issued by highly rated companies.

In discussing bank deposits, I will pay particular attention to *certificates of deposit* (CDs), deposits that are negotiable, since the introduction of CDs often heralds the beginning of deposit deregulation. In the medium-term and long-term end of the market, I will focus on *bonds,* especially those issued by private sector firms.

All of the G-5 countries have long had interbank markets to increase the liquidity of their banking systems. In some countries, nonbanks have direct access to the interbank market. All of these countries have bank deposit and loan markets, but they differ widely in the degree of competition in the setting of interest rates even if attention is confined to wholesale deposits and loans. One important alternative to bank loans is commercial paper, the unsecured notes issued by companies. In most markets, commercial paper is a recent innovation. The key feature of the instrument is that it can be issued independently of banks, so it provides firms with an alternative to bank loans.[1] More traditional instruments, such as bankers' acceptances or commercial bills of exchange, typically require collateral and, more importantly, the endorsement of banks; so the interest rate is normally tied to the bank loan rate. All of the countries have long had markets for medium- or long-term bonds. But in some countries, private sector firms have had only limited access to the bond market. I will discuss how competition from external sources of funding, such as Eurobonds and syndicated loans, has helped to spur deregulation in the national bond markets.

Deregulation can take a variety of forms. In some cases nonbanks, including institutional investors like pension funds and large firms, will be given access to the interbank market directly. In other cases, the deposit and loan rates will become competitively determined. Deposit deregulation may sometimes occur when certificates of deposit are introduced. Sometimes deregulation is preceded by the introduction of nonbank instruments like commercial paper or repurchase agreements (as in the case of the gensaki market in Japan). This chapter will attempt to shed some light on this deregulation process.

A.   A stylized picture of bank competition

The new instruments available in deregulated domestic markets and newly accessible international markets put pressure on regulated banking instruments. In Figure 2.1, three sets of interest rates are illustrated: bank loan and deposit rates, Eurocurrency loan and deposit rates (in the same currency), and commercial paper rates. The loan rates are those charged to prime nonbank borrowers.

---

1. Most firms issuing commercial paper, however, obtain backup lines of credit from banks, at least in the United States. See Rowe (1986). Less highly rated companies even obtain a letter of credit guaranteeing that the bank will repay the commercial paper at maturity if the issuer cannot do so. In that case, the commercial paper becomes more like a bankers' acceptance. For a recent study of the commercial paper markets in other countries, see Alworth and Borio (1993).

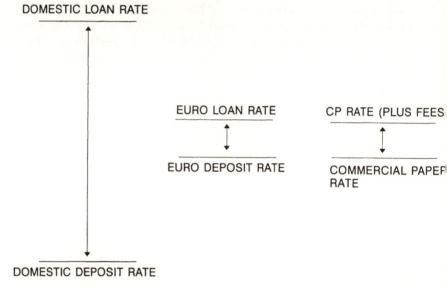

Figure 2.1. Domestic and Eurocurrency rates.

According to this figure, there is a relatively large gap between the loan rates charged by banks in the domestic market and the deposit rates offered by these same banks. The low deposit rates may be due to official ceilings imposed by the government, or they may be due to market conventions associated with collusive behavior by domestic banks. Similarly, the high loan rates may be due to rate-setting rules, although in the case of loan rates these rules are more commonly set not by law but by market convention (which may be sanctioned officially or unofficially by the authorities). The phrase *regulated rates* will be used to describe rates maintained by market conventions as well as those controlled by the authorities, and *deregulation* will refer to the freeing of markets from either rate-setting conventions or official regulations.

The figure also shows a relatively small gap between Eurocurrency loan and deposit rates in the same currency. There is no interest rate regulation in the Eurocurrency markets. The large number of banks in this market, moreover, ensures effective price competition. So the markup of loan over deposit rates for prime borrowers is driven to much lower levels than in the domestic market.

In the absence of capital controls on international transactions, competition from banks in the Eurocurrency market forces domestic banks to abandon their rate-setting conventions. Otherwise both depositors and borrowers switch to the Eurocurrency market. So domestic deposit and loan rates, at least at the wholesale end, have to become competitive with Eurocurrency rates. This suggests that the deregulation of domestic interest rates may be the outcome of forces unleashed when international markets are allowed to compete with domestic markets.

The competitive pressure, however, need not come from outside the country. If the authorities permit parallel markets to develop inside the country, then the effects on regulated rates will be much the same. The introduction of a commercial paper market, for example, undercuts rate-setting conventions in the loan market by giving firms alternative sources of funds. (Only the most highly rated firms have access to this market, however, so banks may keep loan rates high for other firms.) The commercial paper market also offers firms an alternative investment outlet for their short-term funds. Because this market is usually highly competitive, the rate paid by issuers of commercial paper inclusive of underwriting fees is not much higher than the rate received by investors in commercial paper. Whether the competition comes from external or internal markets, banks are unlikely to be able to maintain large margins between deposit and loan rates once markets are deregulated.

B.   Evidence on loan-deposit spreads

The stylized picture of banking spreads depicted in Figure 2.1 is useful in interpreting actual spreads in the national and Eurocurrency markets. The spreads I will examine are those in the wholesale end of the market. In the case of national bank deposits, this means examining interest rates on large-scale time deposits, the actual scale of which varies from country to country. In the case of national bank loans, this means examining interest rates on the lowest-risk (or "prime") loans.[2] Table 2.1 reports the interest rate spreads in the national markets over the 1973–91 period.[3] The definitions of the national deposit and loan rates are given in the table. The spreads range from 0.81 percent in the British market to 3.12 percent in the French market.

Eurocurrency deposits and loans are available only in large denominations. Banks do not report Eurocurrency loan rates for their prime customers, but rates charged on short-term loans to large, highly rated corporations (like the AAA-rated AT&T corporation in the United States) are close to the London interbank offer rate (LIBOR) charged to other banks.

2. As explained later in the chapter, in recent years the highest-rated corporations in the U.S. market have routinely borrowed below prime rate. So the data on U.S. prime rates overestimate the true cost of such loans.
3. Because of the unavailability of data, the sample period ends in April 1986 for French rates and October 1989 for German rates, and begins in 1978 for Euroyen rates.

Table 2.1. *National loan/deposit spreads and Eurocurrency offer/bid spreads (in percent per annum).*

Country	Loan/deposit rate spreads in national markets, 73(1)-91(12)		Offer/bid spreads in Eurocurrency markets, 73(6)-89(12)	
	Average	Sample standard error	Average	Sample standard error
Britain	0.81	0.83	0.25	0.23
France	3.12	1.33	0.34	0.29
Germany	2.29	0.94	0.15	0.06
Japan	2.31	0.84	0.17	0.15
U.S.	1.59	1.00	0.13	0.03

Definitions: Time Deposits
Britain: Three-month time deposits.
France: Three-month time deposits of FF 1 million or over.
Germany: Three-month time deposits in large amounts.
Japan: Three-month time deposits.
U.S.: Three-month negotiable CDs (over $ 100,000).
Bank Loans:
Britain: Clearing banks unsecured overdraft rate for prime borrowers.
France: Overdraft rate for prime borrowers.
Germany: Overdraft rate for prime borrowers.
Japan: Rate on loans of especially high credit standing; prime rate after December, 1988.
U.S.A.: Prime loan rate.
Notes: The French deposit rate series ends in April 1986; the German deposit rate series ends in October 1989; the Euroyen series begins in January 1978.

Sources: All domestic rates are from Morgan Guaranty Trust, *World Financial Markets*, except for the British loan rate which is from OECD, *Financial Statistics Monthly* after 1977(1) and the Japanese deposit and loan rates, which are from the Bank of Japan, *Economic Statistics Annual*. In each of those cases, the WFM series is incomplete. The Eurocurrency rates are end-of-month rates for three-month deposits from Data Resources Incorporated.

So the spread between rates on short-term loans and deposits offered to such corporations will be close to the spread between bid (LIBID) and offer (LIBOR) rates in the interbank Eurocurrency market in London.[4] Table 2.1 reports average offer/bid spreads over the 1973(6)–1989(12) period. In the cases of France, Germany, and Japan, the spreads between national loan and deposit rates are about ten times as large as those between Eurocurrency bid and offer rates in the same currency. Even in the case of Britain, the market with the smallest loan-deposit spread, the national spread is triple the size of the spread in the Eurosterling market.

We also have statistics on medium-term loans tied to LIBOR, although not specifically for the highest-rated firms. The OECD reports the average loan spread above LIBOR paid by *all borrowers* in the OECD area.[5] Over the 1977–92 period, the spread averaged 0.59 percent on loans with an average maturity of about 6.8 years, Since the highest rated firms undoubtedly borrowed at even lower spreads, the Eurocurrency market appears to be very competitive for medium-term loans as well.

So the evidence suggests that the national markets have traditionally had much larger deposit-loan spreads than the corresponding Eurocurrency markets. To understand why this might be true, it is necessary to examine the interest rates more closely. There are at least three possible explanations of the figures in Table 2.1.

First, the national banking markets may be shielded from external competition by capital controls on inflows or outflows of capital. As the next chapter will show, three of the five countries had capital controls during a substantial part of the flexible exchange rate period beginning in 1973. Yet the United States and Germany were free of most controls after 1973.

Second, loan rates may be competitive but government regulations or market conventions may permit banks to offer uncompetitive deposit rates. In this case, we would expect banks to lose many of the large deposits of corporations to the Eurocurrency markets or to alternative domestic markets if such markets exist. The minimum size of Eurocurrency deposits and domestic money market instruments may leave small companies and individuals with access only to bank deposits. Yet if money market funds investing in such instruments are permitted, then even small deposits may not be insulated from market pressures. To ensure that deposit rate setting can be maintained, the authorities have to keep regulations and controls on other markets. If the authorities prohibit alternative nonbank instru-

---

4. For other large firms, the spread between short-term loan and deposit rates is undoubtedly larger. Judging by the spreads for medium-term loans given below, however, short-term spreads for other large firms must still be small, especially compared with spreads in the national markets.

5. OECD, *Financial Market Trends*, various issues.

ments, such as commercial paper and floating rate notes, and maintain controls on international capital flows, then deposit rates can remain uncompetitive. The second section of this chapter will examine the deregulation of deposit rates.

Third, the banks may keep loan rates uncompetitive even though they offer competitive deposit rates. In this case, we would expect the loan market to be abandoned by the largest corporations with access to alternative markets.[6] As in the case of deposit rates, competitive pressure will develop on loan rates if the authorities permit alternative instruments to develop or if they relax controls on international capital flows. The third section of this chapter will examine the deregulation of loan rates.

It is not uncommon for all three types of distortions to coexist. Capital controls make it easier to regulate bank interest rates by eliminating international competition. The regulation of bank deposit rates, moreover, is often justified by the need to control bank loan rates.[7] Because the controls and regulations are so interrelated, it is often difficult to deregulate one market without deregulating others.

II.   Deregulation of deposit rates

In the 1960s and earlier, all five major industrial countries had controls on bank deposit rates. Some controls were established by law and others were maintained by market conventions officially or unofficially sanctioned by the authorities. The controls applied not only to retail (small-scale) deposits but also to the wholesale deposits of large corporations and institutions. Only one country, the United States, had established a market for negotiable certificates of deposit in which interest rates were market-determined, and even that market was subject to interest rate ceilings.

Since the 1960s, deregulation of deposit rates has proceeded at an uneven pace in these five countries.[8] Table 2.2 charts the dates when certificates of deposit were introduced in each market. In only two of the countries, Britain and the United States, did CDs exist prior to the 1970s. In one other country, Germany, time deposit rates were deregulated in the 1960s, even though a CD market was not established until 1986.

---

6. Alternatively, banks may lend below posted prime rates as in the United States. (See below.)
7. The regulation of deposit rates need not affect the pricing of loans if banks treat the interbank rate as the opportunity cost of granting loans. See Baltensperger and Dermine (1987, pp. 86–88).
8. Studies of national banking systems include Hodgman (1974), Mullineux (1987), and Swary and Topf (1992).

Table 2.2. *Introduction of new instruments in national markets.*

Country	Certificates of deposit — Year introduced	Commercial paper — Year introduced	Commercial paper — % of bank credit in 1990
Britain	1968	1986	2.5 %
France	1985	1985[a]	3.9 %
Germany	1986	1991[b]	n.a.
Japan	1979[c]	1987	5.5 %
U.S.	1961[d]	1800s	18.9 %

[a] *Papier commercial* is the traditional name of (collateralized) commercial bills of exchange, so French commercial paper is called *billets de trésorerie*.
[b] Daimler-Benz issued the first commercial paper in February 1991. Floating rate notes were introduced in 1985.
[c] In 1979 the minimum denomination for CDs was set at ¥ 500 million, but in the early to mid-1980s the minimum denomination was progressively lowered.
[d] U.S. CDs were freed of interest rate ceilings under Regulation Q in June 1970 (for thirty to eighty-nine day maturities) and May 1973 (for the remaining maturities).

Sources: For dates when instruments were introduced, central bank publications and OECD *Economic Surveys*. For commercial paper outstanding as a percentage of bank credit, Bank for International Settlements, *61st Annual Report* (10 June 1991), p. 112.

If deposit rates are market-determined, then they should be closely linked to money market rates that are known to be freely determined. Morgan Guaranty Trust's *World Financial Markets (WFM)* reports interest rates on what it terms "representative money markets" in all five countries. In three of the countries (Britain, France, and Germany), the representative rate is on three-month interbank deposits. In Japan, the gensaki rate, the interest rate on repurchase agreements, is used instead.[9] During the 1970s, the gensaki rate was the only short-term rate free to reflect Japanese market conditions. In the United States, the interbank market (for "federal funds") is primarily for overnight funds; so the three-month commercial paper rate is chosen instead.[10]

Table 2.3 compares the interest rate on large-scale time deposits with the representative money market rate. Deposit rates in three of the five countries (Britain, Germany, and the United States) follow closely those in the money market. But in the other two countries (France and Japan), the difference between money market rates and time deposit rates is quite large, at least during part of the sample period. We review each of the five countries beginning with the United States.

A.   *Regulation Q in the United States*

Perhaps the most widely known instance of deposit rate regulation is Regulation Q, which placed ceilings on U.S. time deposit rates including certificates of deposit.[11] For most of that decade, time deposit rates were below the ceilings, which were initially set at 6 percent. But beginning in the credit crunch of 1969, U.S. rates on alternative instruments like Treasury bills and commercial paper rose above the ceilings. Restrained by Regulation Q, time deposit rates became uncompetitive and banks experienced a loss of deposits as investors switched to alternative markets free of the ceilings. The ceilings thus left banks at a competitive disadvantage in attracting funds.

In June 1970, the Federal Reserve decided to remove the ceilings on one category of rates, those on CDs over $100,000 and with 30 to 89 days maturity. In May 1973, moreover, the Fed removed the remaining ceilings on large deposits. Controls on smaller time deposits remained in effect until October 1983, but by that time money market funds had developed to provide even small savers with market rates of return.

To show how market-sensitive the CD rate has been since the removal of Regulation Q ceilings, I compare this rate with the commercial paper rate. Table 2.3 shows that U.S. time deposit rates followed those on the commercial paper market very closely. The interest differential between

---

9. In a typical transaction, a securities firm will agree to sell a government bond to a corporation and repurchase it at an agreed-upon price at a later date. As Suzuki (1987, p. 118) explains, this is equivalent to a corporation lending short-term funds to the securities firm.
10. The term market for federal funds market is limited. See Kreicher (1982).
11. Willemse (1986) describes the market for CDs in the United States.

Table 2.3. *Average interest differentials between money market rates and time deposit rates.*

Country	Instruments	73(1)-80(12)	81(1)-91(12)
Britain	MMR - TD	0.15 (0.02)	0.15 (0.02)
France	MMR - TD	0.34 (0.11)	*81(1)-86(4)* 3.91 (0.32)
	MMR - CD		*88(4)-91(12)* 0.30 (0.03)
Germany	MMR - TD	0.61 (0.09)	*81(1)-89(10)* 0.45 (0.05)
Japan	MMR - TD	4.10 (0.41)	2.76 (0.06)
	MMR - CD		*79(5)-91(12)* -0.30 (0.03)
U.S.	MMR - CD	-0.03 (0.03)	0.20 (0.03)

Abreviations: TD = time deposit rate (as defined in Table 2.2); CD = certificate of deposit rate; MMR = money market rate (see below).

Definitions: Money Market Rates:
Britain, France, and Germany: Interbank rates.
Japan: Gensaki rate (on repurchase agreements).
U.S.: Commercial paper rate.

Notes: The mean differentials are reported in percent per annum. The figures in parentheses are standard errors of these means that have been adjusted for heteroskedasticity and serial correlation. (See the discussion of estimation methods below.)

Sources: Deposit rates, see Table 2.2. All money market rates except the gensaki rate are from MGT, *World Financial Markets*. The Japanese gensaki and CD rates are from Bank of Japan, *Economic Statistics Annual* (database). The other CD rates are from *WFM*.

these two rates ranges from a negligible −0.03 percent in the 1970s to 0.20 percent in the 1980s. As will be shown, moreover, changes in the two rates are highly correlated. Between 1973 and 1991, the correlation coefficient is 0.93. So there is no doubt that rates on large CDs are very competitive with other money market rates.

B.   British and German deregulation of deposit rates

Although deposit rates in both Britain and Germany were regulated in the early 1960s, both countries relaxed their controls prior to 1973. Germany had maintained controls on deposit rates since the banking crisis of 1931. But in April 1967, all controls were lifted including those on small deposits. Although a German CD market was not established until May 1986, bank deposit rates became closely tied to interbank rates. In Britain prior to 1971, a cartel of clearing banks tied deposit rates to Bank rate (the discount rate charged by the Bank of England). The rate on seven-day notice deposits, for example, was held at 2 percent below Bank rate. In September 1971, however, the British authorities instituted a series of reforms designed to make the British financial system more responsive to market conditions. These reforms included the removal of ceilings on bank loans and an end to the policy of supporting long-term government bond rates. As part of these reforms, the authorities pushed banks to "abandon their long-standing cartel arrangements which have provided for uniform deposit rates linked to Bank rate, and also the convention which has governed the relationship of their lending rates to Bank rate." [12] Thus in both Britain and Germany, deposit rates were market-determined by the beginning of the 1970s.

The impact of deregulation is apparent in the interest differentials reported in Table 2.3. In both Britain and Germany, the differentials between time deposit rates and interbank rates are quite small. In Britain, the differential is 0.15 percent in both decades. In Germany, the differential is somewhat larger, ranging from 0.45 to 0.61 percent, but changes in the two series are highly correlated (as will be shown). It is interesting to note that both Britain and Germany have concentrated banking sectors where a handful of banks control a relatively large share of total bank assets. [13]

12. From the Bank of England, *Competition and Credit Control,* as quoted in Hodgman (1974, p. 193).
13. According to the OECD *Economic Survey: United States* (1988), five British banks controlled 45.6 percent of British bank assets in 1986, while six German banks controlled 37.9 percent of German bank assets in 1987. In contrast, the largest five commercial banks in the United States controlled only 12.8 percent of total U.S. bank assets in 1985, although in the United States the restriction on interstate banking limited competition somewhat.

But this degree of bank concentration does not appear to stifle competition in setting deposit rates, at least on large-scale deposits.

C.   The persistence of Japanese controls

In contrast to the previous three countries, Japan continued to maintain control over deposit rates long after 1973. Deposit rates were tied to the discount rate by informal guidelines set by the Federation of Bankers Association. That same association also set the "standard rate" on bank loans. (See Suzuki, 1987.) Figure 2.2 compares the three-month time deposit rate and standard loan rate with the official discount rate set by the Bank of Japan. Although both rates set by banks varied somewhat relative to the discount rate, there is a close correspondence among the three rates with all three rates remaining fixed for months at a time. As Table 2.3 shows, there is no close link between time deposit rates and the market-determined gensaki rate. In fact, the differential between the two rates is an unusually large 4.10 percent in the 1970s.

The first action to deregulate bank interest rates occurred in May 1979 when a market for CDs was authorized. But CDs had a minimum denomination of ¥ 500 million ($ 2.3 million at 1979 exchange rates) and a minimum maturity of three months; so the market was slow to develop. In 1985 the minimum denomination was lowered to ¥ 100 million and the minimum maturity to one month.[14] Since that time, the CD market has surpassed the gensaki market in importance for large investments. Naturally, CD rates have followed the gensaki rates closely. As Table 2.3 indicates, the differential between these rates averaged only 0.30 percent since the CD market was established in May 1979, with the interest rates on CDs actually exceeding the gensaki rate by this amount.

D.   The resurgence of French controls

The French experience departs from the norm of other countries in that deregulation was reversed for a few years during the 1980s. Deregulation of deposit rates proceeded in steps, as in other countries, during the 1970s.[15] By 1979, the unregulated market included one-month deposits for as little as FF 100,000 ($ 25,000, at 1979 exchange rates). But with the advent of the Socialist government in 1981, interest rate controls were reimposed on large time deposits. The minimum amount for unregulated deposits increased from FF 100,000 to FF 500,000 and the minimum ma-

14. Ordinary deposit rates remained regulated.
15. In 1966–67, bank lending rates had been completely liberalized, but deposit rates were kept under control. See de Boissieu (1990).

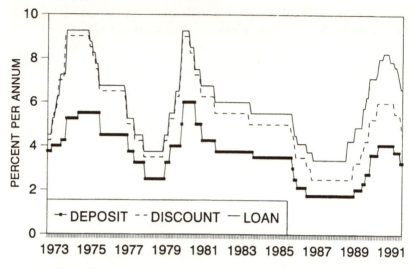

Figure 2.2. Japanese bank interest rates, 1973–91: deposit, loan, and discount rates. (*Source:* Bank of Japan)

turity increased from one to six months. Table 2.3 shows that the interest differential between three-month time deposit rates and interbank rates increased from only 0.34 percent in the 1970s to 3.91 percent in the 1980s.[16]

This retreat toward regulation was reversed in the mid-1980s, however, when the conservatives were returned to power. In March 1985, in fact, the government authorized a CD market as part of its deregulation program. Over the period from April 1988 (when CD quotations were first published by *WFM*) to December 1991, the differential between this CD rate and the interbank rate has been only 0.30 percent. Since May 1986, moreover, interest rates on all time deposits with maturities over three months have been deregulated.

Figure 2.3 shows the effects of regulation and deregulation on time deposit rates. Until 1981, the interest rate on three-month deposits over FF 1 million followed the interbank rate quite closely. When the French government reimposed controls in 1981, the deposit rate fell well below the interbank rate. The gap between the rates continued until the deregulation of the deposit market in May 1986 (at which point the series ends). In the meantime, the CD market was established with freely determined interest rates. The figure shows that from April 1988 (when the published series for CD rates begins), the interbank and CD rates follow closely together.

16. The *World Financial Markets* series for large deposits (over FF 1 million) ends in April 1986 when deposit rates were deregulated.

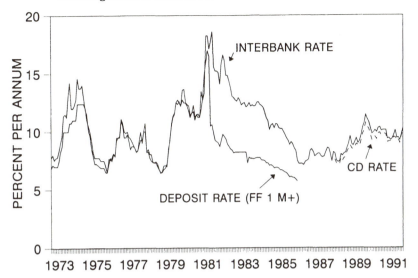

Figure 2.3. French deposit and interbank rates. (*Source:* Morgan Guaranty Trust)

Although Japan and France lagged in deregulation, by the mid-1980s interest rates on large-scale deposits were deregulated in all five of the largest industrial countries. Table 2.3 shows that, in the last half of the decade, the differential between rates on large deposits and money market rates was almost completely eliminated in all of these countries.

III.   Bank loan rates

With deregulation of deposit rates taking place in all five countries, it is to be expected that bank loan rates would also be driven down by competition. If firms have access to alternative sources of funds, such as commercial paper or Eurocurrency loans, then banks will be unable to charge above-market rates for their loans. This section shows how far the deregulation of loan rates has proceeded. I begin by examining innovations in financial markets that have changed traditional bank lending. These innovations include competitive funding from alternative markets and securitization of bank loans. Then I show that, despite these innovations, bank loan rates remain remarkably unresponsive to market conditions. To investigate why this might be true, I offer two detailed case studies of bank loan rates, those in Japan and the United States. Although loan behavior is markedly different in these two countries, in neither country does the loan rate provide a reliable gauge of financing costs.

A.   Innovations in financing

Two innovative trends in financing are fundamentally altering traditional bank lending: the introduction of nonbank instruments such as commercial paper and the securitization of bank claims. The introduction of commercial paper provides firms with a *direct* source of finance independent of banks. Most other sources of short-term financing, such as the discounting of commercial bills, are provided by the banks themselves; so interest rates are normally tied to the bank loan rate. Commercial paper offers firms access to finance at rates that, in the United States at least, have often been below the CD rates offered by banks, let alone the loan rates charged by these banks.

In all of the G-5 countries except the United States, however, the introduction of new instruments to compete with bank loans has proceeded at a slow pace. Table 2.2 charts when commercial paper was first introduced in each country. In four of the five countries, the commercial paper market (or a floating rate note market in the case of Germany) developed only in the mid-1980s. The table also indicates that financing through commercial paper has remained only a fraction of bank financing. Except in the United States, where commercial paper dates from the 1800s, commercial paper was 6 percent or less of bank credit as late as 1990. Thus, although commercial paper may be a longer-term threat to traditional bank lending, so far it has yet to make much of an impact on total financing except in the United States.

The securitization of bank loans has also been an important innovation in financing. Banks have learned to package loans into securities for direct sale to investors (as well as other banks). Securitization began with mortgages in the United States, but has since spread to short-term loans and credit card debt as well. In addition, banks have begun the outright sales of individual loans without packaging into portfolios of loans. The loans are typically those of high-quality commercial borrowers, and the principal sellers of the loans are large money center banks.

Securitization of bank loans broadens the market for fixed income securities beyond traditional instruments like government and corporate bonds. Banking systems where securitization flourishes, moreover, are unlikely to be able to maintain large loan markups indefinitely, since a market willing to absorb packages of bank loans should be equally willing to absorb commercial paper and other instruments issued directly by firms. So, like direct finance, securitization is a trend that threatens bank margins. But securitization is also a trend that has lagged in G-5 countries other than the United States. So in those countries it may only be a trend in the making.

B.   The sluggishness of loan rates

The evidence in Table 2.1 suggests that loan rates have remained considerably above (wholesale) deposit rates even in countries where deposit rates are deregulated. For example, in Germany where time deposit rates have been deregulated since the 1960s, loan rates are on average 2.29 percent above deposit rates. The differential for Britain is much lower at 0.81 percent, but even this differential is large relative to those found in the Eurocurrency markets.

There is also evidence that loan rates respond more sluggishly to changes in market conditions than do deposit rates. In Table 2.4, I compare the behavior of loan rates with that of time deposit rates by examining the correlations between changes in those rates and changes in money market rates. To show the effects of deregulation, I confine the comparisons to the periods *after* the deregulation of deposit rates. Thus in France and Japan, both of whom deregulated deposit rates late in the period, the sample begins only after the introduction of CDs.[17] The correlations in Table 2.4 show a persistent pattern. In all five countries, the correlations between changes in time deposit and money market rates are larger than those between loan rates and money market rates, in most cases much larger. In Germany, for example, the correlation between deposit and money market rates is 0.79, but that between loan and money market rates is only 0.30.

It is also useful to ask whether the introduction of commercial paper has increased competition in the bank loan market. Table 2.5 compares interest differentials between bank loan rates and money market rates before and after the introduction of commercial paper. In the three European countries, the introduction of commercial paper seems to have had only a marginal effect on these differentials, with the French and German differentials remaining over 1 percent. In Britain, the differential has actually increased by a small amount since commercial paper was introduced. These results should not be surprising given that financing through commercial paper remains such a small percentage of bank financing.

In the other two countries, Japan and the United States, the results seem more bizarre. In Japan, the differential between loan and gensaki rates was actually *negative* prior to November 1987 when commercial paper was introduced. In the United States, the differential has averaged 1.49 percent over the whole period despite the long-standing importance of commercial paper in total financing. These two countries deserve further study;

17. In the case of France, CDs were introduced in 1985, but interest rate quotations are available only from May 1988.

Table 2.4. *Correlation coefficients between changes in money market and bank interest rates (after deposit deregulation).*

Country Period		Time deposit and MM rates	Bank loan and MM rates
Britain	73(1)-91(12)	0.96	0.62
France[a]	88(4)-91(12)	0.92	0.24
Germany	73(1)-89(10)	0.79	0.30
Japan[a]	79(5)-91(12)	0.67	0.56
U.S.[a]	73(1)-91(12)	0.93	0.70

[a] The time deposit rate used is the market-determined CD rate.

so the next two sections examine bank lending in Japan and the United States, respectively.

C.   Case study: Japanese loan rates

Prior to 1989, Japanese bank loan rates were quoted relative to a "standard rate," defined as the rate on loans of "especially high credit standing." As has been shown, the standard rate was tied through informal guidelines to the Bank of Japan's discount rate. In January 1989, banks switched to what is formally called a *prime rate,* which is a market-oriented rate tied more closely to the banks' cost of funds than to the discount rate.

While the loan rate was tied by convention to the discount rate, abrupt changes in monetary conditions often left the loan rate in disequilibrium.[18] This would be easy to show if bank deposit rates were set by market forces, but these latter rates were also tied to the discount rate. For most of the 1970s, in fact, the only short-term rate free to reflect current monetary conditions was the gensaki rate, the interest rate on repurchase agreements. As Table 2.4 indicates, the correlation between these rates since the CD market was established in 1979 is only 0.56.

18. For studies of credit rationing and disequilibrium in the Japanese loan market, see Ito and Ueda (1981) and Hamada et al. (1977).

Table 2.5. *Average interest differentials between bank loan rates and money market rates, 1973(1)-1991(12) (before and after introduction of commercial paper).*

Country	Date when commercial paper introduced	Before	After
Britain	1986(4)	0.58 (0.10)[a]	0.70 (0.11)
France	1985(12)	1.34 (0.23)	1.02 (0.14)
Germany	1985(5)[b]	1.73 (0.16)	1.43 (0.18)
Japan	1987(11)	-1.31 (0.17)	0.06 (0.12)
U.S.	1800s		1.49 (0.09)

[a] The numbers in parentheses are the standard errors of the means.
[b] May 1985 is when floating rate notes were introduced to Germany. Commercial paper was not introduced until 1991.

Sources: Same as earlier tables.

More surprisingly, the gensaki rate was systematically higher than the prime rate, 1.31 percent higher prior to 1987 according to Table 2.5.[19] This points to a serious drawback in interpreting the loan series. The cost of Japanese loans is generally higher than the rate quoted because most companies are required to maintain "compensating balances" during the period of the loan. Interest is paid on those compensating balances (because they are typically held in short-term time deposits), but the interest rate is always below that paid on the loans themselves. If i_{Lt}' is the contractual

19. Since the gensaki repurchase contracts are collateralized, there is no reason to believe that the 1 percent differential is a default risk premium.

loan rate, i_{D_t} is the deposit rate, and b_t is the ratio of compensating balances to loans, then the *effective* loan rate, i_{L_t}, is given by:

$$i_{L_t} = \frac{i_{L_t}' - i_{D_t} \times b_t}{1 - b_t}$$

By requiring compensating balances, banks can raise the effective cost of a loan even in the presence of interest rate ceilings on loan rates.

To obtain an estimate of compensating balances, I rely on an annual survey of small to medium-sized companies conducted by the Japanese Fair Trade Commission.[20] This survey gives the ratio of compensating balances to loans as well as the ratio of *total* deposits to loans by these same firms. In evaluating the profitability of loans, banks may take into account the total deposits of firms rather than just those deposits reported (by the firms) as compensating balances. So two measures of compensating balances are developed corresponding to reported compensating balances and total bank deposits.[21] Monthly series for these measures are obtained by interpolating the annual data.

In examining the data, it is useful to consider what biases may be present in these measures of compensating balances. The second measure based on total deposits undoubtedly overstates the true measure because it includes transactions accounts that firms would have to maintain even in the absence of bank loans. On the other hand, both measures may be regarded as overestimates to the extent that larger firms hold a smaller proportion of compensating balances than the small and medium-sized firms in the survey.[22] Unfortunately, there isn't adequate information to suggest which measure is preferable.

Table 2.6 compares the prime loan rates adjusted by the two methods with the gensaki rate. The sample period is divided between the 1970s and 1980s to show whether the behavior of loan rates changed in the 1980s. For each sample period, the mean of the interest differential between the loan rate and the gensaki rate is reported as well as the standard error of this mean. During the 1970s, the loan rate is on average almost 2 percent below the gensaki rate. This differential is reduced when the cost of compensating balances is taken into account, but not even the adjustment by total deposits is sufficient to raise the effective loan rate as high as the

20. Japan Fair Trade Commission, *Survey of Compensating Balances,* 1991. Firms in this survey have capitalization less than ¥ 100 million.
21. These measures are discussed at greater length in Marston (1993). See also Bank of Japan (1991).
22. Large companies presumably have higher credit standing on average than smaller companies and have greater access to alternative forms of financing; so they are not required to maintain the same ratio of compensating balances.

Table 2.6. *Interest differentials between Japanese loan and gensaki rates, 1973(1)-1991(11).*

	Unadjusted prime rate - gensaki	Adjusted by compensating balance ratio	Adjusted by total deposit /loan ratio
73(1)-80(12)			
Mean	-1.87	-1.48	-0.43
SE of mean	(0.28)	(0.25)	(0.21)
81(1)-91(11)			
Mean	-0.40	-0.23	0.83
SE of mean	(0.07)	(0.07)	(0.10)

Sources: Interest rates, see tables above. Compensating balances, Japan Fair Trade Commission, *Survey of Compensating Balances*, 1991.

gensaki rate. During the 1980s, the unadjusted loan rate, as well as the smaller of the adjusted measures, is still on average below the gensaki rate, although the loan rate adjusted by total deposits is now 0.83 percent above the gensaki rate.

What conclusions can be drawn from this analysis? First, it is obvious that it is very difficult to obtain an accurate measure of the loan rate prior to the late 1980s. Without better information about compensating balances, the adjusted loan rates must be regarded as only rough estimates of the true costs of the loans. Second, even if we had reliable estimates, the adjusted loan rates would not tell us the true cost of funds in a *deregulated* environment where loan rates follow other money market rates like the gensaki rate.

D.   Case study: U.S. loan rates

Obtaining a reliable measure of the cost of bank loans in the United States is also difficult, but in this case it is because the meaning of the prime rate itself has changed fundamentally. As firms have obtained greater access to direct financing from the commercial paper market as well as from the Eurodollar market abroad, banks increasingly have lent at rates *below* prime rate to their prime customers. So the prime rate no longer reflects the true cost of funds to prime borrowers.

Consider the relationship between the prime rate and the CD rate. Unlike the comparison between gensaki and Japanese loan rates, this interest rate comparison offers a direct measure of the margin between the deposit and loan rates. Table 2.1 reports the mean differential for the 1973(1)–1991(12) period. If the prime rate were a true measure of the cost of bank loans (to the most creditworthy firms), then bank lending would be profitable indeed, since the average differential over the period is 1.59 percent.[23]

Banks were forced to lend below prime because of competition from other sources of funds. To indicate how severe that competition could be, recall the comparison between the commercial paper rate and the prime loan rate as reported in Table 2.5. Over the 1973–91 period, the differential between these two rates has averaged 1.49 percent. With such a huge gap between the costs of direct and indirect finance, firms (at least those with access to this alternative market) could extract much lower loan rates from banks.

The practice of lending below prime rate has become so routine that the Federal Reserve has begun reporting statistics for loans "made below prime" in its *Survey of Terms of Bank Lending*. Table 2.7 presents statistics summarizing five years of data from this publication.[24] According to this table, loans made below prime constituted between 67.7 and 85.2 percent of total loans between 1984 and 1988. Many overnight and other very short-term loans are tied to the federal funds rate, so it is more instructive to look at loans with a maturity greater than one month. Of these loans, between 43.3 and 57.9 percent were made at rates below prime.

Thus the "prime" rate has ceased to have its original literal meaning of loans to "prime" customers. A court case against First National Bank of Atlanta has even forced banks to be careful in how they describe the prime rate in loan documents. In 1981 a class action suit was brought against First Atlanta by some of its loan customers claiming that it had overcharged prime-based borrowers by tying their loan rates to the prime rate rather than the below-market rate offered to First Atlanta's prime customers. As a result, many banks now refer to the prime rate simply as a "reference rate."

Like the Japanese series, the series for the American loan rate is an unreliable measure of the true cost of funding. But in contrast to the Japanese series, the American series overestimates the true cost of funding, at least for prime customers. The American bank loan market is so competi-

---

23. The spread of 1.59 percent is large compared with spreads of less than 1 percent on Eurodollar syndicated loans to Brazil and Mexico prior to the debt crisis. The U.S. loan rate would naturally be higher than prime for loans to firms with significant credit risk.
24. From Wolfson and McLaughlin (1989) in the *Federal Reserve Bulletin*.

Table 2.7. *U.S. bank loans made below prime rate as percentage of total loans at large U.S. banks.*

Year	Total (%)	Excluding loans of 1 month or less (%)	Spread between prime and CP rate (%)
1984	80.6	57.9	1.99
1985	85.2	52.1	1.94
1986	82.8	53.2	1.75
1987	72.6	46.5	1.58
1988	67.7	43.3	1.67

Source: Wolfson and McLaughlin (1989) in *Federal Reserve Bulletin*, p. 464.

tive that the true spread between loan and deposit rates is likely to be much closer to that of the Eurocurrency market than Table 2.1 indicates.[25]

The two case studies illustrate a more general point about using bank loan rates to measure the cost of financing. In measuring financing costs in a securities market, the terms of that financing are publicly known because the securities must be offered to investors.[26] Bank financing, in contrast, is a bilateral transaction between the bank and firms; so it is more difficult for third parties to determine the true costs of financing. Published prime loan rates thus should be treated with extreme caution.

IV.   Bond financing

A fully deregulated financial system permits all forms of direct financing by firms, including the issue of corporate bonds and other long-term debt securities. In this section, I will examine the national bond markets of the

25. The spread would have to be larger because U.S. bank deposits are subject to reserve requirements; so banks must earn a higher loan rate (or pay a lower deposit rate) to compensate for this cost. In addition, banks must pay FDIC insurance fees on U.S. bank deposits. See Chapter 3.
26. In the absence of disclosure requirements, the underwriting fees and associated up-front costs may not be public knowledge, but the coupon and price are known with certainty.

Table 2.8 *Size of national and international bond markets, end 1992.*

Currency	National bond markets		International bond markets
	$ billions	As percent of all national markets (%)	$ billions
Britain	254.0	1.8	121.3
France	525.0	3.7	64.3
Germany	1,234.0	8.8	168.5
Japan	2,888.6	20.5	207.5
United States	6,676.2	47.5	680.5

Source: Bank for International Settlements, *63rd Annual Report* (14th June 1993).

G-5 countries to determine to what extent bond financing serves as an alternative to indirect financing through bank loans. As in the case of bank loans, the deregulation of the bond markets has been stimulated by increased competition from abroad. I will discuss how the development of the international Eurobond market and the currency swap market has given firms access to alternative sources of longer-term financing.

A.   National and international bond financing

Table 2.8 provides some statistics on both national and international bond markets denominated in the currencies of the G-5 countries. The size of each national bond market at the end of 1992 is reported in billions of dollars and expressed as a percentage of all national markets. In addition, the size of the international (Eurobond) market in the same currency is also reported. The U.S. and Japanese national markets together represent 68 percent of national bond markets worldwide, with the U.S. market alone constituting 47.5 percent of the world total. By contrast, the other three G-5 countries together represent only 14.3 percent of national markets worldwide.

The figures in Table 2.8 do not tell us how large are the *corporate* bond markets in the G-5 countries. We would like to know the extent to which each national bond market provides financing to private firms as compared with local and national governments and other official entities. A study by Salomon Brothers (Fujii, 1992) provides a detailed breakdown for the Japanese bond market. Of the ¥ 147,882 billion bonds outstanding in 1980 ($652.2 billion at 1980 exchange rates), only 6.8 percent were corporate bonds. By 1991, total bonds had risen to ¥ 364,458 billion ($ 2705.5 billion) with the proportion of corporate bonds rising somewhat to 9.0 percent.[27] We also have estimates of the share of corporate bonds in the other national markets for the end of 1988.[28] Corporate issues represented 17.7 percent of total national bond issues in the United States and 19.7 percent in France. The share of corporate issues in the United Kingdom was a much lower 8.5 percent and in Germany a negligible 0.2 percent.

One reason for the share of corporate issues varying so much from market to market is that firms from different countries differ in their reliance on direct financing (through the securities market) as opposed to financing from banks. The OECD reports the stock of liabilities of "nonfinancial enterprises" as part of its flow of funds statistics.[29] Table 2.9 presents a breakdown of financing by nonfinancial firms in four of the five countries. (The OECD does not report comparable figures for the United Kingdom.) The table reports the share of total debt liabilities (excluding trade credits) represented by (1) short-term and long-term loans, and (2) bonds and short-term securities. Sources of funding vary widely across countries. At one extreme is Germany where bank lending provides the bulk of financing and where direct issue of bonds or short-term securities is limited. At the other extreme is the United States where the corporate bond market and commercial paper market both play important roles in financing. In 1976, U.S. firms raised 33.8 percent of their funds from the securities market, whereas the other three countries raised less than 10 percent of their funds from such sources. By 1991, the share of funding from securities had risen in France and Japan to about 15 percent, still far below U.S.

27. The bank debenture market represented 17.6 percent of the total bond market in 1980 and an even larger 20.2 percent in 1991, but bank debentures are strictly controlled with maturities limited until recently to one and five years. The Japanese bond market is discussed more fully later in the chapter.
28. "How Big is the World Bond Market? 1989 Update," *International Bond Market Analysis,* Salomon Brothers Inc. (June 1989), as reported in Solnik (1991).
29. OECD, *Financial Statistics,* Part 2 ("Financial Accounts of OECD Countries"), 1992 and 1993 issues.

Table 2.9. *Sources of funding for nonfinancial enterprises: share of debt (excluding trade credits).*[a]

	1976	1981	1986	1991
United States				
Loans	66.2	67.9	68.7	64.2
Securities	33.8	32.1	31.3	35.8
France[b]				
Loans	90.5	91.6	84.8	83.8
Securities	9.5	8.4	15.2	16.2
Germany				
Loans	94.7	96.6	95.4	96.1
Securities	5.3	3.4	4.6	3.9
Japan				
Loans	94.7	94.2	91.8	86.8
Securities	5.3	5.8	8.2	13.2

[a] The OECD reports all liabilities of nonfinancial firms including trade credits, whereas this table includes only debt in the form of (1) short-term and long-term loans and (2) bonds and short-term securities.
[b] The first set of figures for France is for the year 1977 rather than 1976.

Source: OECD *Financial Statistics*, Part 2 ("Financial Accounts of OECD Countries") 1992 and 1993 issues. There are no corresponding figures for assets and liabilities published for the United Kingdom.

levels, whereas German firms continued to draw only a very small fraction of their funding from the securities market. In France and Japan at least, there is evidently a trend toward greater reliance on the securities market. In both countries, this trend has been facilitated by the continuing deregulation of national markets as well as the liberalization of access to international markets. During the 1980s in France, for example, a credit allocation system giving preferential treatment to particular enterprises has given way to an increasingly deregulated market where debt instruments can be issued in a variety of different forms, including commercial paper, fixed and floating-rate bonds, and bonds with warrants attached. As a

1986 government white paper stated, the reforms aimed to create "a unified capital market, extending from overnight money to the very long-term, open to all economic agents for both spot and forward transactions, and with the possibility of options."[30] Despite these trends, however, U.S. firms still rely on the securities market much more than their counterparts in the other three countries.

The sheer size and trading volume of the U.S. market give it advantages when it comes to trading costs. Table 2.10 compares transaction costs in the U.S. market with those in other markets. The table reports bid/ask spreads in basis points (equal to one-hundredths of a percent) for different types of government bonds depending upon how actively they are traded. The U.S. market has a clear advantage in costs even in the "benchmark" portion of the market (with the most actively traded issues). But its most decided advantage lies in the liquidity of the least traded issues where bid/ask spreads are over fifteen basis points smaller than in any other market.

Firms in need of medium-term financing may turn to international markets to borrow either in their own currency or in foreign currencies. The international or "Eurobond" market developed in the 1960s to provide medium-term financing in dollars and other currencies.[31] Today that market provides over $ 300 billion in new financing in the form of straight fixed-rate bonds, floating rate notes, and equity-related bonds such as convertibles. (See Table 2.11.) Eurobonds usually have maturities of from five to ten years, and are denominated in a variety of currencies including dollars, marks, yen, and ECU, as well as smaller currencies such as Australian dollars. The typical borrower in this market is a large firm (or bank) with a high enough credit standing to be acceptable to the many individual investors who purchase these bonds.[32] A Eurocommercial paper market has also developed in parallel with the national markets in commercial paper. As an alternative to direct finance, the syndicated loan market provides large-scale funding in the form of bank loans at floating interest rates usually tied to LIBOR. Before the debt crisis of 1982, many syndicated loans were extended to firms and government entities in Latin America and Eastern Europe. Since then this market has contracted in size, but it still provides crucial funding to firms without direct access to the credit market.

30. "White Paper on the Reform of Financing of the Economy" (March 1986), as quoted in OECD, *Economic Survey, France* (January 1987), p. 51.
31. U.S. capital controls in the 1960s had the inadvertent effect of stimulating the early development of the Eurobond market because U.S. multinational firms were forced to raise funds outside of the United States.
32. In the last few years, the market has expanded to include firms from less developed countries. Eurobonds issued by Latin American borrowers, for example, totalled $ 12 billion in 1992.

Table 2.10. *Transactions costs in national bond markets: bid/ask spread by liquidity of bond issue (in basis points).*

Country	Benchmark issue(s)	Active issues less benchmark	Traded issues less active	Rest of market
Britain	6	11	16	35
France	10	18	25	40
Germany	5	10	15	30
Japan	8	18	20	50
U.S.	3	4	6	13

Source: Morgan Guaranty Trust, *World Financial Markets* (1989) Issue 5, p. 11.

Table 2.11. *Borrowing in international markets ($ billions).*

	1981	1986	1991
International bond issues	48.8	221.7	316.7
Straight issues	36.9	146.6	255.2
Floating rate	7.5	47.7	19.1
Equity-related[a]	4.4	27.3	42.4
Eurocommercial paper	n.a.	13.9	79.6
Syndicated bank loans	94.6	52.8	87.8

[a] Convertible bonds and bonds with warrants attached.

Sources: For international bond and Eurocommercial paper issues, Bank for International Settlements, *Annual Reports*, various issues. For syndicated bank loans, OECD, *Financial Market Trends*, various issues.

Perhaps the most innovative market to develop in the past 20 years is the swap market, which emerged in the early 1980s. *Currency swaps* are contracts that provide for the exchange of interest and principal payments in two different currencies.[33] *Interest rate swaps* involve the exchange of floating-rate interest payments for fixed-rate payments in a single currency.

Swaps allow firms without direct access to markets in a particular currency to borrow indirectly in that currency by arranging a currency swap. As an example, consider a swap between an American firm that has borrowed at a fixed interest rate in the dollar bond market or at a floating rate in the Eurodollar market and a Japanese firm that has borrowed at a fixed rate in the yen market (either the Japanese or Eurobond market). By the terms of the swap, the American firm would undertake to pay interest payments on the yen debt, in return for which the Japanese firm would pay interest payments on the dollar debt. Each firm would also undertake to swap payments of principal at maturity. Through the swap, the American firm effectively transforms dollar debt into yen debt, while the Japanese firm transforms yen debt into dollar debt.

Table 2.12 provides estimates of the size of the market for swaps reported by the IMF. By 1991 interest rate swaps totaled $ 1,722.8 billion, while currency swaps totaled $ 582.3 billion. To put these figures in perspective, total fixed-rate Eurobonds outstanding at the end of 1991 amounted to $ 1,158.5 billion.[34] The market for swaps has developed to the point that banks and other financial institutions make a market in standard swap contracts. This market is so competitive that margins (in the form of bid/ask spreads) on standard contracts such as DM/$ or ¥/$ have been driven down almost to levels associated with short-term Eurocurrency deposits. In 1987, for example, average bid/ask spreads on five-year currency swaps ranged from 0.13 to 0.18 percent for five major currencies.[35]

So we have several trends at work in the medium-term credit market. First, there is the deregulation of national bond markets to allow greater access for the corporate sector and the introduction of new instruments for all borrowers. Second, there is innovation in the international markets, including the development of the Eurobond, Eurocommercial paper, and swaps markets. For international markets to stimulate deregulation at

---

33. The first publicly announced swap was a dollar/Swiss franc swap between IBM and the World Bank in 1981. For a description of the markets for currency and interest rate swaps, see BIS (1986). A recent paper by Popper (1993) studies arbitrage between medium-term bonds and currency swaps.
34. Bank for International Settlements, *62nd Annual Report* (June 1992), p. 173.
35. Salomon Brothers, *International Market Roundup.* I am grateful to Helen Popper for providing me with the bid/ask quotations.

Table 2.12. *Outstanding interest rate and currency swaps: national principal value ($ billions).*[a]

	Interest rate swaps		Currency swaps[b]	
	1987	1991	1987	1991
Dollar	379.9	831.0	64.6	205.3
Yen	21.1	214.0	22.7	119.2
DM	23.7	152.2	9.1	38.2
Sterling	19.3	147.3	4.2	29.0
Other	32.4	378.3	46.7	190.6
Total	476.2	1722.8	147.3	582.3

[a] The figures exclude interbank transactions.
[b] The currency swap figures are adjusted for double-counting as each currency swap involves two currencies.

Source: Goldstein et al. (1993), p. 25.

home, however, the national authorities must liberalize access by national firms to international markets. Chapter 3 will discuss the liberalization of international capital flows in detail. To see how these three trends interact, the next section provides an in-depth look at the important Japanese market.

B.   Case study: The Japanese bond market

Today the Japanese bond market is the second largest bond market in the world. As Table 2.8 indicates, the Japanese market is a little less than one-half the size of the U.S. bond market. In the early 1970s, however, the market was very limited in size (¥ 20.6 trillion or $ 57.2 billion in bonds outstanding in 1970 compared with ¥ 365.8 trillion or $ 2,888.6 billion in 1992) and overridden with regulations. The government portion of the long-term bond market was small because the rapidly growing economy had allowed the Japanese government to generate enough tax revenues to keep deficit financing to a minimum.[36] The market for bonds that did exist could hardly be called a conventional one. Newly issued government bonds were placed with an underwriting syndicate at below-market rates with the informal understanding that the Bank of Japan would buy the bonds after one year at a price guaranteed to avoid capital losses for the syndicate.[37] There was virtually no corporate bond market except for government-guaranteed issues by electricity companies and the Nippon Telephone and Telegraph Co.[38] The corporate market remained moribund largely because of stringent collateral requirements, which were a legacy of bond market defaults in the 1930s.[39]

The unusual system by which Japanese government bonds were distributed worked well as long as fiscal deficits remained small, but in 1975 the deficit rose to 3.4 percent of GNP (and continued rising to 6.0 percent by 1979). To fulfill its informal guarantee to purchase bonds from the syndicate, the Bank of Japan would have had to increase the monetary base significantly (by 34 percent in 1975 alone by one estimate). Instead, the bond syndicate had to absorb some large capital losses from the recent issues. This led to pressure to reform the system. In April 1977, the syndicate got permission for the first time to sell deficit bonds, although the syndicate was still obliged to hold onto the bonds for one year. By the following year, moreover, the syndicate had managed to negotiate higher yields on new issues so as to eliminate most if not all of the gap between the new issue yields and secondary market yields.[40] But the secondary market for bonds did not become truly active until June 1984 when banks were allowed to trade government bonds in this market.

With the advent of widespread trading in 1984 came a rather unusual phenomenon associated with so-called "benchmark bonds." At any given time, there is always one bond designated as a "benchmark bond" by the major securities firms in the market, which therefore trades at a premium because of its liquidity. According to the Bank of Japan (1988, p. 16), the benchmark bond represents only 1 to 2 percent of total government bonds

36. The Fiscal Law forbid bond issues to cover general account deficits, so any deficit financing had to be approved in a special authorization law. See Feldman (1986) for a good discussion of regulations regarding government bonds. More recent discussions of the Japanese bond markets include Bank of Japan (1988), Fujii (1992), and Mason (1987).
37. The Bank of Japan was prohibited from buying government bonds unless they had been outstanding for one year.
38. NTT required that new subscribers to its telephone service purchase NTT bonds; so these bonds were widely held in Japan.
39. Companies were required to secure the bond issue with property and equipment as collateral.
40. See Feldman (1986, pp. 50–2).

outstanding, but *up to 90 percent* of total spot transaction volume is attributed to the benchmark issue alone. This high liquidity of the benchmark issue has led to yield differentials of as large as 60 basis points between the benchmark bond and other government bonds of nearly equal coupon and maturity.[41]

Government bonds in general are much more liquid than corporate and other types of bonds. Table 2.13 compares figures for bonds outstanding with trading volume. In 1990, government bonds constituted 49.2 percent of the market, but made up 94.8 percent of trading volume. Corporate bonds, in contrast, constituted 3.5 percent of outstanding bonds, but made up only 0.3 percent of trading volume.

As previously stated, corporate bond issues have been discouraged by stringent collateral requirements. The Japanese authorities began to relax these requirements beginning in 1977, but the process was painfully slow.[42] Changes in regulation in 1977 permitted only two Japanese firms to satisfy new capital adequacy requirements and thus escape the stricter collateral requirements. Further relaxation in April 1984 made a total of 20 companies eligible. It was only in November 1990 that the collateral requirements were abolished altogether and replaced by credit rating requirements.

There are now some signs that the corporate market is developing. New straight bond issues increased from ¥ 1.1 trillion in 1988 and 1989 (about $ 8 billion) to ¥ 2.9 trillion in 1990 and ¥ 4.1 trillion in 1991.[43] Over this same period, however, Japanese companies preferred to issue bonds abroad (primarily in the Eurobond market) rather than at home. In the four years 1988–91, new issues of straight corporate bonds in the Japanese market totaled ¥ 9.2 trillion ($ 67 billion at then current exchange rates), while new issues by Japanese borrowers in foreign markets totaled ¥ 13.3 trillion. Takeda and Turner (1992, pp. 78–79) cite several reasons for Eurobonds' being preferred to domestic issues. Among these are the stringent collateral requirements of domestic issues (only recently relaxed) and the greater flotation costs of issuing bonds in the Japanese market (about 40 basis points higher). Added to these factors must be the low degree of liquidity in the Japanese market (especially compared with the dollar portion of the Eurobond market).

The actual pattern of Japanese borrowing in the Eurobond market is of interest in itself. During the last half of the 1980s, Japanese firms typically borrowed in the dollar or other foreign currency Eurobond markets rather than in the yen Eurobond market. Over the 1985–89 period, only 4.4 per-

41. See Bank of Japan (1988, Chart 17).
42. See Japan Securities Research Institute (1992, pp. 86–87) for the chronology of the changes in collateral requirements.
43. Convertible bonds and warrant bonds, on the other hand, declined from ¥ 8.5 trillion in 1989 to ¥ 1.7 trillion in 1991. See Takeda and Turner (1992, Table 27).

Table 2.13. *Japanese bonds outstanding and trading volume by issuer in 1990.*

	Bonds outstanding (as percent of total)	Trading volume (as percent of total)
Government	49.2	94.8
Government-guaranteed	15.6	0.4
Local government	5.9	0.2
Financial debentures	19.0	2.6
Corporate	3.5	0.3
Convertible and warrant	5.2	1.5
Foreign (samurai)	1.6	0.2

Source: Japan Securities Research Institute (1992).

cent of Japanese bond financing abroad was denominated in yen.[44] One reason is that there is a waiting period (90 days from 1986 on) before Japanese investors can purchase yen-denominated bonds (so they are willing to pay a small premium for nonyen issues). Before 1984, yen-denominated issues by Japanese residents were actually prohibited (largely because the Japanese authorities feared that Eurobond issues would undermine the collateral requirements of domestic bonds). Thus foreign firms accounted for most issues of yen-denominated Eurobonds. Japanese firms, after borrowing in foreign currencies, would often arrange currency swaps of foreign currency debt payments for yen debt payments. This complex arrangement was no doubt encouraged by the low interest rates available to Japanese firms able to issue warrants on their equity. Since the fall of the Japanese stock market beginning in 1990, however, the pattern has shifted toward more direct financing by Japanese firms in the yen-denominated Eurobond market. In 1991, the proportion of yen-denominated issues by Japanese borrowers abroad rose to 35.1 from 4.4 percent in the 1985–89 period.

The three trends of deregulation at home, innovation in international markets, and liberalization of access to these markets are evident in the

44. From Table 29 of Takeda and Turner (1992).

case of Japan. Spurred on by competition from the Eurobond market now that barriers to international financing are being lifted, the Japanese market is being gradually deregulated. Table 2.8 indicates that by 1991 Japanese firms' reliance on the securities market rivaled that of France, although still behind financing by U.S. firms. The next chapter will describe how the removal of Japanese capital controls encouraged such deregulation.

V.   Summary

This chapter has examined deregulation and innovation in the financial markets of the G-5 countries. In earlier decades, national markets were riddled with regulations and market conventions, which shielded deposit and loan rates from the normal pressures of supply and demand. Both deposit and loan rates were set independently of interbank rates or other market-determined rates, and were shielded from competition from Eurocurrency rates.

In the last 20 years, deregulation has succeeded in freeing interest rates on deposits in all G-5 countries, at least the large-scale deposits of firms and institutional investors. By the late 1980s, all five countries had established markets in certificates of deposit with rates tied closely to those in the money market. As will be shown in the next chapter, by the late 1980s deposit rates in all five countries were also tied closely to Eurocurrency rates in the same currency.

The deregulation of loan markets, however, has not progressed as far as that of deposit markets. The gap between loan rates and money market rates remains large in most countries. That is partly because competing instruments like commercial paper have been slow in developing. Even if loan markets were competitive, however, posted loan rates might fail to measure the true cost of bank financing. In fact, the evidence from the experience of Japan and the United States suggests that there may be gross errors in using published loan rates to measure financing costs.

The deregulation of national bond markets is also occurring in all G-5 countries, although bond financing remains far more important in the United States than elsewhere. As in the case of the short-term markets, new instruments have been developed that provide alternative sources of medium-term funding for firms. Among these are the international markets in Eurobonds, floating-rate notes and loans, and swaps.

The next chapter examines the extent to which borrowers and investors in the G-5 countries have gained access to international markets.

CHAPTER 3

Liberalization of national capital controls

One of the alleged benefits of flexible exchange rates is that it frees national monetary authorities from balance of payments constraints and thus permits them to relax capital controls. This chapter will show how the switch to flexible exchange rates in the early 1970s led eventually to the removal of controls in all of the G-5 countries, although in some countries liberalization was delayed until much later. The chapter will investigate the effects of the controls by comparing covered interest differentials during control and postcontrol periods.

I.   Covered interest differentials

Covered interest differentials can arise for any of four reasons. First, the securities being considered may differ in default risk.[1] Second, returns on the domestic securities may be regulated so that they fail to reflect domestic market conditions. Third, the market may be segmented by capital controls. Finally, even if no capital controls separate the markets, investors may perceive a political or sovereign risk involving future restrictions.[2]

In the following analysis of interest rates, I will attempt to confine comparisons to securities with equal default risk, although this is not entirely possible. I will also confine my comparisons to short-term assets. It would also be interesting to compare bond yields in the national and Eurobond markets in the same currency, but it is difficult to find bonds with equivalent maturities and levels of default risk. I will use money market rates rather than domestic loan rates because, as explained in the last chapter, loan rates are more subject to regulation and other distortions. The covered interest differentials that I will examine will primarily reflect the joint

---

1. Government securities, for example, are generally regarded as less subject to default risk than private assets. Assets may also differ in tax status and eligibility for discounting at the central bank as well as in other characteristics.
2. Political or sovereign risk arises because of concern that the national authorities of one country might impose controls, taxes, or other regulatory measures on foreign investment in their market or on their residents' investments in other markets.

influence of capital controls and political risk, which I will refer to as the *country premium*.[3]

Capital controls come in two varieties. Governments may restrict resident purchases of foreign assets (and sometimes nonresident outflows as well). Such *outward* controls, which are usually designed to prop up a weak currency, lead to a covered interest differential favoring the foreign market unless there is sufficient flexibility in the controls to permit arbitrage between domestic and foreign markets. Alternatively, governments may restrict nonresident purchases of domestic assets to reduce pressures toward appreciation of the domestic currency. Such *inward* controls may lead to an interest differential favoring the domestic market. Only a few countries like Germany, Switzerland, and Japan have resorted to such inward controls, Japan's controls affecting both inward and outward flows.

The Eurocurrency market operates free of any capital controls. Thus host governments (such as the British government in the case of Eurocurrency transactions in London) permit bank transactions involving foreign currencies by nonresidents even when they restrict transactions involving their own currencies. In addition, political risks are perceived to be of negligible importance in this market. Consider the comparison between Eurodollar and Euromark deposits in London. Investors might perceive that both forms of Eurocurrency deposits are subject to some political risk, although that risk is extremely low since the British authorities are unlikely to tamper with a market that could be moved elsewhere so easily. But even if all Eurocurrency deposits conceivably might be at some risk, there is little reason to believe that the risk is greater for one type of Eurocurrency deposit than it is for another. That is because the British government (or any other government) is unlikely to discriminate among foreign currencies in any extension of controls to the Eurocurrency market. So it is not surprising that *covered interest parity* always holds between any pair of Eurocurrency deposit rates.

Consider the comparison between Eurodollar and Eurosterling interest rates. If the Eurodollar interest rate is adjusted for the cost of forward cover, then the two returns expressed in sterling should be equal:

$$i_{£t} = i_{$t} + f_{£t} \qquad \text{covered interest parity} \tag{3.1}$$

where

$$i_{$t} = \ln(1 + I_{$t}) \text{ where } I_{$t} \text{ is the Eurodollar interest rate}$$
$$i_{£t} = \ln(1 + I_{£t}) \text{ where } I_{£t} \text{ is the Eurosterling rate}$$

3. For previous treatments of capital controls and political risk and their implications for covered interest parity, see Aliber (1973), Frenkel and Levich (1975), Marston (1976), Dooley and Isard (1980), and Bodnar (1993). Frenkel and MacArthur (1988) also use the term "country premium" in their study of covered interest differentials over the 1982–86 period.

$f_{£t} = \ln(F_{£t}/S_{£t})$ where $F_{£t}$ is the forward exchange rate and $S_{£t}$ is the spot exchange rate, both expressed in £/$.[4]

The two returns should be identical except for transactions costs.

If capital controls are effective, then there will be covered interest differentials between national interest rates in any currency and Eurodollar rates covered for exchange risk. But because interest parity holds between Eurocurrency rates, the controls should also result in equivalent interest differentials between national interest rates and the Eurocurrency interest rate in the *same* currency. For example, the deviation of British rates from covered interest parity may be measured in two ways, using either the Eurodollar rate and the forward premium or the Eurosterling rate alone:

$$i_{St} + f_{£t} - i_{Bt} = U_{1t} \qquad (3.2a)$$
$$i_{£t} - i_{Bt} = U_{2t} \qquad (3.2b)$$

The first equation measures the deviation between the covered Eurodollar rate and the British interest rate. The second equation measures the deviation between the Eurosterling rate and the British interest rate. I will use this second measure to examine the effects of capital controls in most of the countries studied.

II.   The effects of national capital controls

In two of the countries to be studied, Germany and the United States, capital controls were lifted in 1973; so capital flows to and from these markets were unrestricted for most of the flexible exchange rate period. In the other three countries, the controls persisted well after 1973. In the case of France, in fact, the controls were strengthened in the 1980s before being lifted only recently. I begin with the British case where it is possible to examine the effects of the controls back to 1961 because the Bank of England started reporting Eurodollar and Eurosterling interest rates at that time. In addition, the Bank reports forward premia so that I can make comparisons between the two measures of controls, Equations (3.2a) and (3.2b).

A.   British controls

The British government maintained a system of controls on resident outflows from before World War II until as late as June 1979. The controls

---

4. The exchange rate for the pound sterling has been inverted to conform with practices in other currency markets.

applied primarily to direct and portfolio investment abroad by U.K. residents, holdings of foreign currency deposits by residents, and foreign currency lending by residents including U.K. banks.[5] Residents could invest abroad only by using foreign exchange obtained from the sale of existing securities or from foreign currency borrowing.[6] These controls did not prevent London from maintaining its preeminence as a financial center because the Bank of England was farsighted enough to allow the Eurocurrency market to develop in London outside the system of controls. Banks in London could accept deposits and make loans denominated in any currency except sterling. Of course, the controls restricted investments by residents in Eurocurrency deposits just as it restricted their investments in markets outside the United Kingdom. The controls also prohibited Eurosterling deposits and loans from being offered by banks located in London, although a Eurosterling market developed in Paris.

Table 3.1 reports monthly interest differentials for the sterling markets for the period from April 1961, when Eurosterling interest rates were first reported by the Bank of England, to June 1979, when British capital controls ended. The underlying data are published by the Bank of England *Quarterly Bulletin*. The British interest rate used is the local authority rate through 1971 and the interbank deposit rate thereafter.[7] The interest rates reported are for three-month maturities expressed in percent per annum; so the differentials are calculated in logs as follows (for the case of the Eurodollar and British interest rates):

$$\{\ln[1 + \frac{I_{s_t}}{400}] + \ln[\frac{F_{\pounds_t}}{S_{\pounds_t}}] - \ln[1 + \frac{I_{B_t}}{400}]\} \times 400 \qquad (3.2a')$$

The table reports differentials between Eurodollar and British rates, between Eurosterling and British rates, and between Eurodollar and Eurosterling rates. The first and last differentials are calculated using the forward premium on the pound, while the second differential omits the forward premium because both interest rates are expressed in sterling. Since British capital controls limited *outflows* of capital, we would expect deviations involving British rates to be *positive* (or equal to zero when the control is not binding).

Table 3.1 illustrates how effective capital controls can be in driving wedges between national and Eurocurrency interest rates. According to this table, interest differentials between the British market and either Euro-

---

5. Artis and Taylor (1989) describe these capital controls in more detail.
6. An investment dollar market grew up with a premium over the official exchange rate reflecting the tightness of the controls.
7. The interest rate on local authority loans was the most representative money market rate in the 1960s.

Table 3.1. *Covered interest differentials in the $/£ markets in percent per annum, 1961(4)-1979(6).*

	Eurodollar minus British[a]	Eurosterling minus British	Eurodollar minus Eurosterling
Number of observations	219	219	219
Avg. differential (standard error)[b] [p-value]	1.12 (0.15) [0.000]	1.04 (0.15) [0.000]	0.08 (0.02) [0.000]
Band for 95 % of Observations	4.23	3.78	0.38

[a] The British interest rate is the three-month rate through 1971 and the three-month sterling interbank deposit rate thereafter.

[b] The standard error of the mean, in parenthesis below the average differential, is corrected for serial correlation and heteroskedasticity. The figure in square brackets is the *p*-value testing whether the average differential is equal to zero.

Source: Bank of England, *Quarterly Bulletin*, various issues.

currency market averaged over 1 percent per annum during the period of the controls. The standard errors of the sample means of these differentials were less than 0.20 percent, so that both of these means are statistically different from zero at the 5 percent level. In the absence of controls, differentials of this size would induce immediate arbitrage activity by bank traders. The fifth row of the table reports the band for interest rate differentials within which 95 percent of the observations fall.[8] That band includes differentials as large as 4.23 percent in the case of comparisons between Eurodollar and British rates and 3.78 percent in comparisons between Eurosterling and British rates. These differentials were large enough to provide firms within the British market with substantial advantages over firms with access only to international markets. During the period of the controls, therefore, multinational firms with operations in Brit-

8. This statistic gives some indication of how distortionary the controls are when they are most binding.

ain as well as elsewhere found it advantageous to finance as much as possible *behind* the British control barrier. Rather than being a high-cost center, the British sterling market offered financing at lower rates, when measured in dollars, than in markets with seemingly low interest rates such as Germany.

The table also shows covered differentials between the Eurodollar and Eurosterling markets. The differentials averaged only 0.08 percent per annum over the period of the capital controls. Although 0.08 percent is statistically different from zero, it is not economically significant since transactions costs are most likely large enough to eliminate any profits from arbitrage activity.[9] Some of the observed differentials were several times as large as 0.08 percent, since the 95 percent band included differentials as large as 0.38 percent. But that is more likely to reflect imperfections in the data rather than genuine arbitrage opportunities open to bank traders. In studying the 1960s and 1970s, researchers have to contend with poorer data than are available today. In the case of the British market, the data are of relatively high quality coming from one source, the Bank of England. But the Bank of England data are not all synchronous, since the Paris market where the Eurosterling quotes originate closes one hour later than the London market where the Eurodollar and exchange rate quotes originate. So the few large differentials observed between the two markets may be due to interest rate movements in Paris in the last hour of trading.

To study the impact of controls in greater detail, I break up the sample period into three subperiods: (1) the last decade of the Bretton Woods period, 1961(4)–1971(4), (2) a period of flexible exchange rates when capital controls were still in place, 1973(1)–1979(6), and (3) the postcontrol period, (1979(7)–1991(3).[10] For each period, I study the differentials between the Eurosterling and British interest rates.

Table 3.2 reports the sample means of the interest differentials between the two markets, the standard errors of these means and their *p*-values, as well as the band within which 95 percent of the observations lie. To show the asymmetric nature of the controls, which inhibited *outward* flows but not inward flows, I report separate statistics for the positive differentials

9. Using bid/ask spreads to measure transaction costs associated with covered interest transactions, Clinton (1988) estimated that transactions costs were as low as 0.06 percent for a six-month period in 1985–6. Whether transactions costs were that low over the entire 29-year period is difficult to say in the absence of better data.

10. The effective end of Bretton Woods is assumed to occur in May 1971 when the mark and guilder began a period of floating and when the Swiss franc was revalued. There was an attempt to reestablish fixed parities in the Smithsonian Agreement reached in December 1971, but the new parities could not be sustained. The Bank of England stopped reporting Eurosterling interest rates in 1989, but Morgan Guaranty Trust's *World Financial Markets* reports Eurosterling rates through March 1991.

Table 3.2. *Interest differentials between the Eurosterling and British markets in percent per annum, 1961(4)-1991(3).*

	Bretton Woods period 1961(4)-71(4)	Flexible rates with controls 1973(1)-79(6)	Flexible rates w/o controls 1979(7)-91(3)
Number of observations	121	78	141
Average differential	0.78	1.50	-0.03
(standard error)	(0.22)	(0.20)	(0.01)
[*p*-value]	[0.001]	[0.000]	[0.015]
Band for 95 % of Observations	4.14	3.78	0.40
Positive observations			
% of observations	72.7	93.6	47.5
Average differential	1.15	1.61	0.06

Notes: See Table 3.1.

Source: Bank of England *Quarterly Bulletin*, various issues. The Bank of England's series for the Eurosterling rate ends in 1989, so the series is updated through March 1991 with data from Morgan Guaranty Trust's, *World Financial Markets*.

of the Eurosterling rate over the British interest rate. If the controls are asymmetric, the differentials should be predominantly positive, especially the large differentials found when the controls are most binding.

In the two periods when the British market was subject to controls, the interest differentials were quite substantial. During the Bretton Woods period, the differential averaged 0.78 percent with the 95 percent band occurring at a differential as large as 4.14 percent. In the flexible period, the average differential was even larger at 1.50 percent. In this latter period, 93.6 percent of the differentials were positive. In both periods, the mean differentials are statistically different from zero at the 1 percent level.

Once the controls were removed in 1979, the differential dropped to −0.03 percent with only 47.5 percent of the differentials being positive. Figure 3.1 illustrates how dramatically different were the differentials in

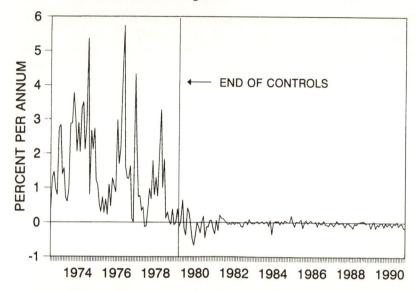

Figure 3.1. Eurosterling-British interest differentials: flexible rate period, 1973(1)–1991(3).

the postcontrol period. This figure shows the differential between the Eurosterling rate and the British interbank rate during the flexible rate period. A vertical line indicates when the controls were removed. Both Table 3.2 and Figure 3.1 show clearly that the controls had a very substantial effect on interest differentials, and therefore on the relative costs of financing in the British and external markets.

B.   U.S. controls

The second set of controls to be studied is the set of controls imposed on U.S. residents in the 1960s. The U.S. balance of payments deteriorated in the 1960s as the dollar became increasingly overvalued relative to other major currencies. In 1963, the Kennedy Administration responded by imposing an interest equalization tax on foreign securities purchased by Americans, but it was only in 1968 during the Johnson Administration that comprehensive capital controls were put in place. These controls restricted outflows of capital by both banks and nonbank residents. For example, under the Voluntary Foreign Credit Restraint Program, there were restrictions on lending abroad by commercial banks and nonbank financial institutions. There were also restrictions on direct investment under the Foreign Direct Investment Program.[11] These controls made it

11. The controls are described in the International Monetary Fund (1975).

PERCENT PER ANNUM

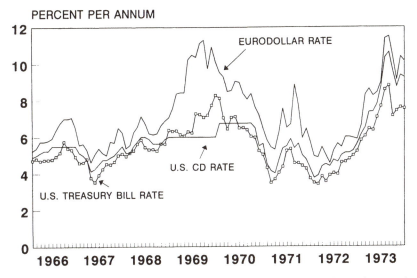

Figure 3.2. Eurodollar and U.S. interest rates: period of controls, 1966(1)–1973(12).

difficult to fund foreign operations from the United States, and led to large differentials between interest rates in U.S. markets and markets abroad, including the Eurodollar market. The effects of the capital controls were complicated by banking regulations that put ceilings on interest rates paid on bank deposits including certificates of deposit (CDs). Regulation Q of the Federal Reserve limited CD rates on three-month deposits to 6 percent through 1969 and 6.75 percent beginning in January 1970.

Figure 3.2 illustrates the combined effects of the controls and Regulation Q ceilings on interest rates in the major dollar markets. The figure shows that the interest rate ceiling resulted in an inversion of the normal relationship between Treasury bill (TB) rates and CD rates. In 1968 through 1970, the TB rate was often above the CD rate when the latter hit its ceiling. The effects of the capital controls are evident in the widening differentials between Eurodollar rates and Treasury bill rates. In 1969, that differential rose to over 4 percent per annum. With controls inhibiting funds flowing from the United States to London, the Eurodollar rate rose far above U.S. rates. A U.S. (or foreign) firm was able to raise funds much more cheaply in the United States, although, because of the controls, these funds could not generally be used for foreign operations.

Table 3.3 reports interest differentials between the Eurodollar and U.S. market for two time periods: (1) the period of U.S. capital controls, 1966(1)–1973(12), and (2) the postcontrol period, 1974(1)–1991(3). The control period extended into the period after the Bretton Woods system

Table 3.3. *Interest differentials between the Eurodollar and U.S. markets in percent per annum, 1966(1)-1991(3).*

	Control period, 1966(1)-73(12)		Postcontrol period, 1974(1)-91(3)
	Eurodollar minus U.S. certificate of deposit	Eurodollar minus U.S. Treasury bill	Eurodollar minus U.S. certificate of deposit
Number of observations	96	96	207
Average differential (standard error) [*p*-value]	1.35 (0.19) [0.000]	1.66 (0.13) [0.000]	0.48 (0.05) [0.000]
Band for 95 % of observations	4.17	3.16	1.44
Positive observations % of observations Average differential	100.0 1.35	100.0 1.66	94.2 0.51

Source: Morgan Guaranty Trust, *World Financial Markets*, various issues.

collapsed; so the division between control and postcontrol periods does not coincide very well with the division between fixed and flexible periods. The interest rates, end-of-month rates for three-month instruments, are drawn from Morgan Guaranty Trust's *World Financial Markets*. For the period of the controls, the table reports two sets of differentials: the Eurodollar-CD differential and the Eurodollar-Treasury bill differential. The latter differential is free of the distortions caused by the Regulation Q ceilings.

The table reveals large differentials during the control period. The differential between Eurodollar and CD rates averaged 1.35 percent with the 95 percent band occurring at a differential of 4.17 percent. The differential involving the Treasury bill rate was of similar size. Both sets of differentials are statistically different from zero at the 5 percent level. The capital controls were evidently binding for much of the period. In the post-control period, in contrast, the differential between the Eurodollar and CD rates averaged 0.48 percent with the 95 percent band occurring at a rate of 1.44 percent. In the next section, I explore why the differential did not become even smaller in the postcontrol period.

Comparing the control and postcontrol periods, it is evident that U.S. controls resulted in raising the relative costs of financing in the Eurodollar market by a little over 1 percent, and even more in 1969 and 1970 when interest differentials reached their peak. By cutting off the Eurodollar market from its national counterpart, moreover, the U.S. controls encouraged the development of the former. Firms that were not allowed to draw on U.S. markets for their financing naturally turned to the Eurodollar market.

C.   *Banking restrictions without capital controls: the U.S. case*

As reported in Table 3.3, the differential between the Eurodollar and CD rates from 1974 to 1991 averaged 0.48 percent. This differential is much smaller than during the control period, but much larger than the average differential in other markets after controls were removed. This differential can be explained in large part by banking regulations that required banks to hold reserves against deposits at U.S. banks and to pay insurance fees on these deposits. For much of the postcontrol period, reserve requirements on large time deposits including CDs were as high as 6 percent, while Eurodollar deposits were exempt from such requirements.[12] In addition, U.S. bank deposits were subject to Federal Deposit Insurance Corporation (FDIC) insurance fees, while Eurodollar deposits were exempt. So interest differentials between the two markets persisted.

Even in the presence of reserve requirements and insurance fees, interest rates in the two dollar markets should be closely linked. Consider the arbitrage activity that any interest differentials might induce.[13] A bank can raise funds in the CD market in New York and invest them in the Eurodollar market. The *effective* rate paid on funds obtained in the CD market (denoted i_{At}') is determined by the CD rate (i_{At}) adjusted for reserve requirements (q_A) and FDIC insurance fees (f_A) as follows:[14]

12. At times the U.S. authorities have imposed reserve requirements on liabilities of U.S. banks to their foreign branches, but not on the dollar deposits of these branches.
13. The analysis of arbitrage margins is based on a paper by Kreicher (1982).
14. The profit from arbitrage per dollar raised in the CD market is

$$[i_{St} \times (1 - q_A)] - (i_{At} + f_A)$$

since only $(1 - q_A)$ of any dollar is available for investment in the Eurodollar market.

$$i_{At}' = \frac{i_{At} + f_A}{1 - q_A} \tag{3.3}$$

The arbitrage margin available to banks is equal to the differential between the Eurodollar rate and the effective rate on CD funds:

$$i_{St} - \frac{i_{At} + f_A}{1 - q_A} = outward\ arbitrage\ margin \tag{3.4}$$

As long as this margin is *positive,* banks can make a profit from such arbitrage activity. If there is no risk involved, then banks will always ensure that Equation (3.4) is equal to zero (or negative), so that i_{At}' provides an *upper* bound on the Eurodollar rate. It is only an upper bound because investors, whose returns are dependent on interest differentials unadjusted for reserve requirements, may drive Eurodollar rates down to CD rates by shifting funds from one market to another.

If Eurodollar rates are low enough relative to CD rates, then *inward arbitrage* can also occur. For much of the postcontrol period, liabilities of U.S. banks to their branches abroad were subject to reserve requirements even though Eurodollar deposits at these branches were not subject to any reserve requirements. If q_s is the reserve requirement on liabilities to foreign branches, then the effective rate paid for Eurodollar funds is $i_s/(1 - q_s)$. Banks will raise funds from their branches if the cost of these Eurodollar funds, inclusive of the reserve requirement, is less than the effective rate paid on CD funds. The *inward* arbitrage margin measures the differential between these two alternative costs:

$$\frac{i_{At} + f_A}{1 - q_A} - \frac{i_{St}}{1 - q_s} = inward\ arbitrage\ margin \tag{3.5}$$

Note that the Eurodollar rate relevant to inward arbitrage is the offer rate rather than the bid rate.

The outward and inward arbitrage margins have been calculated using reserve requirements and FDIC fees applicable in each month of the period from January 1974 to March 1991 (when the Eurodollar series from Morgan Guaranty Trust ends).[15] As will be shown, there are only a few months when *inward* arbitrage is profitable; so the gap between Eurodollar and CD rates is determined primarily by outward arbitrage activity. Consider the following equation relating the Eurodollar rate to the *effective* CD rate:

15. Kreicher (1982) provides a useful chronology of reserve requirement changes, which I have updated. Like Kreicher, I assume that the large marginal reserve requirements in place in the 1979–80 period were not binding on the banks actively involved in arbitrage. Information on FDIC fees was obtained from FDIC annual reports and newspaper articles.

Table 3.4. *Interest rates in the Eurodollar and U.S. (CD) markets: postcapital control period, 1974(1)-1991(3).*

Dependent variable	Independent variables		
i_{St}	i_{At}'	Constant	R^2
Estimate[a]	1.05	-0.42	
(standard error)	(0.01)	(0.11)	0.99
[p-value]	[0.000][b]	[0.000]	
$i_{St} - i_{At}$	$i_{At}'-i_{At}$	Constant	R^2
Estimate	1.26	-0.07	
(standard error)	(0.16)	(0.07)	0.31
[p-value]	[0.098][b]	[0.299]	

[a] These equations are estimated using a generalized method of moments (GMM) estimator. The parameter estimates are the same as obtained with ordinary least squares, but the covariance matrix is adjusted for serial correlation and heteroskedasticity.
[b] The p-values for the coefficients, b_1 and b_2, test whether these coefficients are significantly different from *unity* rather than zero.

Sources: See Table 3.3.

$$i_{St} = a_1 + b_1 i_{At}' + U_{3t} \tag{3.6}$$

where U_{3t} is a disturbance. Table 3.4 reports this equation as estimated over the 1974–91 period. The equation shows that the effective CD rate explains a large portion of the total variance of the Eurodollar rate, although the coefficient of i_{At}', 1.05, is significantly different from one (at the 1 percent level).

A more revealing equation is one that shows how much of the *gap* between the Eurodollar and CD interest rates remains unexplained:

$$i_{St} - i_{At} = a_2 + b_2(i_{At}' - i_{At}) + U_{4t} \tag{3.7}$$

This equation relates the gap to the *difference* between the *effective* CD rate and the CD rate alone. The second equation in Table 3.4 shows that the CD variable has a coefficient, 1.26, which is insignificantly different from one at the 5 percent level. But since the equation has an adjusted R^2 of only 0.31, much of the variance in this interest rate gap remains unexplained.

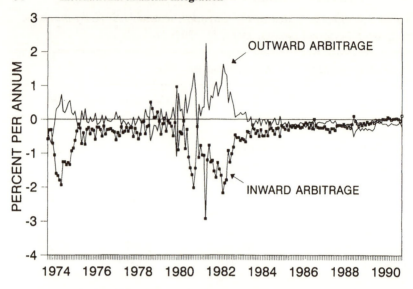

Figure 3.3. Eurodollar-U.S. CD rate differentials: rates adjusted by RR and FDIC fees.

Figure 3.3 tracks the outward and inward arbitrage margins available between 1974 and 1991. A positive margin indicates that arbitrage is profitable (before adjusting for risk). It is evident from the figure that *inward* arbitrage was profitable only for a few months in 1979 and 1980. *Outward* arbitrage, in contrast, is profitable for long periods in 1974–75 and in 1980–83. Both sets of years were free of capital controls; so higher interest rates in the Eurodollar market must be attributed to the market's assessment of risks.

The period of profitable arbitrage in 1974–75 coincides with the Herstatt Bank crisis. During that period, the market demanded risk premiums for bank deposit rates whether the deposits were in the U.S. or Eurodollar markets. The U.S. CD rate at times rose several percent above the Treasury bill rate as investors moved to the safety of government securities.[16] The Eurodollar rate, in turn, rose above CD rates, even when both deposits were at branches of the same bank, because of a perception that Eurodollar deposits were subject to greater default risk. Similar differentials emerged during the 1980–83 period when U.S. bank lending was coming

16. Over the whole postcontrol period, the average premium of CD rates over Treasury bill rates was 0.78 percent. Treasury bills are free of state and local income taxes; so even in the absence of default risk there would be a gap between TB and CD rates. With a marginal state and local tax rate of 5 percent and a CD rate of 10 percent, a gap of 0.50 percent can be attributed to taxes alone. See Cook (1986).

under increased scrutiny, especially after the Mexican debt crisis which began in August 1982.[17] So the "arbitrage margin" referred to may have instead simply been a default risk premium. The interest differential found in the postcontrol period suggests that investigators should be wary about ignoring default premiums when comparing national and Eurocurrency rates.

D.   German controls

As in the British and American cases, the German government resorted to capital controls in an attempt to shield domestic financial markets from international pressures. But German controls were designed to limit inflows rather than outflows of funds. So the controls resulted in a *negative* gap between interest rates in the Euromark market and the German market.

In the late 1960s, the mark came under attack periodically because of a widespread belief that it was undervalued relative to the dollar and other major currencies. In October 1969, the German authorities revalued the mark by 8.5 percent. But when the pressure on the mark resumed in 1971, the authorities imposed new capital controls inhibiting inflows from abroad in an attempt to limit further appreciation of the mark. The authorities introduced controls in stages in an attempt to plug leaks that developed around existing controls. Thus, for example, when banks were prohibited from raising foreign funds through deposits, nonbanks borrowed directly from foreigners. So the authorities imposed the "Bardepot" scheme, which required that a portion of such loans be deposited at the Deutsche Bundesbank in noninterest-bearing accounts. The controls eventually included bans on interest payments to foreigners, the imposition of cash deposits on borrowings abroad (initially 40 percent), restrictions on the purchase of domestic bonds by nonresidents, and, finally, general restrictions on borrowing abroad.[18] The move to flexible exchange rates in early 1973 reduced the incentives to invest in the German market, but it was not until February 1974 that the authorities began to remove the network of capital controls.

Table 3.5 reports evidence on the differential between the Euromark and German interbank rates starting in March 1972 when existing controls were tightened with the imposition of the "Bardepot" requirement. The table reports average interest differentials over three periods: (1)

17. Even without the debt crisis, higher interest rates might have increased default risk on CDs because higher rates increase the risk of default on bank loans.
18. The controls are described in Deutsche Bundesbank (1985) and Dooley and Isard (1980).

Table 3.5. *Interest differentials between the Euromark and German markets in percent per annum, 1972(3)-1991(3).*

	Tight controls 1972(3)-74(1)	Limited controls 1974(2)-81(2)	No controls 1981(3)-91(3)
Number of observations	23	85	121
Average differential	-4.62	-0.30	-0.16
(standard error)	(0.88)	(0.04)	(0.02)
[*p*-value]	[0.000]	[0.000]	[0.000]
Band for 95% of observations	-8.94	-0.93	-0.43
Negative observations			
% of observations	100.1	94.1	81.8
Average differential	-4.62	-0.34	-0.21

Sources: Euromark interest rate: OECD, *Financial Statistics Monthly* (computer diskette) for 1966-75; thereafter from Morgan Guaranty Trust, *World Financial Markets*. German interbank rate: MGT, *WFM*.

March 1972 to January 1974, a period when controls were tightest, (2) February 1974 to February 1981, a period when most controls had been lifted, and (3) March 1981 to March 1991, a period free of controls.

It is evident from the table that the controls were a major impediment to investments during the first period, since the average differential was −4.62 percent and the band for 95 percent of the observations was at −8.94 percent. Differentials that large would be inconceivable in periods free of controls. In this situation it paid multinational firms to finance as much as possible *outside* of Germany and to build up working balances behind the control barrier in Germany. Once the most onerous controls were lifted in February 1974, the differential fell to −0.30 percent during the rest of the decade and to −0.16 percent in the 1980s.[19] So by the early

---

19. The average differentials are statistically different from zero in all three periods. In the two noncontrol periods, however, the differentials are small enough to be attributable to minor differences in risk and other characteristics of the two instruments.

1980s, at least, the mark-denominated markets in London and Frankfurt were effectively integrated.

E.   Tracing the effects of capital controls: the German case

Capital controls are designed to insulate domestic markets from external markets. If the controls are airtight, then arbitrage activity (such as exists between the domestic and external dollar markets) is stifled completely. So it should not be possible to model the effects of the controls. At the other extreme, if controls take the form of a tax on interest earnings, then arbitrage keeps the after-tax interest on the taxed security tied to the tax-free interest on the untaxed security. So the controls can be modeled much like the reserve requirements on U.S. bank deposits. In most countries, capital controls fit neither extreme case. While most controls take the form of outright prohibition of certain types of activities, the effects of the controls on interest differentials depend on how difficult it is for banks and firms to set up alternative transactions that are still permitted within a network of controls.[20]

As previously discussed, the German authorities employed a number of different capital controls in an attempt to limit the appreciation of the mark following the breakdown of the Bretton Woods agreement. The Bardepot control, which required that a portion of foreign loans to nonbanks be deposited at the Deutsche Bundesbank in noninterest-bearing accounts, can be regarded as a tax akin to the reserve requirements on U.S. bank deposits. But other controls, such as the ban on the sale of domestic money market paper, impose unknown costs on German firms and banks. To model such controls effectively, we would have to know how firms and banks raise funds from abroad, if at all, when such bans occur. There are always loopholes in controls, but the costs involved in avoiding the controls are unknown in most cases.

For this reason, Dooley and Isard (1980) modeled the controls with a series of time dummy variables meant to capture the most important of the German controls. I will adopt a similar scheme, although I will not attempt to estimate a portfolio balance equation as they did. The following equations will show how much of the interest differential between Euro-mark and German interest rates can be explained by these control dummy

20. For an explicit model describing the evasion of controls in the context of a dual exchange market, see Gros (1988). Attempts to evade controls may increase over time as agents learn how to set up these alternative transactions, so the effectiveness of any given control may decline over time.

variables. The specific control variables (which differ somewhat from those of Dooley and Isard)[21] are as follows:

1. *Prohibition of interest on nonresident deposits:* Payment of interest was banned from June 1960 until December 1969 (following the appreciation of the mark in October 1969). The ban was reimposed in May 1971 and was not removed until September 1975.

2. *Ban on the sale of domestic money market paper to nonresidents:* This regulation was tied to the prohibition of interest except that it was not removed until August 1981.

3. *Cash deposit requirement for borrowing by nonbank residents from nonresidents (Bardepot):* This regulation, imposed in March 1972, required that borrowers deposit 40 percent of any new credits with the Deutsche Bundesbank in noninterest-bearing accounts. At first, credits under DM 2 million were exempt. The deposit was increased to 50 percent in July 1972, with the exemption reduced to DM 0.5 million. The deposit was reduced to 20 percent in February 1974 before being removed altogether in September 1974.

4. *Authorization for nonresident purchases of bonds:* This requirement was introduced in June 1972 (and extended to equities in February 1973). It was progressively relaxed beginning in February 1974 (with the maturities subject to the controls being lowered each time), but was removed only in March 1981.

5. *Authorization for domestic residents to borrow abroad* (including for trade credits): Introduced in February 1973, it was ended one year later in February 1974.

Each of these controls will be represented by a time dummy variable (labeled $D1$ to $D5$). Except for the Bardepot dummy variable ($D3$), all these variables are equal to one when the control is in effect and equal to zero otherwise. The Bardepot variable is treated as a varying tax on loans, with the tax equaling the percentage of the loan that must be deposited in the Bundesbank. So $D3$ is defined much like the reserve requirement variable in the preceding U.S. equations.

Table 3.6 reports an equation explaining the differential between the Euro-DM rate and the German interbank rate. The equation is of the form:

21. The most important difference is that I omit their variable representing differential reserve requirements on the bank deposits of foreigners. Since these reserve requirements were applied to marginal increases in deposits, it is difficult to know when these reserve requirements were binding.

Table 3.6. *EuroDM-German interbank interest differentials in percent per annum, 1966(1)-1991(3).*

	D1	D2	D3	D4	D5	Const.	R^2
$i_{Mt} - i_{Gt}$	0.11	-0.38	-5.25	0.33	-3.33	-0.26	
	(0.26)	(0.30)	(1.07)	(0.30)	(1.26)	(0.05)	0.71
	[0.680]	[0.210]	[0.000]	[0.269]	[0.009]	[0.000]	

Notes: The figures in parentheses below the coefficients are standard errors. The *p*-values are in square brackets.

Sources: See Table 3.5.

$$i_{Mt} - i_{Gt} = c_0 + \sum_{j=1}^{5} C_j D_j \qquad (3.8)$$

Of the five dummy variables representing capital controls, only two are statistically significant, $D3$ and $D5$. These variables represent controls imposed during the 1972–73 period when the German authorities were attempting to plug all channels for capital inflows in their attempt to prevent the appreciation of the mark. At the height of the controls from February 1973 to January 1974, these two variables alone explain an interest differential of -5.9 percent (compared with an average differential of -6.2 percent).[22]

Figure 3.4 compares the actual interest differential with the fitted values from the estimated equation. The control variables track much but not all of the movement of the differential in 1972–73. Dooley and Isard (1980) attribute most of the unexplained residual in their equation to political risk, the risk that the German authorities might impose even greater controls. I prefer to view the unexplained portion as a measure of our ignorance about how the controls actually affect the placement of funds. If we knew more about how controls work, including the technology for evading controls, we would be able to explain a larger portion of the interest differentials. The fact that dummy variables defined for the control periods explain so much suggests that the controls are driving the differentials. But we fall short of a true explanation of how these controls work.

22. The Bardepot variable (D3) was defined as equal to 0.5 during this period, so its effect is equal to 0.5 times its coefficient.

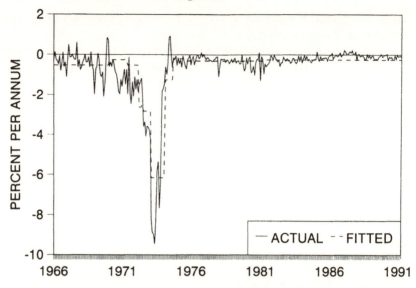

Figure 3.4. Euromark and German interest differential: actual and fitted, 1966(1)–1991(3).

F.   *Japanese controls*

Among the five countries studied, Japan is unique in maintaining controls on both inflows *and* outflows of funds. The Japanese government maintained a system of capital controls throughout most of the 1970s, although the regulations varied in intensity and effect.[23] From November 1973 to June 1974, for example, controls on the *outflow* of funds from Japan were tightened considerably. During this period of the first oil shock, residents were prohibited from holding short-term foreign government securities and were restricted in their holding of foreign currency. As a result, the normally positive forward premium on the yen became a forward discount, which at one point reached 28 percent per annum. With arbitrage between Japan and the external markets curtailed, the Euroyen rate rose far above Japanese interest rates. Between June 1977 and January 1979, in contrast, the controls were generally binding in the opposite direction, limiting inflows of funds to Japan. So during this period, Japanese interest rates exceeded the Euroyen rate by as much as 5 percent.

The study of Japanese capital controls is hampered by the lack of adequate data for both the Japanese and Euroyen markets. As already discussed, in the 1970s most Japanese interest rates were insensitive to market

23. Previous studies of Japanese capital controls include Frankel (1984), Ito (1986), and Otani and Tiwari (1981).

Figure 3.5. Euroyen and gensaki interest rates: January 1973–December 1983.

conditions. Bank deposit rates, for example, were set by banking regulations, while loan rates were tied informally to the discount rate. One important exception was the gensaki rate, the interest rate paid on repurchase agreements, which fluctuated freely in response to market conditions. The gensaki market was rather thin until at least 1975. Indeed, most published sources begin quoting gensaki rates only in the mid-1970s or later. The series I will employ is an unpublished series provided by the Bank of Japan.

Interest rates for the Euroyen market are available only beginning in January 1975 from published sources. Banks quoted Euroyen rates in the early 1970s, but the market was much smaller than the Euromark or Eurosterling markets, which were established in the early 1960s. Prior to 1975, the only way to obtain Euroyen rates was to use the same covered interest parity condition that banks use to generate Eurocurrency quotes. The resulting series, as shown in Figure 3.5, fluctuated sharply in 1973–74, but that is because the forward premium on the yen also fluctuated widely. It is not clear how to interpret these fluctuations. The forward market was limited in size by the "actual demand principle," which required that foreign exchange transactions by Japanese firms be related to certain approved transactions such as export or import payments. On the other hand, the range of variation of Euroyen rates is similar to that of the Eurofranc and Eurolira interest rates in the 1980s when speculative pressure led to large forward discounts on the franc and lira. In the case of those European currencies, forward discounts reflected expectations of possible realignments of these currencies within the European Monetary System. Whether the observed forward discounts on the yen during the oil crisis of 1973–74 reflect expected depreciations of the yen of similar size is difficult to determine.

Table 3.7 reports monthly interest differentials for the yen markets for the period from January 1973 to November 1991. The interest differentials are studied during three subperiods: (1) January 1973 to December 1974, a period when the speculative pressure against the yen was predominant;[24] (2) January 1975 to December 1980, a period when the controls led to a forward premium rather than discount on the yen; and (3) January 1981 to November 1991, a period free of most controls. The second period ends in December 1980, when the Foreign Exchange and Foreign Trade Law was enacted, eliminating most capital controls on short-term assets.[25] Prior to 1975, the Euroyen rate is replaced by the sum of the Eurodollar rate and the forward premium (also defined in logs as $\ln[F_{¥t}/S_{¥t}]$).

Table 3.7 illustrates how effective capital controls can be in driving wedges between national and Eurocurrency interest rates. According to this table, the premium of Euroyen rates over gensaki rates averaged 2.50 percent per annum during the first period of the controls. In several of the months, the differential favoring Euroyen was over 15 percent; so the controls on outflows must have been very effective. During the second period ending in 1980, the average premium dropped to a *negative* 1.18 percent. Here the incentive was to raise money abroad and invest in the Japanese market, but the controls clearly inhibited such activity. With a standard error of only 0.33 percent, this second differential is statistically different from zero. In the absence of controls, differentials of this size would induce immediate arbitrage activity by bank traders. The fifth row of the table reports the band for interest rate differentials within which 95 percent of the observations fall. That band includes differentials as large as 4.47 percent in the 1975–80 period.

Once the controls were removed following the December 1980 law, the differential dropped to 0.25 percent. This differential is statistically different from zero (given a standard error of 0.04 percent), but small enough

---

24. This period is also when no Euroyen quotes are available; so the differential is between the covered Eurodollar rate and the gensaki rate.
25. The December 1980 law established the principle that capital flows were free unless specifically prohibited. Under previous law, capital flows were restricted unless explicitly authorized. As early as May 1979, however, nonresidents were allowed to enter into gensaki agreements. See Ito (1986, p. 226).

Table 3.7. *Interest differentials between Euroyen and gensaki interest rates in percent per annum, 1973(1)-1991(11).*

	1973(1)-74(12)	1975(1)-80(12)	1981(1)-91(11)
Number of observations	24	72	131
Average differential	2.50	-1.18	0.25
(standard error)	(2.45)	(0.33)	(0.04)
[*p*-value]	[0.319]	[0.001]	[0.000]
Band for 95% of observations	17.22	4.47	0.83

Sources: Gensaki rate: three-month rate from Bank of Japan, *Economic Statistics Annual* (databank). Euroyen rate: three-month rate from Morgan Guaranty Trust, *World Financial Markets*, from 1976(1)-91(3); from Bank for International Settlements (databank) from 1975(1)-75(12); calculated using spot and forward rates from BOJ database from 1973(1)-74(12).

to be attributed to transactions costs.[26] Figure 3.5 illustrates how dramatically smaller were the differentials in the postcontrol period. A vertical line indicates when the controls were removed in December 1980. Both Table 3.7 and Figure 3.5 show clearly that the controls had a very substantial effect on interest differentials, and therefore on the relative costs of financing in the Japanese and external markets.

G.   French controls

French controls have an unusual history in that these controls were relaxed in the 1970s only to be tightened considerably after the election of President Mitterand in 1981. The exchange controls date back to a 1939 law, and at their height these controls were extensive enough to cover most

---

26. Transactions costs in the Euroyen market averaged about 0.14 percent in the 1981–88 period. (This estimate is based on bid/ask spreads using DRI data on Euroyen rates.) In addition, there was a 0.16 percent tax on gensaki transactions since gensaki agreements were subject to the securities transaction tax. [This estimate is from Ito (1986, p. 232).]

portfolio investment, direct investment, trade credits, as well as tourist expenditures by French residents.[27]

The controls were detailed enough to restrict the forward cover that exporters and importers could purchase as well as to limit the period during which exports could be financed or import payments prepaid. In 1981, for example, importers were prohibited from buying forward exchange altogether, while exporters could extent credit for only one month (after which foreign financing had to be obtained). In addition, importers could anticipate payment for goods by only two days prior to delivery. Similarly, under the *devise-titre* system, residents who wished to buy foreign securities were restricted to buying the foreign exchange from those residents who already held foreign securities.[28] In a partial liberalization of capital movements, the *devise-titre* system was dismantled in 1971, but, immediately upon election in 1981, President Mitterand reimposed it. Parallel regulations restricted direct investment.

The system of capital controls led to sharp divergences between domestic money market rates and Eurofranc rates in both the 1970s and 1980s. Table 3.8 presents interest differentials between Eurofranc and French interbank interest rates for three periods, the first two of which involved capital controls: (1) the period from 1973 until the Mitterand presidency, which began in April 1981, (2) the period under President Mitterand from May 1981 to March 1986, when the controls were at their height, and (3) the period from April 1986, when the government began relaxing the controls, to the end of the sample period in March 1991. The effects of the controls are evident in the interest differentials reported. During the 1970s, a differential of 1.46 percent separated domestic from foreign interest rates. Since the controls inhibited *outward* flows, the Eurofranc interest rate exceeded the French domestic rate by that percentage. After the controls were tightened in 1981, the differential rose to 2.75 percent on average, with the differential at 9.23 percent at least 5 percent of the period.

One distinctive element of the French controls is that they were in force during the first eight years of the European Monetary System (EMS). Because this system of fixed exchange rates was vulnerable to speculative attacks, a series of realignments led to depreciations of the franc relative to the mark (and other currencies). When a depreciation of the franc was anticipated, speculators would demand Eurofranc loans and sell the franc in the forward market. Both actions drove up Eurofranc rates relative to Euromark rates and relative to French interest rates (the latter being insu-

27. Among studies of French controls are Claassen and Wyplosz (1982), Wyplosz (1988), Giavazzi and Giovannini (1989), and Bodnar (1993).
28. The *devise-titre* was the exchange rate for these financial transactions. It was akin to the exchange rate for the "investment dollar" in the United Kingdom.

Table 3.8. *Interest differentials between Eurofranc and French interest rates in percent per annum, 1973(1)-1991(3).*

	Control period		Postcontrols
	1973(1)-1981(4)	*1981(5)-1986(3)*	*1986(4)-1991(3)*
Number of observations	100	59	60
Average differential	1.46	2.75	0.07
(standard error)	(0.22)	(0.55)	(0.06)
[*p*-value]	[0.000]	[0.000]	[0.290]
Band for 95% of observations	4.27	9.23	0.58

Sources: French interest rate, three-month French interbank rate, Morgan Guaranty Trust, *World Financial Markets*. Eurofranc rate, MGT, *WFM*, from 1976(1)-91(3); OECD, *Financial Statistics Monthly*, prior to 1976.

lated by the controls). Figure 3.6 shows the effects of speculation on the differential between Eurofranc and French interest rates during the EMS period beginning in March 1979. Particularly large differentials emerged prior to the realignments of October 1981, June 1982, and March 1983. Chapter 5 will discuss in detail the behavior of exchange rates and interest rates during these speculative attacks.

The latter half of the 1980s saw a major reversal in French financial policy. As the last chapter indicated, the French government began liberalizing time deposit rates in 1985 with the introduction of CDs in March 1985. In April 1986, the government also began to dismantle the network of capital controls by liberalizing trade credits. Following a realignment of the FF/DM rate by 6 percent in April 1986, the French government abolished the *devise-titre* system in May and removed most restrictions on trade financing in July. By January 1990, all restrictions had been removed on bank loans in francs to nonresidents and on banks' foreign exchange positions.[29] The impact on Eurofranc/domestic interest differentials is ap-

29. In June 1988, the European Community adopted an explicit timetable that called for eliminating all capital controls by July 1, 1990. The French completed their liberalization six months ahead of schedule.

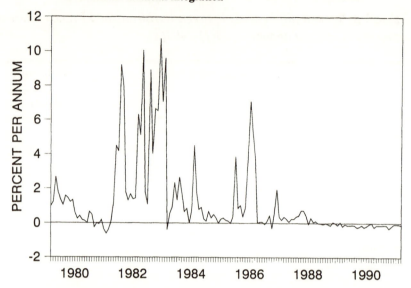

Figure 3.6. Eurofranc and French interest differential: EMS period, 1979(3)–1991(3).

parent in Table 3.8. In the five-year period beginning in April 1986 when restrictions on trade financing were first eased, the differential averages only 0.07 percent. So the London and Paris interbank markets for franc deposits are effectively merged with the remaining average differentials smaller than bid/offer spreads in either market.

III.   Concluding remarks

Although never as airtight as intended, capital controls in the G-5 countries disrupted financial linkages between national and international markets. At times, enormous interest differentials developed between national and Eurocurrency interest rates.

Because of the amorphous nature of the controls, however, it is very difficult to accurately explain how controls affected interest differentials. If the controls had consisted merely of taxes on interest payments, arbitrage operations would have kept Eurocurrency rates tied to (after-tax) domestic interest rates. But since most controls prohibited certain types of capital flows while permitting other flows, interest differentials depended on how easy it was to shift transactions through other channels. Since we know little about how banks and firms avoided controls, it is difficult to model the effects of the controls on interest differentials.

Once the G-5 countries had removed their controls, the national and Eurocurrency markets in each currency became effectively unified. Small differentials between national and Eurocurrency interest rates could still persist, whether due to reserve requirements or other factors. But by the early 1990s, the liberalization of capital flows had proceeded far enough that the distinction between national and international money markets, at least at the wholesale end, ceased to be important.

CHAPTER 4

Nominal interest differentials

If the major financial markets were completely deregulated and international capital flows were liberalized, the only notable interest differentials to be found would be those between currencies. Those interest differentials would depend primarily on expected changes in exchange rates. Today deregulation and liberalization have progressed to the point that such an idealized world is close to reality, at least with respect to some financial instruments in each national market. If we want to study such behavior using historical data, however, we cannot look at past national interest rates because so many of these rates were subject to regulation and control. Instead, we turn to the short-term Eurocurrency markets. These markets have always been free of the controls and conventions that have plagued national markets. For several of the currencies, Eurocurrency interest rates are available from the early 1960s; so it is possible to review interest rate behavior during both fixed and flexible exchange rate periods.

I.   Interest differentials under fixed and flexible rates

Under the Bretton Woods System of fixed exchange rates, which prevailed until 1971, each currency had a fixed value, or par value, relative to the dollar.[1] National monetary authorities were committed to holding their currencies within 1 percent "bands" relative to the par value. The ¥/$ rate, for example, could vary only within 1 percent of its par value of ¥ 360/$. With such fixed exchange rates, interest differentials would not necessarily be eliminated because exchange rates could move within the bands and because the fixed exchange rates themselves could be occasionally realigned. Figure 4.1 illustrates the bands for the DM/$ exchange rate. As is evident in the figure, the German authorities had to revalue their currency twice during the 1960s. In March 1961 the rate was lowered from DM 4.2/$ to DM 4/$, and in October 1969 the rate was lowered further to DM 3.66/$. Later in the chapter I discuss how the market reacts during the period immediately prior to the realignment.

---

1. Strictly speaking, all currencies including the dollar had a fixed value relative to gold, but market participants always focused on the dollar exchange rates.

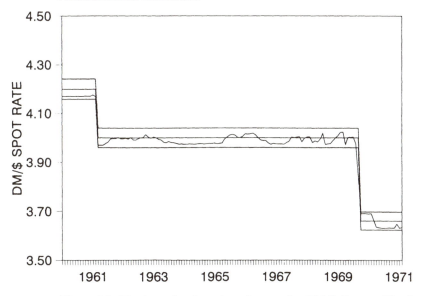

Figure 4.1. Fixed-rate bands and market rate for DM/$: Bretton Woods period, 1960–1971.

Despite occasional realignments, the Bretton Woods period was one of tranquility compared with the period of flexible exchange rates that followed. Figure 4.2 illustrates the movement of two important exchange rates, the DM/$ and ¥/$ rates, over the 33-year period from 1960 to 1992 spanning both exchange rate regimes. In this figure the ¥/$ rate is expressed in 100 ¥ to make the scale comparable to that of the DM/$ rate. It is evident from the figure that the breakdown of the Bretton Woods System in May 1971 is a watershed event that led to much greater variation in exchange rates.[2] The period since 1971 has seen substantial depreciation of the dollar relative to the mark and yen. Those trend depreciations, moreover, have been accompanied by sizable fluctuations around the trend. In the mid-1980s, in particular, the appreciation of the dollar temporarily reversed most of the prior fall of the dollar relative to the mark (with a smaller appreciation relative to the yen). So any trend movements of currencies relative to one another have been accompanied by substantial volatility.

Table 4.1 presents figures for one measure of such volatility, the standard deviation of monthly changes in exchange rates. Although calculated over one-month intervals, the standard deviations are measured in per

---

2. The next chapter studies interest rates and exchange rates in the European Monetary System.

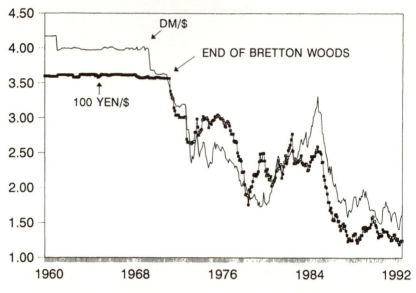

Figure 4.2. Spot rates: DM/$ and yen/$: January 1960–December 1992.

annum terms, as are the interest rates.[3] Standard deviations are reported both for the Bretton Woods period of fixed exchange rates until May 1971 and for the flexible rate period beginning in January 1973.[4] The table examines the dollar exchange rates for the G-5 countries in both nominal and real terms. The real exchange rates are defined as the relative price of non-U.S. to U.S. goods where the price level in each country is represented by the wholesale price index. In the case of the mark, for example, the real exchange rate is defined as $P_{Gt}/(S_{Mt}P_{At})$, where S_{Mt} is the DM/$ exchange rate, and P_{Gt} and P_{At}, are wholesale price indexes for Germany and the United States, respectively.

The table shows that exchange rates were considerably less variable during the Bretton Woods period. In the case of the ¥/$ rate, for example, the standard deviation is only 0.65 percent/annum during the Bretton Woods period, whereas it is 11.48 percent during the 1973–1992 period. The differences are less dramatic for the three other bilateral rates because they

3. If changes in exchange rates are independently distributed over time, then the variances of these changes should be proportional to time. So a variance measured in per annum terms is 12 times that measured in monthly terms. Annualized standard deviations, therefore, are obtained by multiplying by the square root of 12.
4. Several attempts were made to fix exchange rates during the period following the breakdown of Bretton Woods, but most major currencies were floating by early 1973.

Table 4.1. *Standard deviation of monthly percentage changes in dollar exchange rates, 1961(1)-1992(12).*[a]

	£/$	FF/$	DM/$	¥/$
Nominal rates				
61(1)-71(3)	4.42	3.44	2.42	0.65
73(1)-92(12)	11.88	11.99	12.48	11.48
Real rates[b]				
61(1)-71(3)	5.17	3.81[c]	2.95	1.68
73(1)-92(12)	12.13	11.97	12.73	11.32

[a] The standard deviations are measured in per annum terms.
[b] Real exchange rates are defined as the relative price of a country's goods to those of the United States. Wholesale price indexes are used.
[c] France's wholesale price index ends in 1985, so the consumer price index is used instead. The real exchange rate for France relative to the United States is defined using CPIs for both countries.

Source: International Monetary Fund, *International Financial Statistics*.

were all realigned during the 1960s.[5] Similar differences in volatility between the two periods are apparent for real exchange rates. In the case of the real exchange rate between the mark and dollar, for example, the standard deviation is over four times higher in the flexible rate period.

With exchange rates flexible after 1973, interest differentials naturally widened. Eurocurrency interest rates (for three-month maturities) are available beginning in 1963 for three of the five G-5 currencies.[6] The simple differential between the Eurosterling and Eurodollar interest rates (unadjusted for exchange rates) averaged only 1.67 percent/annum during the

5. In addition to the two revaluations of the mark in the 1960s, sterling was devalued from $ 2.80/£ to $ 2.40/£ in November 1967 and the French franc was devalued from FF 4.937/$ to FF 5.554/$ in August 1969.
6. Three-month Eurosterling and Eurodollar rates are available in the Bank of England *Quarterly Bulletin* as early as April 1961. Three-month Euromark and Eurodollar rates are available in the OECD *Financial Statistics Monthly* beginning in January 1963. Eurofranc and Euroyen interest rates are available only beginning in 1973.

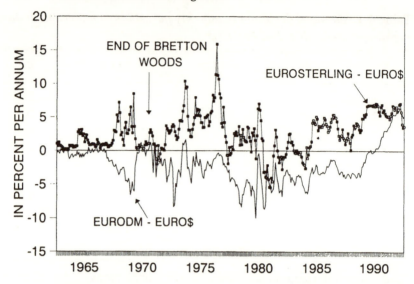

Figure 4.3. Interest differentials in Euro markets: January 1963–December 1992.

Bretton Woods period, compared with 3.20 percent during the period beginning in 1973. Similarly, the differential between Euromark and Eurodollar interest rates averaged −1.12 percent during Bretton Woods and −2.52 percent during the flexible rate period. These average differentials, however, do not tell the whole story. During the 1960s, there were occasionally some large interest differentials between the Eurodollar rate and other Eurocurrency rates. Figure 4.3 presents a graph of the two interest differentials referred to, the Eurosterling-Eurodollar differential and the Euromark-Eurodollar differential. In the three years beginning in 1968, both differentials widened considerably. In fact, the differentials then approached in magnitude those found in the flexible rate period. So financial markets were not entirely tranquil during this period. This should not be surprising since all three European currencies were realigned during the late 1960s.

II.   Risk aversion, market efficiency, and uncovered interest parity

For any individual investor or borrower, the interest differential that matters is one expressed in a single currency (although, as will be seen, this differential is not directly observable). Because almost all currencies are measured as the nondollar price of the dollar (e.g., DM/$ and ¥/$), it is more natural to express returns in nondollar currencies rather than in dollars.[7] Consider, then, a British investor who compares the return on a sterling-denominated deposit with the expected return, measured in sterling, on a dollar deposit. The expected sterling return from investing in dollars involves not only the nominal interest rate on dollar-denominated deposits (I_{s_t}) but also the cost of buying dollars at the current exchange rate $(S_{\pounds t})$ and selling dollars at some future expected exchange rate $(E_t S_{\pounds t+1})$. Thus the expected return on the dollar deposit, expressed in sterling, can be written:

$$\frac{E_t S_{\pounds t+1}}{S_{\pounds t}} (1 + I_{s_t})$$

With exchange rates flexible, the actual future exchange rate $(S_{\pounds t+1})$ can differ widely from its expected value, so the actual return from investing in dollars for a sterling-based investor can also differ widely from its expected value. This chapter will consider how the returns from investing or costs of borrowing in different currencies are related to one another.

A.   Uncovered interest parity

Uncovered interest parity (UIP) states that expected returns on investments in different currencies are the same when measured in a single currency. If the comparison is between Eurocurrency deposits in sterling and dollars, for example, uncovered interest parity requires that the expected return on Eurodollar deposits measured in sterling be the same as the (known) return on Eurosterling deposits:

$$(1 + I_{\pounds t}) = \frac{E_t S_{\pounds t+1}}{S_{\pounds t}} (1 + I_{s_t}) \tag{4.1}$$

Uncovered interest parity can also be expressed in terms of continuously compounded interest rates as follows:

$$i_{\pounds t} = \Delta x_{\pounds t} + i_{s_t}$$

where

$$i_{\pounds t} = \ln(1 + I_{\pounds t})$$
$$i_{s_t} = \ln(1 + I_{s_t})$$
$$\Delta x_{\pounds t} = E_t[\ln(S_{\pounds t+1}/S_{\pounds t})] \tag{4.2}$$

---

7. The major exception is the pound sterling, which is usually measured as the dollar price of the pound. The pound is expressed differently because, prior to the 1970s, the pound was a nondecimal currency; so foreign exchange traders preferred to express exchange rates in terms of other (decimal) currencies. For all statistical tables in this study, the pound-dollar exchange rate is measured in £/$ to conform with practices in other exchange markets.

Equation (4.2) states that the Eurosterling rate should be equal to the Eurodollar rate plus the expected depreciation of sterling relative to the dollar, $\Delta x_{\pounds t}$.[8]

The *expectations theory* of the forward rate, which states that the forward premium is equal to the market's expectation of future depreciation, is closely related to uncovered interest parity. If $f_{\pounds t}$ is the forward premium defined as $\ln(F_{\pounds t}/S_{\pounds t})$, then the expectations theory states that

$$f_{\pounds t} = \Delta x_{\pounds t} \tag{4.3}$$

It is easy to show that the two expressions for the expectations theory [Equation (4.3)] and uncovered interest parity [Equation (4.2)] are identical as long as *covered* interest parity holds.[9] So testing uncovered interest parity is nearly identical to testing the expectations theory of the forward rate, the only difference being due to deviations from covered interest parity attributable to such factors as transaction costs. Some of the previous studies (to be cited) actually tested the expectations theory rather than uncovered interest parity, but the results of testing the latter should be nearly identical.

Actual returns on Eurocurrency deposits will generally not be equal to expected returns because of forecast errors in predicting future spot rates. As will be evident, forecast errors in the exchange market are quite sizable; so differences between expected and actual returns can also be quite sizable in any individual period. The forecast error, $u_{\pounds t}$, in period t is defined as follows:

$$u_{\pounds t} = \Delta s_{\pounds t} - \Delta x_{\pounds t} \tag{4.4}$$

where $\Delta s_{\pounds t} = \ln(S_{\pounds t+1}/S_{\pounds t})$ is the actual percentage change in the spot rate. If the exchange market is "efficient," then this forecast error should be a serially uncorrelated random variable with an expected value of zero.

As Levich (1985) and others have emphasized, it is not possible to test market efficiency by itself because efficiency is always defined relative to some model for pricing assets. The pricing model under discussion here is uncovered interest parity, and in the next section after discussing alternative hypotheses I will present tests of the joint hypotheses of uncovered interest parity and market efficiency.

---

8. The same equation (4.2) can be interpreted alternatively as measuring returns in dollars. In that case, the expected return on the Eurosterling deposit measured in dollars, defined as $i_{\pounds t} - \Delta x_{\pounds t}$, is equal to the certain return on the Eurodollar deposit i_{st}. But as pointed out by Siegel (1972), if expected returns in sterling are equal as in Equations (4.1) or (4.2), then because of Jensen's inequality expected returns cannot be equal when reexpressed in dollars. McCullough (1975) argues that the discrepancy between returns due to Jensen's inequality is empirically insignificant.

9. Recall from Chapter 3 that covered interest parity (for continuously compounded interest rates) can be written as $i_{\pounds t} = i_{st} + f_{\pounds t}$.

Table 4.2. *Decomposition of standard deviations of changes in spot exchange rates, 1973(6)-1992(12) (under assumption of uncovered interest parity).*

Standard deviations (in percent per annum)	£/$	FF/$	DM/$	¥/$
STD of percentage change in spot exchange rate	11.93	11.74	12.09	11.35
STD of interest differential	0.96	1.08	0.90	1.67
STD of forecast error	12.12	11.86	12.18	11.44

Sources: Exchange rates: *International Financial Statistics*; Eurocurrency interest rates: Data Resources, Inc. and Reuters databanks.

In the meantime it is interesting to obtain a preliminary measure of the size of forecast errors. Under the null hypotheses of UIP and market efficiency, this can be done simply by subtracting the interest differential from the actual change in the spot rate using Equation (4.5), which combines Equations (4.2) and (4.4):

$$u_{£t} = \Delta s_{£t} - (i_{£t} - i_{\$t}) \qquad (4.5)$$

Table 4.2 reports the standard deviations of each of the components of Equation (4.5) for the four dollar exchange rates between the G-5 currencies. The Eurocurrency interest rates are for one-month deposits with the data series beginning in June 1973. The series thus begins within a few months after the start of the flexible rate period.[10]

The first row of the table reports the standard deviation of the change in the spot rate expressed in annual terms, while the second and third rows

10. The one-month Eurocurrency interest rate series, obtained from Data Resources Inc., begins only in June 1973. Although any such timing is arbitrary, the flexible rate period is often said to have begun in March of 1973 when Germany permitted its currency to float. I am grateful to Robert Korajczyck for providing the data. The series were updated to December 1992 using Eurocurrency rates from the Reuters database.

give the standard deviations of the interest rate differential and forecast error, respectively. The standard deviation of the change in the spot rate greatly exceeds the standard deviation of the interest differential, an empirical regularity of flexible exchange rates that has been noted by a number of previous authors.[11] For every currency, moreover, the standard deviation of the forecast error is as large as that of the spot rate itself.[12] Thus even if the assumption of uncovered interest parity holds, the interest differential explains only a small fraction of the total variance of changes in exchange rates. The rest of the variance is attributable to forecast errors. With so much "noise" in the exchange rate series, it is not surprising that it is extremely difficult to distinguish between one pricing model (such as uncovered interest parity) and another.

B.   Simple tests of uncovered interest parity

If uncovered interest parity does not hold, then the decomposition of changes in exchange rates is not so easily accomplished. In that case, the interpretation of the error term in Equation (4.5) depends on the particular pricing model employed.

Some of the evidence against uncovered interest parity is quite compelling. Consider a simple test of UIP that has been employed in many previous studies such as Bilson (1981), Cumby and Obstfeld (1984), and Fama (1984).[13] This test involves the regression of the actual change in the spot rate on the interest differential:

$$\Delta s_{\pounds t} = a + b\,\delta_{\pounds t} + v_{\pounds t} \qquad\qquad (4.6)$$

where $\delta_{\pounds t} = i_{\pounds t} - i_{s t}$ is the simple interest differential. Under the joint hypothesis of uncovered interest parity and market efficiency (which ensures that $v_{\pounds t}$ is uncorrelated with $\delta_{\pounds t}$), the coefficient of $\delta_{\pounds t}$, the slope b, should be equal to one and the intercept a equal to zero.

Perhaps because forward exchange rates were more readily available than Eurocurrency interest rates, many past studies regressed $\Delta s_{\pounds t}$ on the forward premium, $f_{\pounds t}$, rather than on the interest differential.[14] Tests in the latter form, which are equivalent to Equation (4.6) as long as covered interest parity holds, are often called "speculative efficiency" tests because

---

11. See Mussa (1979), for example.
12. For all four exchange rates, the standard deviation of the forecast error actually exceeds that of the actual change in the spot rate. This can only be the case if the correlation between the interest differential and forecast error in Equation (4.5) is negative, thus violating one of the assumptions of the model. The correlation coefficient is not statistically significant, however, so I will not discuss this feature in detail.
13. Other studies are cited in the survey by Hodrick (1987).
14. In the 1970s, many studies reported regressions of the *level* of the future spot rate ($S_{\pounds t}$) on the level of the forward rate ($F_{\pounds t}$). Hodrick (1987, pp. 27–31) discusses the econometric

they test the joint hypothesis of market efficiency and the expectations (or speculative) theory of the forward rate. Since covered interest rate parity holds so well for the Eurocurrency markets, tests of uncovered interest parity using Eurocurrency data and tests of speculative efficiency are treated as interchangeable.

Table 4.3 reports regressions for the four dollar exchange rates analyzed previously. The regressions relate the change in each spot rate to interest differentials from one-month Eurocurrency markets. Estimation extends from June 1973 to December 1992. The table reports estimates of a and b together with p-values (in square brackets) for tests of $a = 0$ and $b = 1$. The numbers in parentheses below each estimate are heteroskedasticity-consistent standard errors.[15]

Consider first the estimates of b, the coefficient of the interest differential. All but one of these estimates are negative rather than being equal to one. (The yen is the exception with an estimate of 0.12.) A negative b indicates that an increase in the interest differential, foreign minus Euro-dollar rates, leads to a *fall* in the expected depreciation of the foreign currency rather than an increase as predicted by UIP. A negative coefficient for b is a common finding in tests of this type.[16] Because the exchange rate series are so volatile, however, the standard errors are large. The numbers in square brackets below the estimates for b give the p-value for testing $b = 1$. Only one of the four exchange rates has an estimate for b that is significantly different from one at the 5 percent level. In addition, one of the equations has a constant (a) that is significantly different from zero. The last row of the table reports the Wald-statistic, which tests the joint hypothesis that $a = 0$ and $b = 1$. This statistic is distributed as χ^2 with two degrees of freedom. In the case of the equation for sterling, the joint hypothesis is clearly rejected (with a p-value of 0.000). For the other three currencies, the hypothesis is not rejected at a 10 percent level, although the estimates are numerically far from their theoretical values.

These estimates, therefore, provide little support for the joint hypothesis of UIP and market efficiency, although in only one equation, that for sterling, are the coefficients significantly different from their hypothesized values. The very low R^2s suggest that the equations are explaining only a fraction of the variance of changes in the spot rate.

problems that arise in this specification from the fact that exchange rates in levels are nonstationary or nearly nonstationary.

15. The standard errors are corrected using White's (1980) procedure. For evidence on heteroskedasticity in Eurocurrency returns, see Cumby and Obstfeld (1984). Several studies investigate whether changes in exchange rates follow non-normal distributions, among them Westerfield (1977) and Rogalski and Vinso (1978), while others such as Hsieh (1988) test whether exchange rate changes come from normal distributions whose means and variances change over time. For further discussion, see Hodrick (1987, pp. 24–27).

16. Froot and Thaler (1990, p. 182) cite results from 75 published estimates.

Table 4.3. *Tests of unbiasedness in the Eurocurrency markets,*
1973(6)-1992(12): changes in spot rates related to interest differentials
expressed in percent per annum.

	£/$	FF/$	DM/$	¥/$
Constant (a)	9.11	3.06	-4.31	-3.60
(s.e.)[a]	(3.31)	(3.46)	(3.68)	(2.66)
[p-value][b]	[0.002]	[0.376]	[0.243]	[0.177]
Interest differential	-1.96	-0.65	-0.93	0.12
(s.e.)	(0.71)	(0.96)	(1.08)	(0.55)
[p-value][c]	[0.000]	[0.085]	[0.076]	[0.112]
R^2	.025	.004	.005	.001
Wald-statistic	17.59	3.08	3.17	3.38
[p-value][d]	[0.000]	[0.214]	[0.204]	[0.185]

[a] The numbers in parentheses are heteroskedasticity-consistent standard errors.
[b] The p-value is for the t-test of $a=0$.
[c] The p-value is for the t-test of $b=1$.
[d] The Wald-statistic tests the joint hypothesis $a=0$ and $b=1$. It is distributed as χ^2 with 2 degrees of freedom. The p-value is given below the statistic.

Sources: Same as Table 4.2.

    As a further test of the joint hypothesis, the four dollar exchange rates of the G-5 countries were estimated as one system. Then a Wald test was performed to test whether $b = 1$ in all four equations. The resulting χ^2 statistic is equal to 29.2; so the $b = 1$ restriction is rejected at the 1 percent level.[17] The test based on joint estimation for the four exchange rates thus leads to more definitive results than the tests based on individual equation estimation.
    If the joint hypothesis of uncovered interest parity and market efficiency is rejected in tests of this form, why is it rejected? Many studies have assumed that the rejection occurs because UIP does not hold. These studies

17. The χ^2 statistic has four degrees of freedom. The critical value at the 1 percent level is 13.3.

have then searched for alternatives to UIP based on risk aversion. Because a joint hypothesis has been tested, however, it is not obvious that it is a breakdown of uncovered interest parity that leads to the rejection. So another set of studies have asked whether the rejection of the joint hypothesis could be due to market inefficiencies. Such inefficiencies could lead to systematic forecast errors that bias tests of the joint hypothesis. The next two sections of the chapter discuss these alternatives.

C.   Risk premiums

The most commonly suggested alternative to uncovered interest parity is an asset pricing model with risk-averse investors. If investors are risk-averse, expected returns on different Eurocurrency deposits may differ by a risk premium.[18] In that case, Equation (4.2) is replaced by

$$i_{£t} = i_{$t} + \Delta x_{£t} + \rho_{£t} \tag{4.7}$$

where $\rho_{£t}$ is the risk premium. If $\rho_{£t}$ is positive, for example, investors require a risk premium on the pound sterling relative to the dollar. If the risk premium were known to be constant, then it would be relatively easy to distinguish between the alternative hypotheses (4.2) and (4.7). But most theoretical models of international asset pricing imply that there is a *time-varying* risk premium.[19]

   It is easy to show why a time-varying risk premium complicates the interpretation of tests of uncovered interest parity. Consider Regression (4.6), relating the change in the spot rate to the simple interest differential. If there is a time-varying risk premium, as given by Equation (4.6), the estimate of b should not be equal to one. Using Equations (4.4) and (4.7) the estimated slope is given by[20]

$$
\begin{aligned}
b &= \frac{\mathrm{COV}(\Delta s_{£t}, \delta_{£t})}{\mathrm{VAR}(\delta_{£t})} \\
&= \frac{\mathrm{VAR}(\Delta x_{£t}) + \mathrm{COV}(\Delta x_{£t}, \rho_{£t})}{[\mathrm{VAR}(\Delta x_{£t}) + \mathrm{VAR}(\rho_{£t}) + 2\,\mathrm{COV}(\Delta x_{£t}, \rho_{£t})]}
\end{aligned}
\tag{4.8}
$$

18. Even with risk neutrality, expected returns on Eurocurrency deposits may differ because of the covariance between inflation and the nominal return on deposits. As Frenkel and Razin (1980) and Engel (1984) show, the covariance term drives a wedge between nominal returns in the two currencies, but real returns are the same regardless of how they are expressed. Most observers believe that uncovered differentials cannot be explained by such covariances. See the evidence in Cumby (1988).

19. Among models of international asset pricing are Solnik (1974), Grauer, Litzenberger, and Stehle (1976), Sercu (1980), and Stultz (1981). Three useful surveys are Adler and Dumas (1983), Dumas (1992), and Lewis (1994).

20. This expression only holds, however, if the market is assumed to be efficient. Without that assumption, there would be additional terms in Equation (4.8) involving the covariance between the forecast error and other terms.

As pointed out by Fama (1984), the estimated slope can depart significantly from one to the extent that the risk premium is correlated with the expected change in the exchange rate so that $\text{COV}(\Delta x_{Mt}, \rho_{Mt}) \neq 0$.

As seen in the last section, for many currencies the estimated slope coefficient is not only significantly different from one, but actually *negative*. Fama (1984) provides an interesting interpretation of these results. For b to be negative, the covariance between the expected change in the exchange rate and the risk premium, $\text{COV}(\Delta x_{\pounds t}, \rho_{\pounds t})$, must be negative. But then it is easy to show that the covariance is bounded (in absolute value) by the variance of the risk premium and the variance of the expected change in the exchange rate:

$$\text{VAR}(\rho_{\pounds t}) > |\text{COV}(\Delta x_{\pounds t}, \rho_{\pounds t})| > \text{VAR}(\Delta x_{\pounds t})$$

So the variance of the risk premium is actually *larger* than that of the expected change in the spot rate. If this interpretation is correct, then the risk premium is not only of theoretical interest, but is quantitatively more important than the expected depreciation ($\Delta x_{\pounds t}$) in explaining changes in exchange rates.

A negative b is not necessary for this result. The variance of the risk premium is larger than the variance of the expected change in the spot rate as long as $b < 0.5$. Consider a simple transformation of Equation (4.6):[21]

$$\Delta s_{\pounds t} = a + \delta_{\pounds t} + (b - 1)\delta_{\pounds t} + v_{\pounds t} \tag{4.6'}$$

In this equation, the first three terms represent the expected change in the exchange rate, and the first and third terms represent the risk premium. So the variance of the expected change in the exchange rate is proportional to $(b)^2$, while the variance of the risk premium is proportional to $(b - 1)^2$. For any $b < 0.5$, the variance of the former must be smaller than that of the latter.

Although many studies have attributed the bias found in estimates of UIP equations to a risk premium, there is little *direct* evidence for the existence of such a risk premium. The available evidence is based on either the static capital asset pricing model (static CAPM), which focuses exclusively on asset returns, or the intertemporal model of asset pricing, which examines consumption and asset decisions simultaneously (consumption CAPM).

Adler and Dumas (1983) survey the development of static CAPM beginning with the work of Solnik (1974). As Solnik's work established, the standard, one-factor version of static CAPM generally breaks down when extended to the international setting. In its place is a multifactor model, the exact form of which varies depending on the assumptions. In one com-

---

21. This discussion follows Dumas (1992, pp. 21–22).

mon formulation of international CAPM, investors form two portfolios: The first is common to investors from all countries, while the second is specific to each country's investors. In Solnik's (1974) original version of the model, inflation is nonstochastic; so investors hold equities only in the first portfolio. This means that equity holdings are the same *regardless* of nationality. In actual fact, investors from different countries have a strong *home equity bias*. As shown by French and Poterba (1991) and by Tesar and Werner (1992), most national investors hold equity portfolios with less than 10 percent foreign stocks. In the more general model considered by Adler and Dumas (1983), where the assumption of nonstochastic inflation is relaxed, home equities are held in the second (nation-specific) portfolio in order to hedge inflation risk. But, as Dumas (1992, p. 16) points out, inflation risk is unlikely to be large enough to explain the low degree of international diversification actually observed.

Consumption-based asset pricing models imply that expected returns on a risky asset should be related to the conditional covariance between the intertemporal marginal rate of substitution and the return on the risky asset. Most studies, using either U.S. or international data, have found little support for this model. Perhaps the most promising findings are in Cumby (1988) who uses a version of consumption CAPM due to Stulz (1981). Cumby develops an empirical measure of the conditional covariance of changes in consumption with real asset returns. In the case of three out of five currencies, he is able to reject the hypothesis that the conditional covariances are constant over time (so they are potentially able to explain time-varying risk premia). And he is unable to reject the hypothesis that the conditional covariances are proportional to one another (which means that all the returns could be related to a single benchmark portfolio). But then he investigates whether actual returns can be explained by such conditional covariances by regressing the ratio of returns on two currencies on the ratio of conditional covariances between changes in consumption and asset returns. He finds no significant relationship.

Because it is so difficult to find direct evidence of risk premiums, Hansen and Hodrick (1983) propose a way to test the restrictions of CAPM indirectly.[22] Suppose that returns on assets i and j can be related to returns on a single benchmark portfolio derived from the consumption CAPM. Then the returns on assets i and j should be related to one another. If these returns are regressed on variables currently observed, there will be restrictions on the coefficients in the regressions that can be tested. Hansen and Hodrick are unable to reject the model's restrictions, but Hodrick

---

22. Gibbons and Ferson (1985) independently developed a similar test for U.S. assets.

and Srivastava (1984) are able to reject them using a larger data set and using forward premiums rather than past forecast errors as instruments. Cumby (1988) is also able to reject these restrictions in the study mentioned previously. In a later section, I report the results of such a test using the 20 years of Eurocurrency returns introduced earlier.

So the existing direct and indirect evidence in favor of a risk premium is pretty weak. This has stimulated research that investigates the other key assumption in studies of UIP, the assumption of market efficiency. In the next section I discuss this work in the context of the broader issue of whether forecast errors are systematic.

D.   Systematic forecast errors

Departures from uncovered interest parity can be unambiguously interpreted as evidence of risk premiums only if market efficiency is *assumed* to hold. Like all tests of asset pricing models, tests of uncovered interest parity are joint tests, in this case resting on the two assumptions of UIP and market efficiency. But rejections of a joint hypothesis may be due to breakdowns in either set of assumptions.

Bilson (1981), in fact, chooses to interpret regressions like those in Table 4.3 as evidence of market inefficiencies rather than risk premiums. He shows that trading rules based on the estimated equations yield profits in the postsample period that are statistically and economically significant. In interpreting profits from trading rules, investigators always have to ask whether these profits are simply rewards for risk. Bilson calculates the profit/risk tradeoff: For every dollar the speculator expects to make, the confidence limits range from a loss of approximately $1 to a gain of approximately $3. This represents a very favorable return/risk tradeoff. Hodrick and Srivistava (1984) examine trading rules like Bilson's and find a somewhat less favorable reward/risk tradeoff.[23] In both studies, risk is measured by the standard deviation of returns on the currency position, whereas in theory risk should be measured using an asset pricing model such as the consumption CAPM. So the lack of an empirically acceptable asset pricing model limits progress in assessing such trading rules.

Even if trading rules generate risk-adjusted profits, this by itself does not necessarily imply market inefficiencies. The trading rule profits may be due to systematic forecast errors even though market participants are processing information in a rational manner. There are at least two reasons for systematic, but rational, forecast errors.

23. Hodrick (1987, pp. 70–84) discusses other studies using trading rules.

First, there may be discrete shifts in regimes that are expected but not realized in a particular sample period. This phenomenon has been called the "peso problem" (in reference to the behavior of the Mexican peso prior to its devaluation in 1976).[24] Peso problems can be found in fixed exchange rate periods when parity changes are possible, but they may also occur in flexible rate periods if major shifts in policy regimes are expected. Engel and Hamilton (1990) provide evidence that the dollar has experienced several such regime shifts since the advent of floating in 1973.[25] If market participants anticipate a regime shift, they may systematically overestimate or underestimate changes in exchange rates until the regime shift occurs.

Forecast errors may be systematic also because market participants may be learning about changes in regimes that have occurred. Lewis (1989), for example, develops a model in which market participants update their expectations using Bayesian methods. She shows how departures from uncovered interest parity in the early 1980s are consistent with a model in which market participants reacted to changes in Federal Reserve operating procedures in 1979 by systematically revising their expectations as evidence accumulated about these changes. During this learning process, forecast errors will be systematically related over time. She notes, however, that during the 1980s actual forecast errors did not seem to die out over time, contrary to what should be observed if investors were learning about a once-for-all shift in operating procedures.[26]

To illustrate the potential empirical significance of systematic forecast errors, consider interest differentials during the Bretton Woods period of fixed exchange rates during the 1960s. Three of the Eurocurrency markets have interest rates extending back into the 1960s. Table 4.4 provides some evidence of peso phenomena during the 1960s, specifically prior to the devaluation of sterling in November 1967 and the revaluation of the mark in October 1969. Suppose that a devaluation or revaluation is anticipated in the sense that market participants assign some probability to a change in parity occurring. Then there should be ex post deviations from uncovered interest parity until the change in parity actually occurs. Table 4.4 compares uncovered interest differentials for the whole Bretton Woods period (starting when Eurocurrency data became available) with differentials for the periods ending prior to these changes in parities.[27] The results

24. For a concise discussion of the peso problem, see Froot and Thaler (1990). Rogoff (1979) was among the first to discuss this phenomenon.
25. Nonetheless, Engel and Hamilton are able to reject uncovered interest parity.
26. If the regime shifts frequently, however, then errors might persist indefinitely.
27. In the case of sterling, the period ends in July 1967 because the three-month return beginning at the end of August overlaps with the November devaluation. The mark was

Table 4.4. *Uncovered interest differentials under Bretton Woods, sample periods including and excluding changes in parities, in percent per annum, 1961(4)-1971(4).*[a]

	Eurosterling-Eurodollar		Euromark-Eurodollar	
	Prior to 1967 devaluation 61(4)-67(7)	Bretton Woods period 61(4)-71(1)	Prior to 1969 revaluation 63(1)-69(5)	Bretton Woods period 63(1)-71(1)
Uncovered Differential[b]	1.20	0.15	-1.14	0.01
(s.e.)	(0.30)	(1.27)	(0.37)	(0.70)
[*p*-value]	[0.000]	[0.907]	[0.003]	[0.991]

[a] The devaluation of sterling occurred in November 1967, so the three-month return from the end of August to the end of November 1967 reflects the devaluation of sterling. Accordingly, the sample period excluding the devaluation ends in July 1967. The mark was revalued in October 1969, but it was floated on September 28, so the last observation is in May 1969.
[b] The standard errors are corrected for serial correlation and heteroskedasticity.

suggest that these parity changes may have been anticipated. If the sample period for sterling returns ends prior to the sterling devaluation of November 1967, the average uncovered differential is 1.20 percent in favor of sterling relative to the dollar. The higher return for sterling compensated the dollar-based investor for the expected capital loss due to the devaluation of sterling. If the sample period for the mark ends prior to the mark revaluation in September 1969, the average uncovered differential is 1.14 percent in favor of the dollar relative to the mark. In this case, the higher return for the dollar compensated the investor for the expected gain on the mark due to its revaluation. In both cases, the average interest differentials are statistically different from zero (at the 1 percent level).[28] For

floated on September 28 and formally revalued on October 24, 1969; so the last observation is in May 1969 with the return defined over the May to August period.
28. Using overlapping monthly observations of three-month holding period returns introduces a moving-average term to the residuals. The standard errors of the uncovered interest differentials have been adjusted for serial correlation as well as heteroskedasticity.

both sets of currencies, however, the uncovered interest differentials are very close to zero over the whole sample period. The differential for sterling relative to the dollar is only 0.15 percent and for the mark relative to the dollar only 0.01 percent once the change in parities is included in the sample period.

Systematic forecast errors may help to explain the evidence of bias in the uncovered interest parity relationship as shown in Table 4.3. To see this, consider an alternative to Fama's decomposition of the slope b in Equation (4.6) testing for UIP.[29] If risk premiums are constant rather than time-varying in Equation (4.7), but if forecast errors in Equation (4.4) are systematically related to expected changes in exchange rates, then the slope can be written:

$$b = \frac{\text{VAR}(\Delta x_{\pounds t}) + \text{COV}(\Delta x_{\pounds t}, u_{\pounds t})}{\text{VAR}(\Delta x_{\pounds t})} \qquad (4.8')$$

If a negative slope is reported as in Table 4.3, this may simply reflect a negative covariance between the expected change in the exchange rate and the forecast error. A negative covariance implies that a rise in the exchange rate is associated with a fall in the forecast error in predicting that exchange rate. Lewis (1994) shows how a Bayesian learning process can result in such a negative covariance, thus lending some support to this alternative to Fama's risk premium explanation.

III.   Unconditional and conditional estimates of uncovered interest differentials

The evidence against uncovered interest parity shown in Table 4.3 is compelling. Yet it is difficult to know whether risk premiums or systematic forecast errors account for departures from UIP. In this section I investigate uncovered interest differentials in more detail.

A.   Unconditional estimates

I begin with a simple question too often neglected in the literature on UIP: How large are the departures from UIP *on average*? If UIP differentials are due to risk premiums, how large are risk premiums on average? If UIP differentials are due to forecast errors, how large are forecast errors on average?

---

29. For a similar decomposition, see Froot and Frankel (1989) and Lewis (1994).

Table 4.5. *Unconditional estimates of uncovered interest differentials: one-month and three-month Eurocurrency interest rates in percent per annum, 1973(6)-1992(12).*

One-month Eurocurrency rates	£/$	FF/$	DM/$	¥/$
Simple interest differential	3.24	2.53	-2.32	-2.10
(s.e.)	(0.22)	(0.24)	(0.20)	(0.38)
[*p*-value]	[0.000]	[0.000]	[0.000]	[0.000]
Change in spot rate	2.77	1.41	-2.14	-3.86
(s.e.)	(2.69)	(2.65)	(2.73)	(2.56)
[*p*-value]	[0.305]	[0.596]	[0.432]	[0.133]
Uncovered differential	0.48	1.13	-0.18	1.76
(s.e.)	(2.73)	(2.67)	(2.75)	(2.58)
[*p*-value]	[0.862]	[0.673]	[0.948]	[0.497]

Three-month Eurocurrency rates	£/$	FF/$	DM/$	¥/$
Simple interest differential	3.13	2.58	-2.40	-2.02
(s.e.)	(0.33)	(0.34)	(0.33)	(0.52)
[*p*-value]	[0.000]	[0.000]	[0.000]	[0.000]
Change in spot rate	2.72	1.39	-2.04	-4.06
(s.e.)	(2.50)	(2.40)	(2.44)	(2.33)
[*p*-value]	[0.277]	[0.563]	[0.403]	[0.083]
Uncovered differential	0.41	1.19	-0.35	2.04
(s.e.)	(2.60)	(2.45)	(2.50)	(2.46)
[*p*-value]	[0.875]	[0.628]	[0.888]	[0.406]

Notes: All variables are expressed in percent per annum. The numbers in parentheses are standard errors corrected for heteroskedasticity and serial correlation (the latter in the case of the three-month series). The numbers in square brackets are *p*-values for the coefficients being significantly different from zero.

Table 4.5 presents *unconditional* estimates of uncovered interest differentials for the four currencies considered previously.[30] The top half of the table reports estimates based on one-month Eurocurrency rates, while the bottom half reports estimates for three-month rates. In both cases, the returns are expressed in percent per annum. In the first two rows of each half of the table, the uncovered differentials are decomposed into simple interest differentials (foreign currency minus dollar) and changes in exchange rates. Each row gives the average differential together with the standard error of this estimate and its *p*-value.

Consider first the estimates based on one-month interest rates. There is a clear pattern across the first two rows of data. Currencies with interest rates above that of the dollar, the pound sterling and French franc, depreciate on average against the dollar. Currencies with interest rates below that of the dollar, the mark and yen, appreciate on average against the dollar.[31] In other words, the average interest differential points the right way in forecasting long-run currency changes.[32] This is in contrast to the regression results of Table 4.3, where for most currencies a *rise* in the interest differential is associated with a *fall* in the exchange rate ($b < 0$).

Uncovered interest differentials, defined as the difference between the first two series,

$$(i_{kt} - i_{\$t}) - \Delta s_{kt}$$

for currency *k,* are in the third row of Table 4.5. None of these average differentials is statistically different from zero. So it is not possible to reject the hypothesis that uncovered interest parity holds on average for each set of currencies over the sample period. It is also not possible to reject the hypothesis that all four differentials are jointly equal to zero. The χ^2 statistic for this test is equal to 2.01 with a *p*-value of 0.733.

Two of the one-month uncovered differentials, in fact, are economically as well as statistically close to zero. The uncovered differentials for the pound sterling and the mark are less than 0.50 percent per annum. These differentials are thus comparable to the average differential between the Eurodollar and U.S. CD interest rates discussed in Chapter 3. The other uncovered differentials, for the French franc and yen, are between 1 and 2 percent per annum. If these four uncovered differentials are interpreted as

30. This table updates estimates of uncovered interest differentials in Marston (1992). See also Hodrick (1992).
31. It should be noted, however, that, while all of the simple one-month interest differentials are significantly different from zero, none of the average changes in spot rates are significantly different from zero at even 10 percent levels of significance. Although the point estimates in the first two rows are similar in magnitude, the standard errors associated with the changes in spot rates are much larger.
32. This pattern was previously noted by Froot and Thaler (1990, p. 187).

risk premiums, then the premiums are *on average* quite small, although this would not prevent the risk premium from alternating between large positive and negative values. If the uncovered differentials are interpreted as systematic forecast errors, these errors are on average quite small, although there could be periods when peso phenomena, for example, lead to large positive and negative forecast errors.

The bottom half of the table presents corresponding estimates based on three-month Eurocurrency rates. (Because of the overlapping forecast errors, the standard errors are adjusted for serial correlation as well as heteroskedasticity.) These estimates are reported merely to confirm that the results are not dependent on the specific maturity of the deposit.[33] The estimates are very close to those for one-month deposits. Average uncovered differentials range from -0.35 to 2.04 percent.[34]

B.   Systematic components of the uncovered differential

Even if *average* uncovered interest differentials are close to zero, there may still be systematic variations over time. The systematic component of the differential could be due either to time-varying risk premiums or systematic forecast errors.

Studies such as Giovannini and Jorion (1987), Cumby (1988), and Bekaert and Hodrick (1992) have searched for such systematic components by relating the uncovered interest differential to a variety of variables in the current information set. Consider the following regression for the uncovered interest differential between currency k and the dollar:

$$i_{kt} - \Delta s_{kt} - i_{\$t} = \gamma_k Z_{kt} + u'_{kt} + u_{kt} \qquad (4.9)$$

In this regression, Z_{kt} is a matrix of variables known at time t (including a constant). The error term consists of two elements: the forecast error, $u_{kt} = \Delta s_{kt} - \Delta x_{kt}$, plus a projection error, u'_{kt} associated with projecting the expected or ex ante return, $i_{kt} - \Delta x_{kt} - i_{\$t}$, on the matrix of variables chosen.[35] "Weak form" tests employ only past observations of the dependent variables in the matrix Z_{kt}, in this case past changes in the spot rate as well as past and present interest rates (because current interest rates are known at time t).[36] "Semistrong form" tests use any publicly available data known at time t.

---

33. It would also be interesting to examine uncovered differentials between the 12-month Eurocurrency rates used in Chapter 5, but the available series begins only in December 1980; so there are only 12 independent observations.
34. The χ^2 statistic for all four uncovered differentials being equal to zero is 3.38 with a p-value of 0.496.
35. The projection error thus reflects the econometrician's error in measuring the expected return.
36. The terminology is due to Fama (1970).

A parallel literature examining equity returns attempts to establish that there is a "predictable" component to such returns.[37] If the predictable components of equity and foreign exchange returns are due to risk premiums associated with asset pricing models, then the same variables should be able to predict both sets of returns. Thus recent studies such as Bekaert and Hodrick (1992) and Cumby and Huizinga (1992) have used dividend yields in addition to interest differentials to explain the predictable component of uncovered differentials.

Table 4.6 reports a set of regressions in the same form as Equation (4.9) explaining uncovered interest differentials between Eurocurrency markets. The uncovered differentials are expressed as a function of two sets of variables: the simple interest differential between the currencies concerned $(i_{kt} - i_{st})$ and dividend yields in the equity markets of the two countries. Following Bekaert and Hodrick (1992), I compute the dividend yield as the annualized dividend divided by the current stock index for that country.[38]

The regressions in Table 4.6 indicate that uncovered differentials are systematically related to both sets of variables. In the case of the dividend yields, five of the eight coefficients are statistically significant at the 5 percent level. In the case of the interest differentials, all but one of the four coefficients are significant. The only uncovered differential that seems to be unrelated to current variables is the differential between Eurodollar and Euroyen rates. The table also reports a χ^2 test of the hypothesis that all of the slope coefficients in any equation are equal to zero. Except in the case of the ¥/$ equation, all of the χ^2 statistics are significant at the 1 percent level; so this hypothesis can be rejected in three of four cases. Thus there is strong evidence of a systematic component in the uncovered differentials.

If the sole aim of regressions like those in Table 4.6 is to establish that UIP does not hold, then the choice of instruments to be included in Z_{kt} can be somewhat arbitrary. Any set of variables correlated with expected returns but known at time t will do. But if the aim is to understand the properties of risk premiums or systematic forecast errors, then it is important to choose instruments that explain most of the variation in expected returns. The Q-statistics reported in the table test the hypothesis

---

37. Fama and Schwert (1977) use nominal interest rates to predict stock returns. Keim and Stambaugh (1986), Fama and French (1988), Harvey (1991) and Campbell and Hamao (1992) are among many recent studies using dividend yields to predict stock returns (the latter two studies examining foreign as well as U.S. stock returns).

38. Stock price data are from Morgan Stanley Capital International. A monthly nominal dividend series is first obtained from the dividend price ratio and current stock price index. The annualized dividend is the discounted value of monthly dividends over the past 12 months using the local Eurocurrency rates as a discount factor. The annualized dividend is divided by the current month's stock price index to obtain the dividend yield.

Table 4.6. *Predictable components of uncovered interest differentials:*
Eurocurrency interest rates, 1973(6)-1992(12).

	£/$	FF/$	DM/$	¥/$
Constant	-0.30	-0.03	0.11	0.18
(s.e.)	(0.15)	(0.16)	(0.13)	(0.13)
[*p*-value]	[0.049]	[0.836]	[0.398]	[0.163]
Interest differential	4.55	2.67	2.72	0.70
(s.e.)	(0.88)	(1.15)	(1.17)	(0.60)
[*p*-value]	[0.000]	[0.021]	[0.021]	[0.245]
U.S. dividend yield	0.83	0.57	1.04	-0.27
(s.e.)	(0.34)	(0.44)	(0.37)	(0.29)
[*p*-value]	[0.016]	[0.193]	[0.005]	[0.357]
Foreign dividend yield	-0.44	-0.49	-1.21	-0.04
(s.e.)	(0.19)	(0.18)	(0.33)	(0.34)
[*p*-value]	[0.023]	[0.006]	[0.000]	[0.909]
$\chi^2(3)$	27.52	11.39	18.94	3.92
[*p*-value]	[0.000]	[0.010]	[0.000]	[0.270]
R^2	.078	.058	.075	.022
$Q(3)$	1.45	2.88	2.02	3.21
[*p*-value]	[0.693]	[0.411]	[0.568]	[0.360]
$Q(12)$	7.60	8.24	13.12	13.13
[*p*-value]	[0.816]	[0.766]	[0.360]	[0.360]

Notes: The numbers in parentheses are heteroskedasticity-consistent standard
errors. The $\chi^2(3)$ statistic tests the joint hypothesis that the coefficients of the
three information variables are equal to zero. $Q(3)$ and $Q(12)$ are Q-statistics
testing for serial correlation in 3 or 12 lags, respectively. The Q-statistics are
distributed as χ^2 with degrees of freedom equal to the number of lags.

that the residuals in the regressions are serially uncorrelated.[39] Tests of the autocorrelation coefficients on three- and 12-month lags of the residuals are reported. The low serial correlation in the regressions suggests that the instruments chosen explain most of the systematic variation in the uncovered differential.

The interpretation of these regressions depends on whether departures from UIP are due to time-varying risk premiums or systematic forecast errors. Consider the interpretation in terms of risk premiums. The fitted values of three of the regressions, all except the regression for the yen (which is statistically insignificant), are displayed in Figures 4.4–4.6. The fitted values represent the ex ante returns on each set of currencies. The dashed lines provide 95 percent confidence intervals for the estimates.[40] Several characteristics should be noted. The ex ante returns alternate between positive and negative values; so the risk premiums alternate between the dollar and other currencies. The risk premiums are thus time-varying. The confidence intervals around these ex ante returns are sometimes rather wide, but there are periods when the ex ante returns are significantly positive or significantly negative for all three currencies. But the ex ante returns may be varying too much, since the amplitude of the fluctuations in ex ante returns is very large. There are several periods when ex ante returns on the £, FF, and DM exceed 20 percent per annum.[41] And ex ante returns swing between large negative and positive values within a few months. It is difficult to believe that these swings are consistent with an asset pricing model of any type.

C.   *The latent variable test of CAPM*

There is some evidence against interpreting the fitted values of Table 4.6 as risk premiums. This evidence is based on the latent variable test developed by Hansen and Hodrick (1983) and Gibbons and Ferson (1985). Suppose that expected returns are explained by a single-factor model of the following form:

$$i_{kt} - \Delta x_{kt} - i_{\$t} = \beta_{kt}[E_t r_{pt} - i_{\$t}] \qquad (4.10)$$

where r_{pt} is the return on a benchmark portfolio. If the benchmark portfolio were observable, equations in the same form as Equation (4.10) could

---

39. See Ljung and Box (1978). The Q-statistics are distributed as χ^2 with degrees of freedom equal to the number of lags.
40. The standard errors are calculated according to a formula in Mishkin (1981), which assumes that the variances of the forecast errors are large relative to the variances of the projection errors. See also Cumby (1988).
41. Similar amplitudes are found by Cumby (1988) using forward premiums (and forward premiums squared) as instruments.

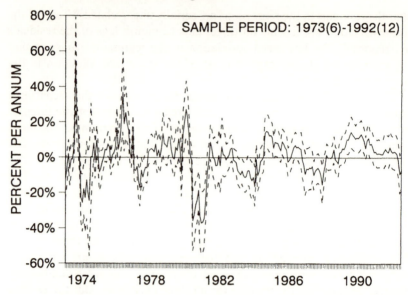

Figure 4.4. Ex ante returns on sterling.

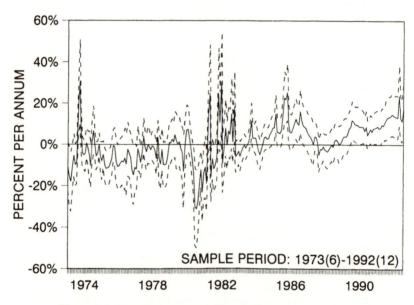

Figure 4.5. Ex ante returns on French franc.

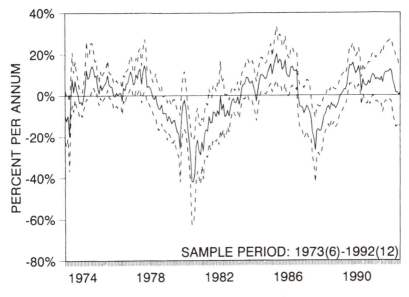

Figure 4.6. Ex ante returns on Deutsche mark.

be estimated using actual returns. Since this portfolio is not observable, Equation (4.10) is used instead to derive restrictions on equations relating the uncovered interest differential to observable variables. The first step is to take the ratio of the uncovered differentials for the French franc and pound in order to eliminate the benchmark return in Equation (4.10). The result is Equation (4.11), which relates the uncovered differentials on the two currencies to one another as follows:

$$i_{F_t} - \Delta x_{F_t} - i_{s_t} = \frac{\beta_{F_t}}{\beta_{\pounds_t}} (i_{\pounds_t} - \Delta x_{\pounds_t} - i_{s_t}) \tag{4.11}$$

If Equation (4.11) is combined with Equation (4.9), with actual returns replacing expected returns plus a forecast error, then the result is a system of four equations:

$$i_{\pounds_t} - \Delta s_{\pounds_t} - i_{s_t} = (\gamma_\pounds Z_{\pounds_t} + u'_{\pounds_t}) + u_{\pounds_t}$$

$$i_{F_t} - \Delta s_{F_t} - i_{s_t} = \frac{\beta_{F_t}}{\beta_{\pounds_t}} (\gamma_\pounds Z_{\pounds_t} + u'_{\pounds_t}) + u_{F_t}$$

$$i_{M_t} - \Delta s_{M_t} - i_{s_t} = \frac{\beta_{M_t}}{\beta_{\pounds_t}} (\gamma_\pounds Z_{\pounds_t} + u'_{\pounds_t}) + u_{M_t}$$

$$i_{\yen_t} - \Delta s_{\yen_t} - i_{s_t} = \frac{\beta_{\yen_t}}{\beta_{\pounds_t}} (\gamma_\pounds Z_{\pounds_t} + u'_{\pounds_t}) + u_{\yen_t} \tag{4.12}$$

If the additional assumption is made that the ratio of the betas is *constant* over time, then the coefficients in Equation (4.12) should be proportional to each other, $\gamma_k = (\beta_{kt}/\beta_{\pounds t})\,\gamma_{\pounds}$.

Four equations in the same form as (4.12) were estimated with the independent variables consisting of share yields and interest differentials from all five currencies. In the unrestricted version of these equations [in the same form as Equation (4.9)], there are ten regressors, including the constant in each equation, and 40 unrestricted parameters. With the proportionality restrictions imposed, there are $10 + (4-1) = 13$ restricted parameters; so there are 27 parameter restrictions to be tested. The test statistic, distributed as $\chi^2(27)$, is equal to 53.2 with a *p*-value of 0.002. Thus there is less than a 1 percent probability that the null hypothesis of a benchmark return can be accepted. This test using the present 20-year data set confirms earlier results in Hodrick and Srivastava (1984).[42]

The rejection of the benchmark model does not necessarily rule out the possibility that time-varying risk premia explain excess returns. The test itself relies on the assumption that the ratio of the betas in Equation (4.12) is constant, even though time-varying beats are consistent with a variety of asset pricing models.[43] More definitive tests of risk premiums may have to await the development of a viable international asset pricing model that can be tested directly.

D.   Tests for stability of equations

The equations reported in Table 4.6 suggest that there is a systematic relationship between variables known in the current period and future uncovered returns. But according to the evidence just presented, that relationship is not a result of a stable link between uncovered returns and an unobservable benchmark portfolio. An alternative explanation of the results in Table 4.6 is that there are systematic forecast errors in predicting uncovered returns. It is perhaps implausible that forecast errors would be stable over the 20-year period examined in Table 4.6, since this would imply that market participants were ignoring persistent profit opportunities. But it is possible that forecast errors could persist for shorter periods if there were changes in regimes occurring. As explained earlier, such

42. Other studies that test the latent variable model include Giovannini and Jorion (1987), Campbell and Clarida (1987), Cumby (1988), and Lewis (1990). Among these studies, only Campbell and Clarida fail to reject this model at some time horizon, although Lewis shows that the model cannot be rejected when longer holding periods are examined.

43. In his study of excess returns on five currencies, however, Cumby (1988) finds that he cannot reject the hypothesis that the ratio of the betas is constant over time.

changes in regimes could lead to peso problems in the period prior to the regime shift and to learning phenomena following the shift. But in that case the coefficients reported in Table 4.6 should not be stable over time.

To investigate this possibility, I split the sample period into subperiods to test whether the coefficient estimates in Table 4.6 are constant over time. I test for the possibility of structural breaks at particular dates in the sample when there are said to be changes in regime either as a result of shifts in government policy or changes in private behavior. Two possible periods when structural breaks may have occurred are investigated:

1. *November 1979:* At the end of October, the Carter Administration began to intervene actively in the foreign exchange market in an attempt to bolster the dollar. These actions were followed by the Federal Reserve Board's shift in operating procedures towards monetary targets.[44]

2. *October 1981:* As described in Lewis (1989), there was a large shift in money demand in the United States beginning in October 1981 without a corresponding rise in money supply to accommodate the shift in velocity. This shift in money demand led to a sustained rise in the dollar.

Both structural shifts have to do with U.S. rather than foreign phenomena. In the next chapter, I will study shifts in behavior associated with the start of the European Monetary System. Such shifts are not investigated here because they should affect inter-European exchange rates primarily.

The equations estimated are of the same form as Equation (4.9), as reported in Table 4.6. Thus each equation relates the uncovered interest differential between currency k and the dollar to three information variables, the share yields in the U.S. and foreign markets, and the simple interest differential between the two currencies (as well as a constant).[45] Traditional Chow tests for the stability of coefficients between periods are not appropriate in the presence of heteroskedasticity. Instead, I rely on a χ^2 test described in Hodrick and Srivastava (1984). If γ_{ki} is the estimated coefficient vector for subsample T_i and if Ω_{ki} is the variance, then the test statistic is

$$(\gamma_{k1} - \gamma_{k2})' \, \Omega_k^{-1} \, (\gamma_{k1} - \gamma_{k2})$$

where $\Omega_k = (\Omega_{k1}/T_1) + (\Omega_{k2}/T_2)$. This test statistic is distributed as χ^2 with degrees of freedom equal to the number of parameters estimated (four in this case).

44. Hodrick and Srivastava (1984) also investigated structural breaks in November 1979.
45. Similar results are obtained if the information variables include share yields and interest differentials from the other markets (as in the latent variable tests). Variables from third countries contribute little to such equations.

Table 4.7. *Tests for structural breaks in equations for uncovered interest differentials in Eurocurrency interest rates, 1973(6)-1992(12).*

	£/$	FF/$	DM/$	¥/$
November 1979				
$\chi^2(4)$	12.1	23.6	4.84	6.39
[*p*-value]	[0.017]	[0.000]	[0.304]	[0.172]
October 1981				
$\chi^2(4)$	14.4	10.3	5.87	4.90
[*p*-value]	[0.006]	[0.036]	[0.209]	[0.288]

Notes: The $\chi^2(4)$ statistic tests for shifts in the coefficients of equations in the same form as Table 4.6. The month listed is the first month of the second period.

Table 4.7 reports the χ^2 tests for the two potential regime shifts. For two of the currencies, the pound sterling and French franc, there is evidence of a structural shift in parameters whether the break occurs in November 1979 or October 1981. For both currencies it is possible to reject the hypothesis of constant parameters at the 5 percent level. The hypothesis of no structural break cannot be rejected for either of the other currencies, although the result for the yen is difficult to interpret because the underlying equation for the yen displays so little explanatory power. Thus, for two currencies, the systematic link between future uncovered returns and current variables is unstable over time.

On the basis of this evidence and that of the latent variable tests, it would be tempting to conclude that systematic forecast errors, rather than risk premiums, explain uncovered differentials. Unfortunately, the instability of the coefficients in the equations for uncovered returns may also undermine the conclusions drawn from the latent variable tests. The rejection of the latent variable model may simply be due to the instability of the underlying equation linking uncovered interest differentials to variables in the current information set. Without a stable Equation (4.9), coefficients in the constrained equations of Expression (4.12) may vary over time leading to a rejection of the latent variable model itself (4.10).

Thus the challenge of distinguishing between the two rational explanations of uncovered differentials remains. The next section makes one last attempt to distinguish between these two models by introducing survey evidence on exchange rate expectations.

E.   Survey data on exchange rate expectations

In testing asset pricing theories, most investigators adopt the assumption
of rational expectations (or market efficiency) in order to use realized returns in place of expected returns. Direct measures of expectations from
survey data allow an investigator to test asset pricing theories without
having to adopt the rational expectations assumption. In several papers
Frankel and Froot use survey data on foreign exchange expectations to
investigate risk premiums in the foreign exchange market.[46]

One hypothesis that Frankel and Froot investigate is whether there
is any systematic bias in an equation relating the expected change in
the exchange rate to the forward premium. You will recall from the
"speculative efficiency" regressions of Table 4.3 that the forward premium
(or simple interest differential) is a biased determinant of *actual* changes
in exchange rates. If forecast errors are assumed to be random white noise,
then the bias in the forward rate coefficient indicates the presence of a
time-varying risk premium. In Froot and Frankel (1989), the authors ran
regressions relating *expected* changes rather than actual changes in exchange rates to the forward premium. If $\Delta x'_{kt}$ is the expected change in
the exchange rate reported in survey data, then the regression takes the
form:

$$\Delta x'_{kt} = a' + b'f_{kt} + v'_{kt} \qquad (4.6'')$$

Like in the analogous Regression (4.6) using actual changes in the exchange rate, the coefficient b' is expected to be equal to one. But unlike in
the previous regressions, no assumption of market efficiency is required.[47]
The hypothesis is the simple one that there is no time-varying risk premium that would bias the coefficient b' away from one. The results as
reported in Table IV of Froot and Frankel (1989) are quite definitive. Using three separate surveys, from the *Economist,* Money Market Services,
and American Express, the authors find that the coefficient b' is significantly different from one in only two of nine regressions. So the bias found
in conventional regressions seems to disappear when direct measures of
expectations are introduced. If the coefficient b' in Equation (4.6'') is truly
equal to one, then the risk premium must be constant (equal to the estimate of a'). And the results reported in Table 4.6, showing that there are
predictable components of uncovered differentials, must be attributed to
systematic forecast errors rather than time-varying risk premiums (subject
to the important qualification that the survey estimates must be unbiased
estimates of the true market expectations).[48]

46. See especially Frankel and Froot (1987) and Froot and Frankel (1989).
47. The error term, v'_{kt}, represents measurement error in estimating the (true) market expec-
     tation.
48. Frankel and Froot (1987) discuss some of the limitations of survey estimates.

To investigate these implications further, I ran two additional sets of regressions using the same survey data.[49] With a direct measure of exchange rate expectations, $\Delta x'_{kt}$, it is possible to obtain direct measures of two key variables defined earlier in the chapter, the forecast error and risk premium:

$$\text{Forecast error:} \quad u_{kt} = \Delta s_{kt} - \Delta x'_{kt}$$

$$\text{Risk premium:} \quad \rho_{kt} = f_{kt} - \Delta x'_{kt}$$

where, as before, f_{kt} is the forward premium and Δs_{kt} is the actual change in the exchange rate. By studying the behavior of these two series, it should be possible, in principle at least, to distinguish between the two explanations of uncovered differentials: systematic forecast errors and risk premiums.

Recall the equations in Table 4.6 showing the systematic link between uncovered interest differentials and three information variables: the simple interest differential and dividend yields in the two national markets. In the first set of regressions, the forecast error rather than the uncovered interest differential is related to these same information variables in equations of the form:

$$\Delta s_{kt} - \Delta x'_{kt} = \lambda'_{kt} Z_{kt} + \varepsilon'_{kt} \tag{4.13}$$

where λ'_{kt} is a vector of coefficients. If any of the coefficients of the information variables is significantly different from zero, then we have direct evidence that forecast errors are systematic.

Forecasts for a monthly horizon are available from Money Market Services (MMS) for three of the four exchange rates (all except the FF/\$ rate) for the period 1982(11)–1987(12).[50] The forecasts were collected by telephone once a week after October 1984 and once every two weeks before that. I have taken the survey from the last day of the month or the next closest day following. This ensures that the information variables used in the equations, which are end-of-month variables, were observable to market participants at the time of the survey. Equations in the form of (4.13), estimated using a GMM estimator, are reported in Table 4.8.[51]

For all three currencies, there is evidence that the forecast errors are systematically related to the information variables. Although many of the individual coefficients are insignificantly different from zero, a Wald test

---

49. These series were kindly provided by Kenneth Froot.
50. This was the only survey with forecasts for a one-month horizon. Note that the Frankel and Froot survey data set includes market data (spot and forward rates) properly aligned with the forecasts.
51. Because some of the forecast errors from one-month overlap with those from the succeeding month, I have allowed for serial correlation in the estimation.

Table 4.8. *Regressions of forecast errors derived from survey data on current information variables, 1982(11)-1987(12).*

	£/$	DM/$	¥/$
Constant	0.26	-0.98	-0.56
(s.e.)[a]	(0.39)	(0.27)	(0.32)
[p-value]	[0.506]	[0.001]	[0.085]
Interest			
differential	-13.94	-11.19	-10.21
(s.e.)	(3.73)	(6.30)	(5.17)
[p-value]	[0.001]	[0.081]	[0.053]
U.S.			
dividend yield	-1.43	-0.17	-0.21
(s.e.)	(1.99)	(1.03)	(1.15)
[p-value]	[0.475]	[0.869]	[0.853]
Foreign			
dividend yield	1.41	1.74	3.46
(s.e.)	(2.03)	(0.84)	(2.64)
[p-value]	[0.489]	[0.041]	[0.195]
$\chi^2(3)$[b]	32.26	21.23	10.31
[p-value]	[0.000]	[0.000]	[0.016]
R^2	.286	.165	.120

[a] The numbers in parentheses are heteroskedasticity-consistent standard errors.
[b] The $\chi^2(3)$ statistic tests the joint hypothesis that the coefficients of the three information variables are equal to zero.

for the hypothesis that all of the information variables are jointly insignificant is rejected with the p-value of 0.016 or less.

Before drawing any conclusions from these regressions, however, consider an alternative set of regressions relating the *risk premium* to these same information variables. If systematic forecast errors alone account for systematic deviations from UIP, then the risk premium should be unrelated to these information variables in an equation of the form:

$$f_{kt} - \Delta x'_{kt} = \lambda''_{kt} Z_{kt} + \varepsilon''_{kt} \tag{4.14}$$

Table 4.9. *Regressions of risk premiums derived from survey data on current information variables, 1982(11)-1987(12).*

	£/$	DM/$	¥/$
Constant	0.37	-0.17	0.07
(s.e.)[a]	(0.11)	(0.11)	(0.14)
[p-value]	[0.001]	[0.134]	[0.609]
Interest differential	-4.80	-1.62	-2.44
(s.e.)	(1.29)	(2.60)	(1.87)
[p-value]	[0.000]	[0.535]	[0.199]
U.S. dividend yield	-1.71	-0.39	-0.89
(s.e.)	(0.63)	(0.35)	(0.43)
[p-value]	[0.008]	[0.261]	[0.040]
Foreign dividend yield	1.18	0.92	3.58
(s.e.)	(0.61)	(0.26)	(0.85)
[p-value]	[0.059]	[0.001]	[0.000]
$\chi^2(3)$[b]	14.56	19.21	34.09
[p-value]	[0.002]	[0.000]	[0.000]
R^2	.297	.145	.300

[a] The numbers in parentheses are heteroskedasticity-consistent standard errors.
[b] The $\chi^2(3)$ statistic tests the joint hypothesis that the coefficients of the three information variables are equal to zero.

In Table 4.9, I report regressions for the risk premium for the same three currencies. The results are once against quite definitive. In each of the equations for the three currencies, the risk premium is systematically related to information variables. A Wald test rejects the hypothesis that the three coefficients of the information variables are jointly insignificant.

Tables 4.8 and 4.9 together account for the variation in the uncovered interest differential studied earlier, since the uncovered differential can be decomposed into the following (using covered interest parity):

$$(i_{kt} - i_{st}) - \Delta s_{kt} = f_{kt} - \Delta s_{kt} = (f_{kt} - \Delta x'_{kt}) - (\Delta s_{kt} - \Delta x_{kt}) \qquad (4.15)$$

The two expressions on the right side of Equation (4.15) are the risk premium and forecast error, respectively. The results reported in Tables 4.8 and 4.9 suggest that both elements of the uncovered differential are systematically related to variables known to market participants. So the earlier evidence that uncovered interest differentials are related to such variables can now be interpreted more precisely (under the assumption that the survey responses represent true market expectations). It is *both* systematic forecast errors *and* risk premiums that account for the results reported in Table 4.6.

F. *Some tentative conclusions*

The evidence presented in this chapter allows us to draw a few tentative conclusions about uncovered interest differentials:

1. As established by many previous studies, forward premiums or simple interest differentials are *biased* predictors of actual changes in exchange rates. Over the sample period studied, the coefficient relating changes in exchange rates to the forward premium or interest differential is negative rather than positive.

2. Despite this bias, uncovered interest differentials between the Eurodollar and other G-5 Eurocurrencies have been quite small *on average* over the past 20 years. *Unconditional* estimates of uncovered interest differentials range from -0.35 to 2.04 percent over the 1973(6)–1992(12) period.

3. Month-to-month movements in uncovered interest differentials are very large. Most of the variation is due to forecast errors. The key question addressed in this chapter and in previous studies is whether any of the variation is systematic.

4. Regressions of these uncovered differentials on variables currently known to investors show that there is an important ex ante component of these differentials. *Conditional* estimates of uncovered interest differentials have very low R^2s, ranging from 0.022 to 0.078, but in the case of three differentials the information variables are statistically significant. Unfortunately, these regressions give no clue as to whether the ex ante component is due to a time-varying risk premium or to systematic forecast errors associated with regime shifts or simply to market inefficiencies.

5. It is difficult to directly test for a risk premium, but previous authors have shown how to specify a latent variable model implicitly

linking these ex ante differentials to a benchmark portfolio. This latent variable model is rejected by the data.

6. The regressions linking uncovered differentials to current variables are unstable over time, perhaps because of structural regime shifts associated with changes in monetary policy or in private behavior.

7. Exchange rate expectations obtained from survey data provide direct measures of forecast errors and risk premiums. But *both* measures are shown to be related to current variables, so that there is evidence of both systematic forecast errors *and* time-varying risk premiums. It is not possible to rule out either potential source of systematic variations in the uncovered differentials.

In the next chapter, I examine how European exchange rate arrangements affect uncovered interest differentials. After reviewing evidence concerning inter-European interest differentials, I will assess the overall effect of uncovered differentials on the relative costs of financing in the G-5 countries.

CHAPTER 5

Exchange rates and interest rates
in the European Monetary System

The five currencies of the G-5 countries include two, the French franc and Deutschemark, that have been tied together in the European Monetary System (or EMS) throughout most of the period under study. The EMS was established in March 1979 to provide a "zone of monetary stability" in Europe where exchange rate movements would be limited to narrow bands of 4½ percent around central parities. Countries such as France and Germany wanted to limit the movement of inter-European exchange rates because so much trade took place within the European Economic Community.[1] This chapter examines the effects of the EMS on exchange rate and interest rate behavior in the major European countries.

I.   Exchange rate experience in the EMS

The French and German authorities have followed exchange rate policies distinct from that of their fellow EEC member, the United Kingdom. While all three countries became members of the EMS from its inception in 1979, the British at that time refused to join the crucial Exchange Rate Mechanism (ERM), which fixes inter-European rates within the 4½ percent bands. Sterling floated freely until as late as October 1990 when Britain joined the ERM, adopting wider 12 percent bands.[2] The chapter shows to what extent this British decision to stay out of the ERM affected sterling's relative performance during the 1980s.

The chapter focuses on the FF/DM and £/DM exchange rates. But to better understand behavior in the EMS, two other currencies are also studied: the Italian lira and Dutch guilder (commonly designated by DFL or

1. Giavazzi and Giovannini (1989) discuss the motivation behind establishing the EMS including the need to stabilize agricultural prices supported by the common agricultural policy of the European Economic Community. Among other studies of the EMS are Ungerer et al. (1986), Guitián et al. (1988), and Giovannini (1990). Additional references follow.
2. The 4.5 percent bands provide for movements around the central rate of ±2.25 percent and the 12 percent bands provide for movements of ±6 percent. For technical reasons, the bands actually require that upper and lower bands be slightly different from ½ of the width of the band (see Grabbe, 1991, pp. 39–41), but I will continue to refer to ±2.25 percent limits.

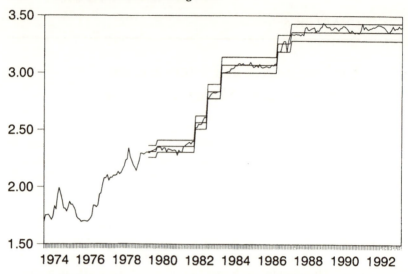

Figure 5.1. FF/DM spot exchange rate, 1973–1992: market and EMS rates.

Dutch florin).[3] The experience of the French franc in the EMS falls somewhere between the extremes of these other two European currencies. The guilder enjoyed remarkable stability relative to the mark, while the lira experienced eight devaluations before dropping out of the ERM completely in September 1992.

Figure 5.1 traces movements in the FF/DM rate over the entire sample period from June 1973 to December 1992. Up until March 1979, the franc and mark floated freely except for a brief period prior to January 1974 and from July 1975 to March 1976 when the so-called "snake," a precursor of the EMS, was in effect. When the EMS was established in March 1979, a central rate of FF2.3095/DM was chosen with bands of ±2.25 percent. These bands are shown explicitly in the figure. On six different occasions, realignments of the franc or mark occurred that changed the FF/DM central rate. In each case the franc was devalued relative to the mark. Notice, however, that the last realignment in January 1987 ushered in a tranquil period lasting through the end of the sample period (although, as will be discussed, the franc came under pressure in September 1992).

Figure 5.2 shows movements in the DFL/DM rate over the same period. This exchange rate, which varies only between DFL 1/DM and DFL 1.16/

3. In the last few years, the designation for the guilder has changed to NLG, but I have retained the more traditional DFL designation, which prevailed for most of the sample period.

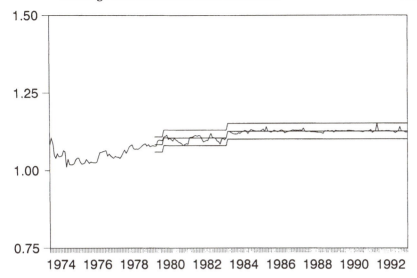

Figure 5.2. DFL/DM spot exchange rate, 1973–1992: market and EMS rates.

DM, displays remarkable stability over the whole sample period. (Figure 5.2 is scaled to make it roughly comparable to that of Figure 5.1, so that the stability of the FF/DM and DFL/DM rates can be compared.) During the period prior to 1979, the guilder first appreciated then depreciated relative to the mark, ending at about the same rate as it began. Since the EMS started, there have been only two realignments involving this rate, the last one being in March 1983.

In Figure 5.3, the lira/DM rate seems to depreciate at a steady rate before and after the establishment of the EMS. When the EMS was established, Italy was allowed to join with ±6 percent rather than ±2.25 percent bands. But despite the wider bands, the lira had to be realigned eight times during the period. The exchange rate appears to follow a nearly steady upward trend from 1973 throughout most of the EMS period. With the 1987 realignment, however, the lira began to stabilize within its bands. And in 1990, those bands were narrowed to ±2.25 percent, with the new upper band coinciding with the band established in 1987. This new period of stability was interrupted in September 1992 when speculation against the lira and pound forced both currencies out of the ERM. A later section of the chapter will examine in detail this speculative episode.

Figure 5.4 shows the fourth European exchange rate, the £/DM rate. Sterling floated freely through the 1970s and 1980s. When the EMS was established, the Prime Minister at that time, Margaret Thatcher, decided

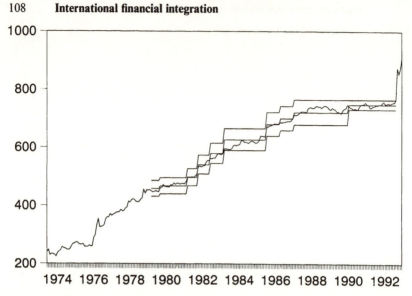

Figure 5.3. Lira/DM spot exchange rate, 1973–1992: market and EMS rates.

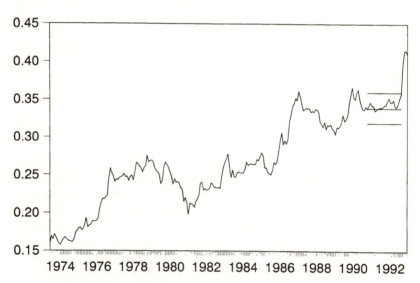

Figure 5.4. £/DM spot exchange rate, 1973–1992: market and EMS rates.

Table 5.1. *Standard deviations of monthly percentage changes in Deutschemark exchange rates, 1973(6)-1992(12).*[a]

	FF/DM	Lira/DM	DFL/DM	£/DM
1973(6)-79(2)				
Pre-EMS	7.25	10.61	3.85	9.47
1979(3)-92(12)				
EMS	3.56	5.05	1.89	9.50
Recent	*87(1)-92(12)*	*87(1)-92(7)*[b]	*87(1)-92(12)*	*90(10)-92(7)*[c]
Period	1.92	2.24	1.71	4.18

[a] The standard deviations are measured in per annum terms.
[b] The Lira dropped out of the Exchange Rate Mechanism (ERM) in September 1992, so the recent period is measured only up through July 1992 (since the August 1992 figure measures the change in exchange rates from the end of August until the end of September).
[c] Sterling joined the ERM in October 1990 and dropped out of the ERM in September 1992, so the recent period is measured only from October 1990 to July 1992.

Sources: Exchange rates: *International Financial Statistics*; Eurocurrency interest rates: Data Resources, Inc. and Reuters Databanks.

against tying sterling to the other European currencies within the ERM. As the figure shows, this decision left sterling free to fluctuate widely relative to the mark (and hence relative to other currencies in the ERM). The rate fell below £ 0.20/DM (or rose above DM 5/£) in early 1981 as sterling appreciated relative to all major currencies including the dollar. Later in 1986–87 sterling depreciated sharply to over £ 0.36/DM. When John Major brought Britain into the ERM in October 1990, sterling was fixed at £ 0.339/DM (or DM 2.95/£), although the 12 percent bands provided some flexibility for the new policy. The market rate stabilized for almost two years before sterling had to drop out of the ERM again in the currency crisis of September 1992.

The figures show long-term trends in three of the four exchange rates, the exception being the DFL/DM rate where relative stability prevailed. Table 5.1 examines the month-to-month variation in the same four exchange rates as measured by the standard deviations of the percentage changes in these rates. The first three exchange rates listed are those of currencies that joined the ERM in 1979, while the fourth exchange rate is that of sterling, which did not join until October 1990. For the first three exchange rates, the standard deviations in the EMS period are one-half the size of those in the pre-EMS period. The DM exchange rate for sterling, in contrast, is as variable in the EMS period as in the pre-EMS period.

As already indicated, the period since the January 1987 realignment was one of notable stability until interrupted by the speculative crisis of September 1992. This stability is demonstrated in Table 5.1 in the comparison between standard deviations for this recent period (post-January 1987) and the whole EMS period. In the case of the FF/DM rate, the standard deviation is 1.92 percent in the recent period compared with 3.56 percent in the EMS period as a whole. The standard deviation for the FF/DM rate for the recent period, in fact, is as low as that of the DFL/DM rate (which remained stable throughout the whole EMS period). Equally remarkable is the stability of the Lira/DM and £/DM rates, the latter measured from October 1990 when sterling joined the ERM. In the case of these currencies, the standard deviations are measured only up to the month before they dropped out of the ERM. If the standard deviations are measured through December 1992, they are as high in the recent period as in the whole period since 1979.[4]

II.   Uncovered differentials in the EMS

This brief review of EMS history will be useful in interpreting the behavior of interest rates within Europe over the past 13 years. One question to be addressed is whether the European Monetary System has helped lead to a convergence of European interest rates. Of particular interest is the question about whether the attempt to fix exchange rates has kept *total* returns from diverging as much within Europe as they have between Europe and the United States. The existence of exchange rate bands around the central rates of the ERM may lead to what Krugman (1987) calls a "honeymoon effect," which stabilizes exchange rate expectations. But if the exchange rate bands lack credibility among market participants, interest differentials can persist despite an official commitment to fix rates.

---

4. The standard deviation for the lira/DM rate over the period from January 1987 to December 1992 is 6.22 percent and that of the £/DM rate over the period from October 1990 to December 1992 is 8.24 percent.

A.   Standard tests of uncovered interest parity

It is useful to begin with a preliminary study of interest differentials within Europe to help to establish whether inter-European returns behave differently from those elsewhere. All of the returns reported in Chapter 4 were based on dollar exchange rates. It is possible that returns measured in marks or other European currencies might conform more closely to uncovered interest parity than do dollar-centered rates. This section repeats two sets of tests for uncovered interest parity, expressing returns in terms of marks rather than dollars.

Table 5.2 presents tests of unbiasedness for mark-centered exchange rates in the same form as Table 4.3. These tests involve regressing the percentage change in the spot rate for currency k relative to the mark (Δs_{kt}) on the interest differential between these two currencies (δ_{kt}).

$$\Delta s_{kt} = a + b\delta_{kt} + v_{kt} \tag{5.1}$$

where $\delta_{kt} = i_{kt} - i_{Mt}$. Three European cross exchange rates are studied, the £/DM, FF/DM, and DFL/DM rates. (Eurolira interest rates are not available until October 1980.) For purposes of comparison, the ¥/DM rate is also included.[5]

The results of the estimation contain only one surprise. The equation for the FF/DM rate has a coefficient for the interest differential b, very close to unity and an intercept a, insignificantly different from zero.[6] The Wald-statistic jointly testing $b = 1$ and $a = 0$ has a p-value of 0.376; so the joint hypothesis of uncovered interest parity and market efficiency cannot be rejected at conventional significance levels. If all tests of unbiasedness were as consistent with the null hypothesis, the search for the elusive risk premium might never have been undertaken. Unfortunately, the other mark-centered rates conform more closely to findings for dollar-centered rates. The joint hypothesis can be rejected for the £/DM and DFL/DM rates at 5 percent significance levels. The joint hypothesis cannot be rejected for the ¥/DM rate, but the equation has as little explanatory power as its ¥/$ counterpart.

Equations in the same form as Table 5.2 were also estimated for the EMS period alone. The results, not reported here, are similar to those of Table 5.2 in that the FF/DM rate has a coefficient for the interest differen-

---

5. Equations for the DM/$ exchange rate were previously reported in Table 4.3.

6. This result for the FF/DM rate is consistent with a study by Bjorn Isberg (1993) who examines tests of unbiasedness using cross rates defined relative to the mark, pound sterling, and Swedish kroner. Isberg also finds positive coefficients for other mark-centered rates such as the Austrian schilling, Belgian franc, Spanish peseta, and Swedish kronor. Rose and Svensson (1992) also report similar results for the FF/DM rate.

Table 5.2. *Tests of unbiasedness for DM exchange rates, 1973(6)-1992(12): changes in spot rates related to interest differentials expressed in percent per annum.*

	£/DM	FF/DM	DFL/DM	¥/DM
Constant (a)	11.72	-1.68	0.93	-1.78
(s.e.)[a]	(4.77)	(2.18)	(0.62)	(2.31)
[*p*-value][b]	[0.015]	[0.444]	[0.133]	[0.443]
Interest				
differential	-1.22	1.08	-0.85	0.27
(s.e.)	(0.81)	(0.49)	(0.42)	(0.48)
[*p*-value][c]	[0.006]	[0.878]	[0.000]	[0.135]
R^2	.010	.054	.027	.001
Wald-statistic	7.58	1.95	19.63	3.12
[*p*-value][d]	[0.023]	[0.376]	[0.000]	[0.210]

[a] The numbers in parentheses are heteroskedasticity-consistent standard errors.
[b] The *p*-value is for the *t*-test of $a=0$.
[c] The *p*-value is for the *t*-test of $b=1$.
[d] The Wald-statistic tests the joint hypothesis $a=0$ and $b=1$. It is distributed as χ^2 with 2 degrees of freedom. The *p*-value is given below the statistic.

tial *b* which is close to one, and the other two European rates have estimates of *b* that are negative. The one important difference is that the estimate of *b* for the ¥/DM rate, which should not necessarily be affected at all by the establishment of the EMS, is now negative rather than positive, a shift in behavior that is difficult to rationalize.

It is also interesting to examine unconditional estimates of uncovered interest differentials for mark-centered rates. Table 5.3 reports average uncovered differentials on one-month Eurocurrency deposits for the entire sample period and for the EMS period alone. The differentials are measured (in percent per annum) as the return on Eurodeposits in currency *k* minus the return on Euromarks, $i_{kt} - i_{Mt} - \Delta s_{kt}$. We might expect uncovered differentials to become much smaller once currencies are fixed within the EMS, but this is not the case for the FF/DM differential. The uncov-

Table 5.3. *Unconditional estimates of uncovered interest differentials for European exchange rates, 1973(6)-1992(12).*[a]

	Currencies in exchange rate mechanism for whole EMS period			Outside ERM[b]
	FF/DM	Lira/DM[c]	DFL/DM	£/DM
1973(6)-92(12)				
Differential	1.31		0.61	0.66
(s.e.)	(1.09)		(0.62)	(2.18)
[*p*-value]	[0.231]		[0.328]	[0.763]
1979(3)-92(12)				
Differential	1.76	2.41	0.20	1.60
(s.e.)	(0.88)	(1.50)	(0.53)	(2.60)
[*p*-value]	[0.046]	[0.109]	[0.698]	[0.540]

[a]All variables are expressed in percent per annum. The numbers in parentheses are the heteroskedasticity-consistent standard errors. The numbers in square brackets are p-values for the coefficients being significantly different from zero.

[b] Britain has been a member of the EMS since its inception, but joined the Exchange Rate Mechanism (ERM) only in October 1990.

[c] The series for the Eurolira interest rate begins only in October 1980, so the estimate for the ERM period is for October 1980-December 1992.

ered differential between Eurofranc and Euromark deposits is actually larger in the EMS period, although the difference is not statistically significant. During the EMS period, the higher interest rate on Eurofranc deposits evidently more than compensated investors for the six realignments of the FF/DM rate that occurred in the EMS period. In the case of the guilder/DM rate, in contrast, the uncovered differential is much smaller in the EMS period, although this difference in estimates once again is not statistically significant. The third currency fixed in the ERM from the beginning, the lira, has no Eurocurrency interest rate series for the pre-EMS period. The average excess return on the lira over the period from October 1980 (when the Eurolira series begins) is equal to 2.41 percent per annum. As in the case of the franc, the higher interest rate on Eurolira deposits more than compensated investors for the frequent realignments of the lira/DM rate and for the depreciation of the lira relative to the mark, which occurred after the lira dropped out of the ERM in September 1992. Results for the £/DM rate are also reported in the table for the whole period and for the EMS period beginning in March 1979, although sterling did not join the ERM until October 1980. It is interesting to note that the excess return on sterling relative to the mark is no larger than that of the franc relative to the mark despite the fact that the FF was in the ERM from the beginning in March 1979.

B.   *A simple test of EMS credibility*

If in the 1980s uncovered interest differentials for the FF/DM rate were on average just as large as those for the £/DM rate, did the ERM bands for the franc lack credibility among market participants? This question may seem difficult to answer in the absence of direct measures of exchange rate expectations. But studies by Svensson (1991a) and Giovannini (1990) have proposed a simple test of credibility that relies only on observed interest rates and exchange rates.[7]

The test of ERM credibility involves comparing the Eurofranc interest rate with two limiting values of the Eurofranc rate consistent with the FF/DM exchange rate remaining within its ERM bands. Because ERM realignments are expressed in arithmetic terms (new rate/old rate − 1) rather than as log percentage changes, the ERM bands will be expressed in terms of the level of the exchange rate S. Suppose that S^U is the upper band for the FF/DM exchange rate in the ERM, S^L is the lower band, and S_t is the current market exchange rate. If the ERM bands are credible, then the return *in francs* on Euromark deposits can be bounded as follows:[8]

$$I^U_{Ft} = [(1 + I_{Mt})\left(\frac{S^U}{S_t}\right) - 1] \tag{5.2a}$$

$$I^L_{Ft} = [(1 + I_{Mt})\left(\frac{S^L}{S_t}\right) - 1] \tag{5.2b}$$

Both of these limiting values, which have been called "credibility bounds" by Giovannini, are observable, since the variables on the right sides of Equations (5.2a) and (5.2b) are observable.

Svensson (1993b) proposes two alternative concepts of credibility.[9] *Absolute credibility* means that the probability distribution of future exchange

---

7. Svensson (1991a) cites prior work by Gronvik (1986) and Porter (1971).
8. Recall that the continuously compounded Euromark rate, i_{Mt}, is related to the simple Euromark rate, I_{Mt}, as follows: $i_{Mt} = \ln(1 + I_{mt})$.
9. Svensson's (1993b) analysis is framed in terms of inflation targets rather than exchange rate bands, although (as he pointed out in private correspondence) the two concepts of credibility can be readily applied to exchange rate bands.

rates lies entirely within the bands S^L and S^U. *Credibility in expectation* means that the *expected* exchange rate (although not necessarily all of the probability mass) lies within the bands. These two concepts of credibility can be applied to the interest rate *credibility bounds* in Equations (5.2a) and (5.2b) just as readily as to the exchange rate bands themselves.

If the actual Eurofranc rate, I_{Ft}, is found outside the credibility bounds defined in (5.2a) and (5.2b), then absolute credibility can be rejected. To see this, suppose that the Eurofranc rate is above its upper bound in (5.2a). Then if the bounds had absolute credibility, there would be an arbitrage profit to be made from borrowing Euromarks and investing in Eurofrancs.[10] Such an arbitrage profit is inconsistent with a well-functioning financial market; so absolute credibility must be rejected. If the Eurofranc interest rate is within the credibility bounds, however, then this alone does not prove that there is absolute credibility, since agents could still assign positive probability to the exchange rate lying outside its bands.

Credibility in expectation leads to a more definitive test, but only in the case where *uncovered interest parity* is assumed to hold. Svensson (1992) argues that UIP is more plausible in a fixed rate system than in a free floating system. He develops a theoretical model of the risk premium that divides it into two components corresponding to movements of the exchange rate within existing bands and devaluations of the central rate. Svensson argues that movements within the bands are likely to generate only negligible risk premiums as long as the bands are narrow enough. Risk premiums associated with devaluations are potentially much larger, but he uses rough estimates of the parameters in his model to bound these risk premiums at about 20 percent of the devaluation itself.

If UIP does hold and if there is credibility in expectation, then the Eurofranc rate must lie within the bounds,

$$I_{Ft}^L \leq I_{Ft} \leq I_{Ft}^U$$

If the Eurofranc rate lies outside the bounds, then credibility in expectation (as well as absolute credibility) can be rejected.[11] On the other hand, if the Eurofranc rate lies inside the bounds, then this constitutes evidence in favor of credibility in expectation (even though, as already discussed, no conclusion can be drawn regarding absolute credibility).

What evidence about credibility do we find? Figure 5.5 shows a time series for the one year Eurofranc rate between December 1980 when the

10. With no probability that the exchange rate will move outside its bands, this is a true arbitrage (i.e., riskless) profit since the cost of borrowing Euromarks (measured in francs) must be below the return on Eurofrancs.
11. The assumption of UIP is crucial to this result, since the presence of a risk premium could push the Eurofranc rate outside the bounds even though credibility in expectation held.

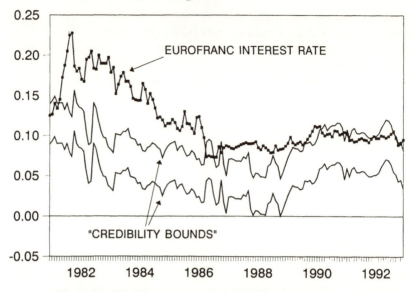

Figure 5.5. Eurofranc rate and its "credibility bounds": 1-year interest rate, 1980(12)–1992(12).

series first became available and December 1992.[12] The upper and lower bounds calculated using Equations (5.2a) and (5.2b) are labeled "credibility bounds" in the figure. It is evident that the FF/DM parity lacked credibility among market participants throughout most of the sample period. Up through 1990, the Eurofranc rate was almost always above the upper limit. At times the differential between the Eurofranc interest rate and the upper bound reaches 10 percent/annum. It is only in the 1990–92 period that the interest rate settles between the upper and lower bounds.

Contrast the experience of the franc with that of the guilder. In Figure 5.6, the Euroguilder rate is always between the upper and lower credibility bounds defined for the DFL/DM rate. So the guilder evidently enjoyed credibility in expectation (though not necessarily absolute credibility).[13] Recall from Figure 5.2 that the DFL/DM central rate was realigned in March 1983 (representing a devaluation of the guilder's central rate). The

12. The figure is an updated version of a figure presented in Giovannini (1990). Note that if shorter maturities are examined, such as the one-month series used throughout the rest of this chapter, the implied credibility bounds are proportionately wider because small capital losses on depreciations translate into large *per annum* losses. So interest differentials for short maturities are unlikely to violate their credibility bounds except in extreme circumstances.
13. There may have been some probability assigned to exchange rates beyond the bands, even though the expected DFL/DM rate is within its bands.

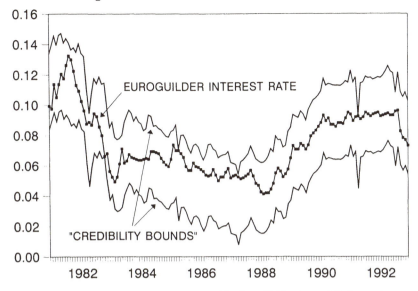

Figure 5.6. Euroguilder rate and its "credibility bounds": 1-year interest rate, 1980(12)–1992(12).

market rate did not jump discontinuously at the realignment date, however; so it may not be surprising that the Euroguilder interest rate stayed within its bounds even during the realignment period.[14] The case of the Eurolira (not shown) corresponds more closely to that of the Eurofranc. The lira entered the ERM with 12 percent rather than 4.5 percent bands, so the credibility bounds are much wider for the Eurolira rate. Despite the wider bounds, however, the one-year Eurolira interest rate was often above its upper credibility bound except for periods during 1986–87 and 1990–92.[15]

It is useful to ask whether the lack of ERM credibility revealed in Eurofranc rates was justified by subsequent events. Table 5.4 analyzes interest rates and exchange rates at the time of five of the six realignments of the FF/DM rate.[16] The second column gives the excess one-year Eurofranc rate ($I_{F_t} - I_{F_t}^U$) at the end of the month preceding the realignment. The third column gives the percentage realignment taking place that month.

14. The credibility bounds become narrower as the maturity lengthens; so it is possible that the guilder interest rates violated the credibility bounds for maturities greater than one year.
15. Note that the Eurolira rate again rose above the upper credibility bound several months prior to the September 1992 currency crisis.
16. The first realignment in September 1979 occurred before the one-year Eurofranc series begins.

Table 5.4. *Excess Eurofranc rates compared with percent realignments and actual depreciations of the FF/DM exchange rate.*

Date of realignment	Excess Eurofranc rate[a] $(I_{Ff}\text{-}I^U_{Ff})$	Percent realignment of FF/DM bands	Actual depreciation of FF/DM rate[b]	
			To end of month of realignment	To end of year after realignment
10-5-81	10.43	8.76	4.91	17.82
6-14-82	11.38	10.61	6.55	15.19
3-21-83	10.62	8.20	5.69	8.65
4-7-86	3.32	6.19	3.53	8.24
1-12-87	3.80	3.00	0.31	1.52

[a] The interest differential is measured at the end of the month preceding the realignment.
[b] The actual depreciation is measured from the end of the month preceding the realignment to the end of the month of the realignment or, alternatively, one year from the end of the month preceding the realignment.

The fourth and fifth columns give the rate of depreciation of the market rate for two intervals: from the end of the previous month to the end of the month of realignment and from the end of the previous month to 12 months later (at the maturity of the deposit). For four of the five realignments, the excess Eurofranc rate exceeds both the percentage realignment and the actual depreciation during the month of the realignment. (The exception is April 1986.) But for three of the five realignments, the excess Eurofranc rate falls short of the actual depreciation over the year-long holding period. For these three realignments, investors suffered a capital loss on holding francs (relative to marks), which exceeded the excess Eurofranc rate.[17] The realignment of March 1983, however, led to a depreciation over the next year that fell short of the 10.62 percent excess Eurofranc rate. A similar result occurred following the realignment of January 1987.

17. The capital loss also exceeded the Eurofranc-Euromark interest differential.

So investors were generally justified in demanding realignment premiums on the Eurofranc rate, at least in the periods immediately preceding the actual realignments. Still, there is evidence that, over the *whole* EMS period, the premium may have been excessive. The average uncovered interest differentials between one-month deposits reported in Table 5.3 suggest that the premiums for the Eurofranc (and Eurolira) rates were *on average* in excess of subsequent deposits. These premiums may reflect expected realignments larger than actually occurred or may reflect risk premiums demanded by market participants for investing in a depreciation-prone currency.

III.   Exchange rate bands: stabilizing or not?

A monetary system in which investors demand realignment premiums is a far cry from the system described by Krugman (1991) in his celebrated article on "target zone" behavior. Although economists had long tried to model fixed exchange rate systems, Krugman was the first to show how the commitment to intervene at the fixed rate bands affected exchange rates within these margins. He did this by introducing option pricing methods into the analysis of exchange rates. The result was an elegant statement of exchange rate dynamics within a fixed exchange rate system.

A.   Target zone models

Krugman formulated his model of exchange rate bands based on two assumptions: (1) The exchange rate bands are fully credible, and (2) central banks intervene only when the exchange rate approaches these bands. He showed that under these conditions the bands create an S-curve relationship between the exchange rate and its fundamental determinants. This stabilizing (or "honeymoon") effect of the bands implies that a rise in the exchange rate toward the upper bands leads to a *fall* in the expected change in the exchange rate. If uncovered interest parity holds, then there should be a fall in the interest differential as well. In the case of the FF/DM rate, for example, a depreciation of the franc towards its upper band should induce a fall in the expected depreciation of the franc and a fall in the franc-mark interest differential. Krugman emphasizes that these dynamics depend crucially on the exchange rate bands being fully credible.

Attempts to verify this negative correlation between the exchange rate and interest differential have met with only limited success. Svensson (1991b) finds a negative correlation for the Swedish target zone. But Bertola and Caballero (1992) find a positive correlation for France in the ERM. Flood, Rose, and Mathieson (1991), using daily data so that they can analyze subperiods of the ERM, find both positive and negative correlations between exchange rates and interest differentials depending on the subperiod.

Bertola and Svensson (1993) suggest a way to reconcile these conflicting results by introducing into the target zone analysis the possibility of devaluations. Suppose that variations in exchange rates are primarily due to changes in the expected rate of devaluation; then a rise in the exchange rate may be associated with an *increase* rather than a decrease in the interest differential. Because the central rate lacks credibility, the exchange rate bands lose their stabilizing influence.

B.   *Empirical models of target zones*

Whether exchange rate bands are stabilizing or not is thus an empirical question. The previous section showed that interest rate differentials are often too large to be consistent with credible bands. This suggests that the interest differentials may reflect both anticipated devaluations of the central rate and movements in the market rate relative to the central rate. Define c_{kt} as the natural log of the central rate, $c_{kt} = \ln(C_{kt})$, and define e_{kt} as the log of the ratio of the market rate to the central rate, $e_{kt} = \ln(S_{kt}/C_{kt})$. Then the expected change in the market exchange rate for currency k, Δx_{kt}, can be decomposed into the expected devaluation plus the expected movement of the market rate relative to the central rate.[18]

$$\Delta x_{kt} = E_t(c_{kt+1} - c_{kt}) + E_t(e_{kt+1} - e_{kt}) \tag{5.3}$$

It is important to keep both elements of this decomposition in mind, since the movement in e_{kt} can be large even in the month when a devaluation occurs. Recall that in Table 5.4, the actual depreciation of the FF/DM rate in any month when a realignment occurs falls short of the realignment of the central bands. In several cases, the implied movement of e_{kt} is quite substantial. In June 1982, for example, the franc's central rate was raised by 10.61 percent, but the market rate rose by only 6.55 percent. So the position of the market rate within the new bands was about 4 percent lower than within the old bands. As shown in Figure 5.1, the franc went from the top of the prerealignment bands to the bottom of the postrealignment bands.

Under the assumption of uncovered interest parity, expected devaluations can be related to the interest differential and expected movement in e_{kt} as follows:[19]

$$E_t(c_{kt+1} - c_{kt}) = \delta_{kt} - E_t(e_{kt+1} - e_{kt}) \tag{5.4}$$

18. Recall that Δx_{kt} measures the expected change in the spot rate, $E_t(\Delta s_{kt})$, where $\Delta s_{kt} = \ln(S_{kt+1}) - \ln(S_{kt})$.
19. Bertola and Svensson (1993) suggest this decomposition.

Neither of the expected changes in Equation (5.4) are observable directly, but a paper by Chen and Giovannini (1993) shows how to investigate these expectations indirectly. These authors relate an ex post measure of this expression, $\delta_{kt} - (e_{kt+1} - e_{kt})$ to variables in the current information set, Y_{kt}, which may influence expectations of devaluation:

$$\delta_{kt} - (e_{kt+1} - e_{kt}) = \lambda_k Y_{kt} + u_{kt} \qquad (5.5)$$

The disturbance term u_{kt} has two components: the forecast error $(e_{kt+1} - E_t e_{kt+1})$ and an error term due to the imprecise measurement of expectations. Under the usual rational expectations assumption, the former is orthogonal to any variable included in Y_{kt}. As Chen and Giovannini argue, the forecast error is likely to swamp the error due to mismeasurement because the variance of the unpredictable component of exchange rates is so high.

Among the variables that Chen and Giovannini include in the set of information variables are two that directly relate to the credibility of the bands:

e_{kt}: the log of the current spot rate relative to the central rate
τ_{kt}: the time elapsed since the last realignment of currency k

in which case the equation takes the form:

$$\delta_{kt} - (e_{kt+1} - e_{kt}) = a_0 + a_1 e_{kt} + a_2 \tau_{kt} + u'_{kt} \qquad (5.5')$$

The authors argue that, if the bands are not credible, an upward movement away from the central rate should lead to an increase in expected devaluation.[20] On the other hand, the longer the time period since the last realignment, the more credible the bands become. So the expected devaluation should be positively related to e_{kt}, and negatively related to τ_{kt}.

Rose and Svensson (1993) suggest a different approach to estimating devaluation expectations called the *drift adjustment method*.[21] They estimate equations for the expected movement in $(e_{kt+1} - e_{kt})$, then subtract the estimates from the interest differential, δ_{kt}. Their estimated equation relates the actual change in e_{kt} to two variables, the current level of e_{kt} and the interest differential:

$$e_{kt+1} - e_{kt} = b_0 + b_1 \delta_{kt} + b_2 e_{kt} + u''_{kt} \qquad (5.6)$$

Equations in the form of (5.6) provide a direct measure of mean-reversion in the series for e_{kt}, mean-reversion being one implication of the Krugman model. (The coefficient of e_{kt} is negative if there is mean-reversion, but equal to zero if e_{kt} follows a random walk.) Equations in the form of (5.5'),

---

20. In contrast, if the bands are credible and if UIP holds, the dependent variable should have an expected value of zero, so that the coefficients in Equation (5.5') should be equal to zero (unless forecast errors are systematically related to e_{kt} or τ_{kt}).

21. See also Rose and Svensson (1991) and Svensson (1993a). For an alternative model of realignment, see Collins (1992).

on the other hand, provide a more direct measure of devaluation expectations than does this drift-adjustment method.

Table 5.5 reports equations in the same form as those of Chen and Giovannini. Two versions of Equation (5.5′) are reported, one with dummy variables defined for each subperiod between realignments. Equations for the franc and lira only are reported, since the guilder-mark central rate remained virtually unchanged throughout the 1980s (and the pound stayed out of the ERM until 1990). In all four equations for the franc and lira, the two credibility variables suggested by Chen and Giovannini play an important role in the equation. The coefficient of e_{kt} is positive (and statistically significant), indicating that a rise in the FF/DM rate or Lira/DM rate relative to its central rate is associated with *increased* expectations of devaluation. Under this interpretation, the bands lack credibility and the honeymoon effect predicted by the Krugman model is contradicted by the evidence.[22] In all four equations, the coefficient of τ_{kt} has its postulated negative sign, suggesting that the exchange rate bands do gain credibility over time. This result is somewhat surprising because it could be argued that the elapse of time permits inflation differentials to accumulate, resulting in cumulative losses in competitiveness for the country with higher inflation. To investigate this possibility, I specified a variable measuring the *cumulative* change in relative prices between country k and Germany, but this variable was totally insignificant in the French equation and had the wrong (negative) sign in the Italian equation.[23]

Like most studies of exchange rate bands, Chen and Giovannini (1993) explicitly assume uncovered interest parity. Since the evidence against UIP is so overwhelming in the case of the freely fluctuating dollar exchange rates, however, it makes sense to investigate UIP for the mark-centered ERM exchange rates. So I report the following set of regressions, which investigate uncovered interest differentials rather than devaluation expectations alone. The equations take the form:

$$\delta_{kt} - \Delta s_{kt} = \gamma_k Z_{kt} + \epsilon_{kt} \qquad (5.7)$$

where Z_{kt} is a matrix of variables in the current information set. As in the case of the regressions in Chapter 4 of the same form, significant coeffi-

22. It should be noted that a positive correlation between expectations of devaluation and e_{kt} is also consistent with the model of Bertola and Svensson (1993), where e_{kt} is determined by devaluation expectations that are completely exogenous.
23. Chen and Giovannini also include a relative price variable in their regressions. This variable is defined not as the cumulative change but is this period's change in relative prices. They also include a number of other variables that could potentially influence expectations of devaluation, but find that most are insignificant. I have kept the number of variables to a minimum since I want to use the same set in the second set of regressions in Table 5.6.

Table 5.5. *Expected devaluations of the franc and lira in the EMS.*

	FF/DM rate 1979(3)-92(12)		Lira/DM rate 1980(10)-92(7)	
	Constant included	Regime dummy variables included[a]	Constant included	Regime dummy variables included
Constant	0.09		0.14	
(s.e.)	(0.02)		(0.03)	
[*p*-value]	[0.000]		[0.000]	
e_{kt}	0.43	0.57	0.22	0.34
(s.e.)	(0.10)	(0.10)	(0.07)	(0.09)
[*p*-value]	[0.000]	[0.000]	[0.003]	[0.000]
τ_{kt}	-0.03	-0.02	-0.05	-0.04
(s.e.)	(0.01)	(0.01)	(0.02)	(0.02)
[*p*-value]	[0.000]	[0.001]	[0.009]	[0.064]
R^2	0.185	0.318	0.098	0.262
$\chi^2(2)$	21.95	34.20	10.37	15.02
[*p*-value][b]	[0.000]	[0.000]	[0.006]	[0.001]

[a] Not reported.
[b] The χ^2-statistic tests the joint hypothesis that the coefficients of e_{kt} and τ_{kt} are jointly equal to zero. The *p*-value is given below the statistic.

cients may indicate the presence of time-varying risk premiums or systematic forecast errors. Among the variables included in the information set are the credibility variables previously defined. So in addition to the share yields and interest differentials found to be significant in the dollar-centered regressions of Chapter 4, I include credibility variables found to be significant in the Chen and Giovannini (1993) study.

Table 5.6 reports regressions explaining excess returns on currency k in the same form as Equation (5.7). Equations for all four European exchange rates are reported. The equations are reported for the full EMS

Table 5.6. *Predictable components of uncovered interest differentials during EMS period, 1979(3)-1992(12).*[a]

	FF/DM	Lira/DM[b]	£/DM	DFL/DM
Interest				
differential	-1.19	0.67	2.03	4.49
(s.e.)	(0.74)	(0.39)	(0.56)	(1.19)
[*p*-value]	[0.109]	[0.089]	[0.000]	[0.000]
Local				
dividend yield	0.24	-0.06	0.06	-0.29
(s.e.)	(0.10)	(0.13)	(0.08)	(0.35)
[*p*-value]	[0.024]	[0.619]	[0.503]	[0.410]
German				
dividend yield	-0.33	-0.36	-0.01	0.51
(s.e.)	(0.16)	(0.41)	(0.09)	(0.33)
[*p*-value]	[0.035]	[0.386]	[0.928]	[0.129]
e_{kt}	0.25	-0.06	0.33	-0.39
(s.e.)	(0.08)	(0.07)	(0.11)	(0.65)
[*p*-value]	[0.002]	[0.430]	[0.002]	[0.552]
τ_{kt}	-0.02	0.03	0.00	0.11
(s.e.)	(0.01)	(0.04)	(0.00)	(0.08)
[*p*-value]	[0.010]	[0.444]	[0.267]	[0.139]
R^2	0.090	0.084	0.217	0.097
$\chi^2(5)$	13.13	8.99	29.67	21.71
[*p*-value][c]	[0.022]	[0.109]	[0.000]	[0.001]

[a] A constant was included in the estimation, but is not reported.
[b] The equation for the lira/DM rate begins in October 1980 when the Eurolira series begins.
[c] The χ^2-statistic tests the joint hypothesis that the coefficients of the five independent variables are jointly equal to zero. The *p*-value is given below the statistic.

period through December 1992, even though in the cases of the lira and pound the EMS credibility variables are defined only for the periods when these currencies were within the ERM.

There is evidence of predictability in the excess returns on all four currencies in Table 5.6. In the case of the excess return on the franc, in particular, the two dividend yields as well as the two credibility variables are all statistically significant at the 5 percent level. According to this equation, a rise in e_{kt} is associated with a *rise* in the excess return on the franc. As explained above, this could be due either to a rise in the risk premium on the franc or a forecast error. A rise in τ_{kt} leads to a fall in the excess return on the franc, suggesting that the risk premium (or forecast error) is systematically related to the time elapsed since the last devaluation. In the case of the lira/DM rate, in contrast, neither of the credibility variables is statistically significant. In fact, the interest differential is the only significant variable (at the 10 percent level), even though the Wald-statistic testing the joint significance of the independent variables has a p-value of only 0.109. The excess return on the guilder also has no significant relationship to the credibility variables; if there is any risk premium on the guilder, it is not associated with these EMS credibility variables. The coefficient of e_{kt} in the £/DM equation is statistically significant, but this variable is defined only for the October 1990–July 1992 period. So of the three currencies that entered the ERM in 1979, it is only the excess return on the franc that is significantly related to e_{kt} and τ_{kt}.

What conclusions can be drawn from Tables 5.5 and 5.6? In the cases of the franc and lira, there is evidence that the ERM bands fail to play a stabilizing role. An increase in e_{kt} is associated with an increased expectation of devaluation or a rise in the risk premium (or possibly both). But the longer bands are in effect, the more credible they become. In the case of the franc, it is possible to be more precise about how the bands work. The finding that e_{kt} is statistically significant in both Tables 5.5 and 5.6 indicates that it is not just expectations of devaluation that vary with e_{kt}. According to Table 5.6, excess returns on the franc are also systematically related to movements of the franc within its bands. So there is evidence that increases in e_{kt} are associated with larger risk premiums on the franc or alternatively with excess returns on the franc due to forecast errors. For both the franc and lira, the ERM bands *do* matter, even if they work differently than in Krugman's original model.

IV.   Recent behavior in the EMS

The realignment of January 1987, which lowered the value of the franc and lira by 3 percent relative to the mark and guilder, signaled the beginning of a tranquil period of over five years when speculation against the major currencies virtually ceased. During this period, interest rates on the franc and lira (as well as the pound once it joined the ERM) converged towards German levels. Inflation differentials vis-à-vis Germany also fell for these same currencies. Confidence in the ERM was strengthened by the Basle-Nyborg Agreement of September 1987, in which central bank governors agreed to extend the use of the VSTFF (the very short-term financing facility) to finance intramarginal foreign exchange intervention. (Prior to that agreement, financing was available only when exchange rates reached the bands.) But probably more important than any explicit agreement was the increasing perception that the French and Italian authorities were determined to avoid any further realignments of their currencies and hence were committed to monetary policies more closely in line with those of Germany.[24]

A.   The convergence of European interest rates

The enhanced credibility of the EMS central rates led to a widespread belief in the gradual convergence of European interest rates. According to this view, interest rates on currencies like the franc and lira would converge with those on the mark (as well as other strong currencies like the guilder). If the EMS evolved toward European monetary union, in fact, the convergence might result in full equalization of European interest rates. Figure 5.7 suggests that the convergence strategy had some empirical basis, since interest differentials between the lira, franc, or pound relative to the mark fell significantly during much of the post-1987 period. French and Italian interest rates began converging toward mark rates in 1988, French rates becoming almost equal to mark rates by 1991. Sterling did not join the ERM until October 1980, but sterling interest rates converged steadily towards mark interest rates thereafter. This convergence was undoubtedly helped along by the increase in German interest rates both before and after the reunification of the two Germanys. Note that Italian interest rates began rising again relative to mark rates even before the September 1992 crisis.

The convergence view gave rise to portfolio strategies designed to take advantage of the ERM's newly found credibility. These strategies involved investing in the high-yielding weaker currencies like the pound and lira,

---

24. Giavazzi and Giovannini (1989) argue that the EMS became a mark-centered regime even before 1987 despite rules about foreign exchange intervention designed to avoid the asymmetric features of the Bretton Woods system, which centered around the dollar. See also Giavazzi and Pagano (1988), Fratianni and von Hagen (1990), and De Grauwe (1992).

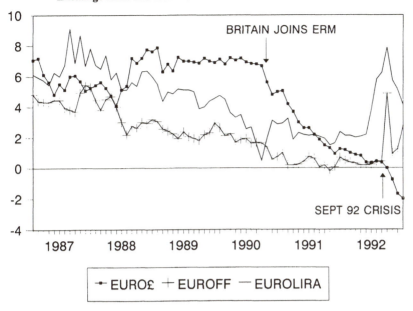

Figure 5.7. Interest differentials relative to Euromark: 1-month Euro-rates, 1987(1)–1992(12).

trusting that the ERM parities would hold firm.[25] A so-called "cross hedge" strategy guarded against depreciations of European currencies relative to the dollar by borrowing marks at the same time as investing in the pound or lira.[26] It should be pointed out that the convergence strategy was based on the implicit assumption that the market was inefficiently pricing the weaker European currencies. If risk premiums are ignored,[27] uncovered interest parity states that interest differentials can persist only if the market as a whole expects a depreciation of the higher interest rate currency large enough to offset the interest differential. So the convergence strategists were betting that the rest of the market was wrong in insisting on a devaluation premium for the lira and pound.

25. Goldstein et al. (1993, p. 10) estimates that such convergence strategies may have involved as much as $ 300 billion. This IMF study provides a detailed analysis of market behavior before and during the crisis of September 1992.
26. This was a popular strategy of the American global income funds that emerged in the three years prior to the September 1992 crisis. See *The Economist* (October 10, 1992, p. 97–98) for a postmortem on these funds.
27. If the higher interest rates on the lira and pound reflected risk premiums, then the convergence strategy simply represented a choice of higher expected return to compensate for the higher risk. It is unlikely that portfolio managers, particularly those managing global income funds, perceived their strategies in those terms.

Table 5.7. *Unconditional estimates of uncovered interest differentials for European exchange rates from January 1987.*

	FF/DM	Lira/DM	DFL/DM	£/DM
1987(1)-92(7)				
Differential	1.83	3.07	0.40	5.20
(s.e.)	(0.85)	(0.98)	(0.75)	(2.70)
[*p*-value]	[0.035]	[0.003]	[0.594]	[0.059]
1987(1)-92(12)				
Differential	1.93	-0.01	0.34	2.20
(s.e.)	(0.81)	(2.53)	(0.71)	(3.22)
[*p*-value]	[0.021]	[0.995]	[0.627]	[0.496]

Note: All variables are expressed in percent per annum. The numbers in parentheses are the heteroskedasticity-consistent standard errors. The numbers in square brackets are *p*-values for the coefficients being significantly different from zero.

Chapter 4 discussed the importance of peso-type phenomena in foreign exchange markets where anticipated jumps in exchange rates may not occur in a given sample period. The period prior to September 1992 may be such a period. Consider the evidence on uncovered differentials presented in Table 5.7. This table measures the excess return on four currencies relative to the mark over the period since January 1987 (the last realignment prior to September 1992). The top half of the table reports returns until July 1992 (measuring returns through the end of August), while the bottom half reports returns through the end of December 1992. The excess return on the lira conforms most closely to the peso model. Prior to dropping out of the ERM, a Eurolira deposit earns 3.07 percent more than a Euromark deposit when both are measured in marks. But this excess return is eliminated by December 1992. The excess return on the franc, in contrast, is not eliminated, perhaps because the market was anticipating a realignment that did not occur (at least by the end of the sample period). The guilder return is very close to that of the mark and is unchanged when extended to the end of 1992. Finally, the pound provides a large 5.20 percent excess return through July 1992, but still gives an excess return of 2.20 percent through the end of that year. Recall, however, that the pound did not join the ERM until October 1990. When measured over the October 1980–July 1992 period, the excess return is actually −0.76 percent, while it is −7.65 percent when measured from October 1990 through the end of 1992. So, when applied to the period when sterling was in the ERM, the convergence strategy was unprofitable even *before* the September crisis, largely because sterling's 6 percent bands permitted substantial depreciation against the mark even before realignment.

B.   The Maastricht Agreement and its aftermath

Those betting on the convergence of European interest rates were undoubtedly heartened by the signing of the Maastricht Agreement in December 1991, which set out a timetable for a single European currency. Maastricht called for a single European currency and a European Central Bank by 1999 at the latest.[28]

The agreement set forth certain preconditions that countries would have to fulfill to be approved for entry into the new system. Among these were requirements that the inflation rate of each country entering be within 1.5 percent of the rates of the three lowest-inflation countries, that each country's government deficit be within 3 percent of its GDP, and that government debt be within 60 percent of GDP.[29] Among the major countries, Italy had a projected budget deficit for 1992 of 11.3 percent of GDP, Britain 4.6 percent, and Germany 3.4 percent. Only France met the Maastricht requirement with a budget deficit of 2.3 percent of GDP.[30] As far as inflation is concerned, Italy's projected inflation rate was 5.2 percent compared with a 2.3 percent rate for the lowest-inflation countries (which included France). Italy was also an outlier (among the major countries) as far as government debt is concerned with an outstanding debt equal to about 100 percent of GDP.[31] Britain, in contrast, satisfied both the inflation and debt criteria.

In explaining the crisis to follow, what may be more important than the *current* rate of inflation is the *cumulative* loss of competitiveness since the last realignment.[32] After reviewing the evidence of cumulative changes in

28. Kenen (1992) analyzes the Maastricht Agreement and the problems of transition to a full European monetary union.
29. There was also a requirement that long-term interest rates be no higher than 2 percent above the three lowest-inflation countries and that no devaluations should have occurred within two years of entry. These latter requirements would be easier to satisfy if the currencies gained credibility from having met the inflation and fiscal requirements.
30. *The Economist* (September 19, 1992), p. 89.
31. In a paper published over a year before the September 1992 crisis, Froot and Rogoff (1991) cited relative price trends, continuing budget deficits, and growing current account deficits as evidence that the lira was seriously overvalued.
32. De Grauwe (1992) emphasizes the importance of cumulative changes in competitiveness in his monograph on monetary integration. See also Froot and Rogoff (1991).

competitiveness, Eichengreen and Wyplosz (1993) conclude that Italy's inflation since the last realignment in 1987 had led to a substantial deteriora-
tion of competitiveness vis-à-vis Germany. French competitiveness, in
contrast, was virtually unchanged. The evidence is more ambiguous for
Britain. (In the next chapter I will examine relative price trends using a
variety of different measures.) Eichengreen and Wyplosz also cite reunification as a direct cause of tension within the ERM because the increase
in domestic spending associated with the reunification required a real appreciation of the mark (rather than constant relative prices between Germany and other EMS countries).[33] In his comment on their paper, Branson (1993) suggests that this reunification spending may have been the
primary cause of tension within the ERM because the high German interest rates induced by the spending put heavy pressure on all of the other
European currencies.

Whatever the cause of the underlying tension, hopes that the Maastricht
Agreement would win quick approval were shattered in June 1992 when it
was rejected in a Danish referendum. Soon after, Italian interest rates began rising, spurred also by events in Italy that led to the downgrading of
Italian government debt by Moody's from AA1 to AA3 in July.[34] In contrast, French and British interest rates remained close to German levels
until September. The event that seemed to serve as a catalyst for speculative activity was the French referendum on Maastricht scheduled for September 20. By late August, French polls suggested that the vote on the
agreement would be very close. Speculators believed that if Maastricht
was rejected by the French, it would probably have to be scuttled and
plans for European monetary union postponed indefinitely.

C.   Speculative profits in September 1992

Speculative attacks follow certain patterns. Once the probability of a major realignment emerges, speculators begin taking positions against the
vulnerable currency. The speculative positions can take a variety of forms,
but a simply strategy in this case was to borrow in the Eurocurrency market of the vulnerable currency and invest in Euromarks. (Note that this is
the opposite of the convergence strategy.) The carrying cost of such a position can be sizable if the monetary authorities of the country whose cur-

33. Recall the real appreciation of the dollar that followed expansionary fiscal policy in the
    United States during the Reagan Administration.
34. The study by Goldstein et al. (1993, p. 52) cites several reasons for the downgrading
    including the delay in forming a government, the continued crisis in public funding, a
    wealth tax included in the July budget package, and the liquidation of a major state
    holding company.

rency is under attack allow interest rates to rise. In the September crisis, the Swedish authorities allowed overnight rates to approach 500 percent/ annum. When the pound, franc, and lira came under attack, however, interest rates on the pound and franc remained almost fixed, while rates on the lira rose from 15 to 23 percent (for seven-day deposits) between early August and the last trading day before the lira realignment on September 13.

Table 5.8 shows a breakdown of speculative profits from one-week positions starting at the end of July 1992. In all cases, the position involves borrowing the currency under attack for one week (in the Eurocurrency market) and investing in one-week Euromark deposits. The profits are expressed in dollars to make them comparable across currencies and are measured in percent/*week*. In examining returns over a single week, it is important to include transactions costs in measures of profits; so bid and ask rates from the *Financial Times* are used.[35] If S_{kt}^b and S_{kt}^a are the bid and ask rates for currency k measured in $k/\$$ and if I_{kt}^b and I_{kt}^a are the bid and ask rates for Eurocurrency deposits, then the profit from a speculative position is as follows:

$$[1 + I_{Mt}^b \left(\frac{7}{360}\right)](\frac{S_{Mt}^b}{S_{Mt+1}^a}) - [1 + I_{kt}^a \left(\frac{7}{360}\right)](\frac{S_{kt}^a}{S_{kt+1}^b}) \qquad (5.8)$$

The interest rates are measured per annum; so they must be deannualized using the factor $(7/360)$.[36]

In the second column of Table 5.8, I present the pure interest rate return from a speculative position holding exchange rates fixed; since the weaker currencies bore higher interest rates, this negative term represents the carrying cost of the position. The third column gives the total return (interest plus currency gain) in percent/week. In the weeks prior to the September 13–16 crisis, the interest carrying costs range from about 0.01 percent for short positions in sterling and the franc to over 0.10 percent for short positions in the lira.[37] Interest carrying costs are so low for the former currencies because, as Figure 5.7 shows, interest rates on sterling and the franc had declined to levels close to Euromark rates by August 1992. In some weeks, the carrying cost was more than offset by the depreciation of the pound, franc, or lira within its bands with the mark, so that the specu-

---

35. Large trades may be executed at more favorable prices than the quoted bid and ask rates; so Equation (5.8) may underestimate true profits from speculation. See the discussion of foreign exchange trading in Lyons (1993).
36. The Eurocurrency market uses a 360-day year; so interest rates are deannualized using the factor, number of actual days in contract/360.
37. If the Eurolira rate is 15 percent/annum and the Euromark rate is 9 percent/annum, then the carrying cost is $(0.15–0.09)(7/360) = 0.00117$ percent/week.

Table 5.8. *Profits from speculation through September 1992 crisis measured in dollars in percent/week (borrow from £, FF, or lira seven-day Eurocurrency market and invest in DM market).*

Friday to Friday starting	Interest only	Total return (interest plus capital gain)	Cumulative return
Sterling			
7-31	-0.017	0.426	0.426
8-7	-0.005	0.277	0.705
8-14	-0.004	0.449	1.157
8-21	-0.009	0.229	1.388
8-28	-0.006	-0.525	0.856
9-4	-0.005	0.220	1.078
Crisis week			
9-11	-0.007	6.055	7.199
French franc			
7-31	-0.019	-0.141	-0.141
8-7	-0.006	0.056	-0.086
8-14	-0.007	0.013	-0.073
8-21	-0.007	0.175	0.102
8-28	-0.011	-0.322	-0.220
9-4	-0.009	-0.175	-0.394
Crisis week			
9-11	-0.010	0.374	-0.022
Lira			
7-31	-0.158	-0.162	-0.162
8-7	-0.090	0.176	0.013
8-14	-0.123	0.033	0.046
8-21	-0.123	0.218	0.264
8-28	-0.130	-0.313	-0.050
9-4	-0.182	-0.241	-0.291
Crisis week			
9-11	-0.318	7.806	7.493

Source: Financial Times, various issues.

lative position actually gained small profits even in the absence of a re-alignment. The last column, however, shows that the *cumulative* profits of a position held from the end of July until September 11 were still negative for two of the three currencies: -0.394 percent for the franc and -0.291 percent for the lira. But they were close enough to zero to constitute a *one-way bet* against the vulnerable currencies.[38] Ironically enough, a short position in sterling actually brought profits of 1.078 percent for the specu-lator even before sterling had to drop out of the ERM, simply because sterling began to weaken when it was still considerably below its 6 percent upper band against the mark.

In the last week listed in the table, which begins on Friday, September 11, speculators scored a major victory because the pound and lira dropped out of the ERM, the pound on September 16 and the lira one day later. Those short in sterling gained 6.055 percent while those short in lira gained 7.806 percent. (Speculators against the franc were disappointed with a 0.374 percent gain because the franc's central rate was successfully defended.) Positions held for the entire seven-week period were also very profitable, even for the high-interest lira. When the costs of holding the lira position from the end of July are taken into account, the cumulative profits are substantial at 7.493 percent.

Over the remaining two weeks of September, short positions in sterling and the lira were rewarded with further profits of 7.099 percent and 4.955 percent, respectively. But those profits were not gained from bets against the ERM, since both currencies were by then floating freely.

D.   The temporary reemergence of capital controls

During most of the 1980s, the French national markets were shielded from attacks on the franc by extensive capital controls. As shown in Chapter 3, the French controls kept speculative pressure confined largely to the Eurofranc market in London so that the premium of Eurofranc over French national interest rates sometimes soared to double-digit levels. The Italian authorities maintained controls as long as the French; so a similar differential developed between Eurolira and Italian interest rates. By the time that the speculative attack occurred in September 1992, however, all French and Italian capital controls had been removed.[39] British and Ger-

---

38. The term "one-way bet" also refers to the belief that there was virtually no chance that the lira, pound, or other vulnerable currencies would rise rather than fall in value in a realignment.

39. The Single Europe Act mandated the removal of all controls by July 1, 1990 (with some exceptions for countries like Spain). France removed its last controls in January 1990, Italy in July 1990.

man controls had been removed much earlier. So (in principle at least) speculators were free to borrow the franc or pound or any other vulnerable currency.

The classic defense against a speculative attack is to raise interest rates in the market whose currency is under attack. Governments may delay such action because high interest rates can impose substantial costs on an economy.[40] The British did not attempt to raise rates until the very day, September 16, when sterling succumbed to the attack and withdrew from the ERM. Prior to the withdrawal decision that day, the Bank of England raised its minimum lending rate from 10 percent to 12 percent and announced a rise to 15 percent for the next day. As a result, Eurosterling rates soared: the one-month rate was quoted at 15 percent bid and 30 percent ask.[41] In the chaos of that one trading day, gaps may have appeared between the British interbank and Eurosterling interbank rates; according to the *Financial Times,* the British one-month interbank rate closed at 11 percent bid and 30 percent ask. In any case, both Eurosterling and British rates fell back to normal the following day after sterling began floating.

The French franc, however, came under attack soon after the pound and lira had dropped out of the ERM. In this case the rise in interest rates was more prolonged. The French voted in favor of the Maastricht Treaty on Sunday, September 20, but the 51 percent majority voted did little to dissuade speculators from attacking the franc. Over the next two weeks, the French authorities defended their currency by raising interest rates sharply. One-month interbank rates soared to 14 percent from 10 percent, while overnight rates rose to over 20 percent. What is more puzzling is that higher French interest rates were accompanied by an increasing differential between Eurofranc and French interest rates as if capital controls were still in place. Figure 5.8 shows that one-month Eurofranc rates rose on one day to 5 percent above French interbank rates of the same maturity. Smaller gaps of 1 to 2 percent occurred on other days. *The Economist* attributed this differential to implicit barriers to capital possibly involving "moral suasion" by the French authorities who encouraged French banks to keep funds at home.[42] Figure 5.8 also suggests that there

40. Eichengreen and Wyplosz (1993) argue that high interest rates impose unduly burdensome costs on an economy, especially if its mortgage rates are indexed (as in Britain), its government debt is excessively large (as in Italy), or its banks are vulnerable (as in several European countries).
41. *Financial Times* (September 16, 1992). The seven-day Eurosterling rate was 24 percent bid and 30 percent ask.
42. *The Economist* (October 10, 1992), p. 97. This article also noted that money market rates rose 3 or 4 percent above prime lending rates in the French market. Obstfeld (1993a) also discusses these differentials between Eurocurrency and national interest rates.

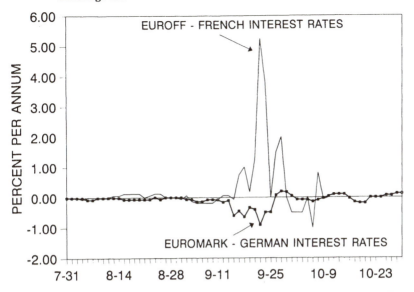

Figure 5.8. Eurocurrency minus national interest rates: 1-month Euro-rates, August–October 1992.

may have been implicit controls on *inflows* to the German market, since Euromark rates fell below German money market rates. Goldstein et al. (1993, p. 56) attributes this phenomenon to a "gentlemen's agreement" between the Bundesbank and German banks, which limited the onlending of Euromark deposits from German branches in London to their head offices in Germany.

So there is evidence that informal controls remain in some European countries. They may be inactive in normal times, but in a crisis the authorities may maintain some control over even arbitrage activity. In the case of the FF/DM rate, these controls may have been effective enough to help stave off a realignment of the franc in September and October of 1992. Whether the reemergence of controls is a one-time phenomenon remains to be seen.

V.   Concluding remarks

This chapter has made it clear that the European Monetary System has fallen somewhat short of its objective to date. It has not managed to stabilize exchange rates between European currencies. The frequent realignments of the first eight years of the EMS led to steady depreciations of the franc and lira. Nor did the financial market have much confidence in the system, since it demanded realignment premiums on franc and lira interest rates. When the franc and lira depreciated within their bands, moreover, these realignment premiums only increased. It is true that the 1987 realignments were followed by five years of stable exchange rates. But the events of September 1992 shattered the calm, reminding everyone about how vulnerable currencies are to speculative attack.

Yet in the aftermath of this speculative crisis, it is easy to forget the achievements of the EMS. These achievements include a narrowing of inflation rate and interest rate differentials, particularly since 1987 (although differentials also narrowed for the other G-5 countries). There is evidence that, after the realignments of January 1987, market participants were beginning to accept the view that the monetary policies of the major countries were going to converge. For five years prior to the crisis, interest rates on the franc, lira, and pound *did* start to converge with those of the mark. That the convergence was incomplete is an indication that the markets recognized that differences in national policies persisted, particularly in the case of Italy.

It may be true that full coordination of national policies could lead to stable exchange rates even in the absence of monetary union. The stability of the guilder-mark rate is evidence in favor of this proposition. Yet speculative attacks against the franc provide evidence to the contrary. France *had* lowered inflation to German levels and had matched if not exceeded the fiscal performance of Germany; yet the franc was attacked as vehemently in late September of 1992, as had the pound and lira been earlier in the month. So there is some doubt that policy coordination alone will keep exchange rates stable.

What are the implications of these findings for relative returns and relative financing costs within Europe? Exchange rates between the major currencies have been variable enough to keep uncovered returns measured in any given currency from being equalized. The evidence shows that uncovered interest differentials persist among the major European countries. In fact, departures from uncovered interest parity within the EMS are as large on average as those between EMS and non-EMS currencies. So the EMS, at least to date, has not been able to narrow differences in nominal financing costs between firms from different countries. The next chapter will consider whether departures from UIP inside and outside Europe are also reflected in real interest differentials.

CHAPTER 6

Real interest differentials

In many settings, financing and investing decisions can be based on nominal interest rates. But with high or variable inflation rates, it is often useful to examine real interest rates, that is, interest rates adjusted for expected inflation. This chapter offers evidence on real interest rates faced by the Group of Five industrial countries over the past 20 years. The real interest rates that will be studied include one-month and three-month Eurocurrency rates as well as three-month national loan rates. Two measures of real interest rates for government bonds will also be discussed.

The chapter examines the conditions under which "real interest parity" holds, in which case real borrowing costs and real returns to investment are the same across countries. One of the two key conditions that ensures real interest parity involves relative prices, the so-called "purchasing power parity" condition. So the first section of the chapter reviews the evidence on purchasing power parity. For some currencies, estimates of real interest rates vary widely depending on the composition of the price indexes used to deflate nominal returns. So the chapter will distinguish between estimates of real interest rates based on the broad-based consumer price index and those based on other price indexes, such as the producer price index for the manufacturing sector alone.

I. Purchasing power parity: theory and evidence

Purchasing power parity has a long tradition in international finance originating with classical writers like Ricardo. It was Gustav Cassel, however, who brought the doctrine into prominence in this century through a series of studies in the 1920s.[1] Since then the theory has been subjected to a variety of tests for numerous sets of countries and a variety of time periods. It has often fared badly in these tests, but the theoretical simplicity of this concept makes it among the most resilient in economics.

1. See Cassel (1921). Frenkel (1978) describes the historical origins of PPP.

A.   *Traditional formulations of PPP*

PPP is usually formulated in two alternative ways. The *absolute* form of
PPP states that prices in two different countries should be equal when
expressed in a single currency. If P_{kt} is the price of country k's goods, P_{At}
is the price of U.S. goods, and S_{kt} is the level of the exchange rate (currency
k price of the dollar), then the absolute form of PPP states that $P_{kt} = P_{At}$
S_{kt}, or in natural logs, $p_{kt} = p_{At} + s_{kt}$. For this form of PPP to be meaning-
ful, the prices must be those of individual goods or baskets of goods with
identical weights across countries.[2] If individual goods are involved, the
phrase "law of one price" is often used in place of PPP. This form of PPP
is unlikely to hold even for homogeneous commodities, however, since any
tariffs or transport costs would cause departures from PPP.[3]

The *relative* form of PPP states that *changes* in prices are related between
countries. These changes can be defined relative to a base year or from
one period to the next. If the changes are measured from period to period,
the relative form can be expressed in logs as follows:

$$\Delta p_{kt} = \Delta p_{At} + \Delta s_{kt} \tag{6.1}$$

where Δp_{kt} is the inflation rate in country k, $\Delta p_{kt} = \ln(P_{kt+1}/P_{kt})$, and Δs_{kt}
is the rate of depreciation of currency k relative to the dollar, $\Delta s_{kt} =$
$\ln(S_{kt+1}/S_{kt})$. This form is less restrictive than the absolute form, since barriers to trade such as tariffs and transport costs need not necessarily lead
to a breakdown of PPP as long as the tariffs or transport costs are proportional to prices.[4]

Departures from even this less restrictive form of PPP are so frequent,
however, that institutions like the IMF and Morgan Guaranty Trust regularly report series for real exchange rates, which measure the ratio of one
country's price to that of other countries. Figure 6.1 displays real exchange
rates based on consumer price indexes for three of the four G-5 exchange
rates relative to the dollar. The real exchange rates are defined as the relative price of country k's goods to those of the United States (with prices
defined relative to a base year):

$$N_{kt} = \frac{P_{kt}/(P_{At}\, S_{kt})}{P_{k0}/(P_{A0}\, S_{k0})} \tag{6.2}$$

2. Kravis et al. (1975) constructed such price indexes in order to provide PPP-based measures of real income. Conventional price indexes measure prices relative to an arbitrary
   base year with weights varying from one country to the next.
3. For evidence against the law of one price, see Isard (1977) and Richardson (1978).
4. A tariff on American goods that remains at 10 percent of value, for example, would lead
   to a constant wedge between the absolute level of prices in country k and the United
   States, but would not affect the relative form of PPP.

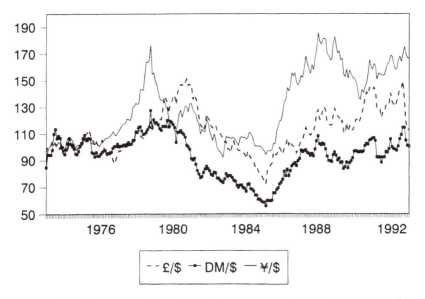

Figure 6.1. Real exchange rates (1973=100): relative consumer prices (foreign/U.S.).

Thus a rise in the index represents a real appreciation of currency k relative to the dollar. In the figure, each rate is defined relative to the base year of 1973. Since the price indexes are expressed in arbitrary units and the base year chosen is inevitably arbitrary, it is the *changes* in the real exchange rates that are of interest, not the absolute levels in any given year. It is evident from the figure that all three real exchange rates vary by 50 percent or more over the 20-year period from 1973 to 1992.

An alternative way to express the relative form of PPP is in terms of year-to-year or month-to-month percentage changes in the real exchange rate, $\Delta n_{kt} = \ln(N_{kt+1}/N_{kt})$. If PPP holds in relative form, the change in the real exchange rate should be equal to zero, or[5]

$$\Delta n_{kt} = \Delta p_{kt} - \Delta p_{At} - \Delta s_{kt} = 0 \tag{6.3}$$

Figure 6.2 shows percentage changes in the real exchange rate between the mark and dollar over the 20 years ending in 1992. The figure shows that the real exchange rate, representing the relative price of German to American goods, can change from month to month by 5 or 10 percent (where the changes are measured per month rather than per annum). Similar vol-

---

5. When expressing the change in the real exchange rate between periods t and $t + 1$, the base period prices drop out of the expression.

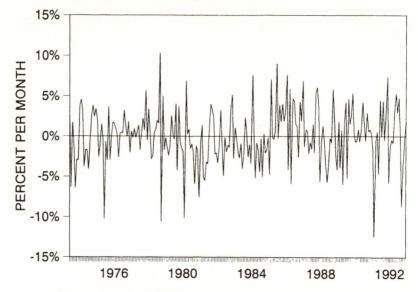

Figure 6.2. Monthly changes in DM/$ real exchange rate: relative consumer prices (German/U.S.).

atility is found between the relative prices of British or French or Japanese goods and American goods.

Whether formulated in absolute or relative form, PPP fares poorly when confronted with data. Yet it is possible that PPP holds in the long run even though deviations from PPP are the rule rather than the exception in the short run. Before considering long run evidence on PPP, consider an alternative formulation developed by Richard Roll.

B.   The efficient markets version of PPP

Purchasing power parity was given a new lease on life when Roll (1979) formulated an "efficient markets" version of PPP. Roll reasoned that market participants (or, more accurately, speculators) would respond to any perceived profit opportunities arising when the *expected* prices of any storable commodities diverged between markets. If the expected price of a commodity originating in the United States is lower than that of a commodity originating in country k, expressing both prices in a common currency, then speculators will buy in the United States and deliver in k. As a result, the expected prices of the two commodities expressed in the same currency will be equalized.

Roll pointed out that such equalization of expected prices can take place even in the absence of shipping between countries. Consider speculators from the United States who perceive a profit opportunity from purchasing country k's good at time t and reselling it at time $t + 1$. The *nominal* return from such speculation in the other country's commodity but expressed in dollars is given by $\ln\left[(P_{kt+1}/S_{kt+1})/(P_{kt}/S_{kt})\right]$ or $\Delta p_{kt} - \Delta s_{kt}$. If American speculators use the inflation rate of their own good to deflate this return, then the *real* return is given by:

$$R_{kAt} = (\Delta p_{kt} - \Delta s_{kt}) - \Delta p_{At} \qquad (6.4)$$

According to Roll, in an *efficient market* the expected return from such speculation should be equal to zero, or

$$E_t R_{kAt} = (\pi_{kt} - \Delta x_{kt}) - \pi_{At} = 0 \qquad (6.5)$$

where π_{kt} is the expected inflation rate in country k, $\pi_{kt} = E_t \Delta p_{kt}$, and Δx_{kt} is the expected change in the exchange rate (currency k/\$). This ex ante or *expectational* form of PPP is similar to UIP in being an outcome of efficient speculation. Instead of speculating by investing in interest-rate-bearing assets, the speculator invests in storable commodities.

This description of market behavior seems plausible when confined to the prices of homogeneous commodities, but Roll extends it to the price level as a whole. So speculators are assumed to be able to respond to any profit opportunities arising when the United States' price index is expected to be lower than country k's. If π_{kt} is the expected inflation rate of a broad-based price index like the consumer price index (CPI), then Equation (6.5) says that speculators will respond to any profit incentives to drive the expected inflation rates of two countries to equality (when expressed in a common currency). In any modern industrial economy, price indexes consist of much more than homogeneous, storable commodities. The market basket making up the consumer price index, for example, has a large component of nontraded services, which are in most cases neither homogeneous nor storable. The basket also includes many differentiated manufactured goods. Not only do the prices of these goods vary from producer to producer (and hence from country to country), but the same producer may charge different prices for the same good from country to country. Such "pricing to market" is a common occurrence in any market characterized by imperfect competition and barriers to complete arbitrage.[6]

In any case, Roll points out that all of the standard implications of efficient markets apply to deviations from PPP. Define the expected change in the real exchange rate as

---

6. For evidence on pricing to market, see Knetter (1989) and Marston (1990).

$$E_t \Delta n_{kt} = \pi_{kt} - (\pi_{At} + \Delta x_{kt}) \qquad (6.6)$$

where the expected inflation rates now apply to general price indexes rather than individual commodities. If all expected profit opportunities are eliminated by speculators, then $E_t \Delta n_{kt}$ should be equal to zero. If the market is efficient, moreover, then forecast errors in predicting inflation and exchange rates should be random, so that changes in n_{kt} should be random as well. The real exchange rate next period should be equal to today's real exchange rate except for a random error term, ω_{kt}:

$$n_{kt+1} = n_{kt} + \omega_{kt} \qquad (6.7)$$

If ω_{kt} has the usual error properties, an expected value of zero and no serial correlation, the real exchange rate is said to follow a *random walk* (or, more precisely, a martingale). Whenever this property of real exchange rates holds, PPP ceases to provide a long-term anchor for the exchange rate, since the real exchange rate can wander far from its initial values. (The variance of n_{kt} is infinite.) The absolute form of PPP fails to hold, while the relative form of PPP holds only in expected value terms.

It should be noted that the real exchange rate also follows a random walk in models without speculation in commodities.[7] Adler and Lehman (1983) derive Equation (6.5) using a financial arbitrage rather than commodity arbitrage argument. (This study will be discussed later in the chapter when real interest parity is examined.) In some conventional macroeconomic models with price flexibility, the real exchange rate follows a random walk as long as underlying real economic disturbances themselves follow random walks.[8] Rogoff (1992) develops an intertemporal model with international borrowing and lending in which the real exchange rate follows a random walk even when the underlying shocks are stationary. So if the real exchange rate is found to be a random walk, this need not imply that the Roll model is valid. On the other hand, all of these models share the perhaps unappealing characteristic that relative prices can take any value.

Whether justified in terms of efficient markets theory or not, this random walk characterization of real exchange rates fares well in simple empirical tests.[9] Consider a regression of the change in the real exchange rate on the current (log) level of this rate:

7. Dumas (1992), on the other hand, develops a model of commodity speculation where because of shipping costs deviations from the law of one price do not follow a Martingale event though capital market efficiency has been assumed.
8. For example, this would be true of the flexible price model described in Marston (1985).
9. Although the following discussion is confined to nonstructural models of the exchange rate, it should be noted that the random walk model outperforms several structural models based on sticky price behavior. See Meese and Rogoff (1988).

$$\Delta n_{kt} = a_0 + a_1 n_{kt} + \omega'_{kt} \tag{6.8}$$

This regression provides the basis of a unit root test to determine whether a_1 is equal to zero. Under the null hypothesis of a random walk, conventional t-statistics are biased downwards, but Dickey and Fuller (1979) provide adjusted t-statistics that will be used here. The following estimated equation allows for a deterministic time trend as well as for lagged changes in the real exchange rate (in the event that there is serial correlation in the residuals):

$$\Delta n_{kt} = a_0 + a_1 n_{kt} + a_2 \Delta n_{kt-1} + a_3 t + \omega''_{kt} \tag{6.9}$$

In this so-called augmented Dickey-Fuller test, the crucial parameter is still the t-statistic for testing whether $a_1 = 0$.

Table 6.1 reports two sets of unit root tests: one to test for a unit root in n_{kt} [as in Equation (6.9)] and the other to test for a unit root in the *change* in n_{kt}. If n_{kt} is a random walk, then we should find that n_{kt} has a unit root or is nonstationary, while Δn_{kt} is stationary. The tests are performed for two different real exchange rates, one defined using consumer price indexes and the other using producer price indexes for manufactured products. (France stopped publishing either a wholesale price index or producer price index for manufactures in 1985; so only the real exchange rate based on the consumer price index is reported.) In each case, the t-statistic for a_1 is reported along with its p-value.[10] The results of the estimation are clearcut. In all cases, a unit root for n_{kt} cannot be rejected at conventional significance levels, while a unit root for Δn_{kt} can be rejected. So it is not possible to reject the hypothesis that the real exchange rate follows a random walk.

How are these results to be interpreted? If the real exchange rate is indeed a random walk, then as previously discussed, there is no long-run equilibrium for the real exchange rate. On the other hand, small departures from random walk behavior change the economics of the real exchange rate radically. Consider a simple alternative to a random walk involving a *stationary* autoregressive process for n_{kt}:

$$n_{kt+1} = b_0 + b_1 n_{kt} + v'_{kt} \tag{6.10}$$

The autoregressive process is stationary if b_1 is less than unity. In this case, the real exchange rate follows a *mean-reverting* process, which drives it towards its long-run equilibrium value, $b_0/(1 - b_1)$, with the speed of adjustment depending on b_1. Abuaf and Jorion (1990) calculate the half-life of n_{kt}, defined as the number of months (years) required to return half-way

---

10. The p-values are based on an expanded set of critical values for the Dickey-Fuller tests as reported in MacKinnon (1990).

Table 6.1. *Tests for unit roots in real exchange rates, 1973(6)-1992(12).*

CPI	£/$	FF/$	DM/$	¥/$
Levels				
t-statistic[a]	-2.108	-1.516	-1.537	-1.862
[*p*-value][b]	[0.604]	[0.874]	[0.872]	[0.741]
Changes				
t-statistic[c]	-10.001	-9.912	-9.732	-10.359
[*p*-value]	[0.000]	[0.000]	[0.000]	[0.000]

PPI for manufacturing	£/$		DM/$	¥/$
Levels				
t-statistic	-2.303		-1.549	-1.925
[*p*-value]	[0.488]		[0.868]	[0.718]
Changes				
t-statistic	-10.124		-9.933	-10.656
[*p*-value]	[0.000]		[0.000]	[0.000]

[a] The *t*-statistics are for the coefficient a_1 in Equation (6.9).
[b] The *p*-values are based on the critical values for Dickey-Fuller tests as reported in MacKinnon (1990).
[c] These *t*-statistics test for a unit root in Δn_{kt} rather than n_{kt}.

Sources: Consumer price indexes and exchange rates: *IFS*; British and German producer prices in manufacturing: OECD, *Main Economic Indicators*; Japanese PPI in manufacturing: Bank of Japan, *Price Indexes Annual*; U.S. PPI in manufacturing: *Survey of Current Business*.

to equilibrium in monthly (annual) data. If the monthly autoregressive parameter is 0.98, then the half-life is 34 months.[11] If the autoregressive parameter is 0.96, then the half-life declines to 17 months. In either case, this near-random walk behavior leads to significant mean reversion within the space of a few years.

11. The half-life is given by $\ln(1/2)/\ln(b_1)$. See Abuaf and Jorion (1990, p. 159).

There is evidence that random walk tests have limited power relative to stationary alternatives. Using Monte Carlo methods, Hakkio (1986) shows that such tests have difficulty distinguishing random walk behavior from ARIMA models of the real exchange rate, while Lothian and Taylor (1992) show that such tests have limited power relative to simple autoregressive alternatives like Equation (6.10). The latter study shows that random walk models can be rejected using almost 200 years of annual data for the \$/£ and FF/£ real exchange rates, even though they cannot be rejected using data from the post-Bretton Woods period.[12] ARIMA or simple autoregressive models are no more rooted in economic theory than random walk models, but they do allow the real exchange rates to revert towards some long-run equilibrium value.

C.   Conditional estimates of changes in real exchange rates

One implication of the efficient markets version of PPP is that no information available at time t should be useful in predicting Δn_{kt}. Roll himself investigates this property of efficient markets in his study of ex ante PPP. Rather than testing for unit roots in n_{kt}, he tests whether lagged values of Δn_{kt} are significant determinants of Δn_{kt}. If the ex ante version of PPP holds, then Δn_{kt} should be uncorrelated not just with its lagged values, but with any variables currently known at period t. Consider the following regression relating changes in the real exchange rate, Δn_{kt}, to variables in the current information set W_{kt}:

$$\Delta n_{kt} = \lambda_k W_{kt} + v_{kt} \qquad (6.11)$$

If the efficient markets version of PPP holds, then λ_k should be insignificantly different from zero.

Table 6.2 reports tests of $\lambda_k = 0$ for the real exchange rates of the G-5 countries. Two alternative real exchange rates are examined, those based on the CPI and the PPI in manufacturing. The regressions relate the log change in the real exchange rate to variables known at time t. In choosing which variables to include in the information set, W_{kt}, there is less guidance than in the case of uncovered interest differentials in Chapter 4 where variables found in studies of equity returns could be used. Cumby and Huizinga (1992) estimate equations in the same form as (6.11) using forward premia and lagged inflation rates as information variables. Mishkin (1984) uses various functions of time (T, T^2, etc.) in his study of PPP deviations and real interest differentials. Here I have chosen to use the simple interest differentials, $i_{kt} - i_{st}$, and lagged inflation differentials over the

---

12. See also studies of long-term real exchange rate behavior by Frankel (1986), Abuaf and Jorion (1990), Diebold, Husted, and Rush (1991), and Glen (1992).

Table 6.2. *Tests for predictable components of changes in real exchange rates, 1973(6)-1992(12).*

Currencies	CPI $\chi^2(8)$ [p-value]	PPI in manufacturing $\chi^2(6)$ [p-value]
£/$	32.89 [0.000]	27.07 [0.000]
FF/$	13.90 [0.084]	
DM/$	22.01 [0.005]	13.63 [0.034]
¥/$	10.60 [0.226]	6.71 [0.348]

Notes: The χ^2-statistic tests the joint hypothesis that the coefficients of the information variables are equal to zero.

past 12 months for all four countries. So there are eight information variables in each equation (six in the case of the equations based on manufacturing prices).

Table 6.2 reports a χ^2 statistic for each exchange rate testing whether these eight variables are jointly significant. The results provide strong evidence of a systematic component in real exchange rates. In the case of the CPI-based real exchange rates, the hypothesis of $\lambda_k = 0$ is rejected at the 1 percent level for the £/$ rate and DM/$ rate and at the 10 percent level for the FF/$ rate. The evidence against the null hypothesis is almost as strong in the case of the real exchange rates based on prices in manufacturing. Of the four exchange rates, only the ¥/$ rate appears to be unrelated to current information variables.

The findings in Table 6.2 contrast with those in Roll's (1979) study wherein changes in real exchange rates were totally unrelated to their lagged values for a period, 1957 to 1976, spanning both fixed and flexible rate periods. But they are consistent with the findings of Cumby and Huizinga (1992) using data from the flexible rate period, 1975 to 1989. They are also consistent with a study by Cumby and Obstfeld (1984) for the 1975–81 period, in which they estimated an equation relating the inflation differential, $\Delta p_{kt} - \Delta p_{At}$, to the current change in the exchange rate, Δs_{kt}.[13]

Thus we are left with mounting evidence against the random walk hypothesis. The evidence in Table 6.2 suggests that for all except one currency the real exchange rate moves systematically over time. The evidence of autoregressive behavior in studies using longer (annual) time series, moreover, suggests that there are mean-reverting elements in real exchange rate series. There is also a third set of evidence about systematic movements in real exchange rates to which I now turn.

D.   Sectoral changes in relative prices

In most economies, inflation rates are higher in the sector producing nontraded goods and services than in the traded sector. This pattern can be seen in the inflation rates for the major industrial countries if consumer price indexes, which include goods and services from both nontraded and traded sectors, are compared with producer price indexes (PPI) for manufacturing.[14] Table 6.3 reports average inflation rates for four of the five G-5 countries (France being the only country without a PPI index for manufacturing). In all four countries, the inflation rate for the CPI exceeds that of the producer price index in manufacturing. In the United States, the differential between inflation rates is 0.85 percent per year, while it is about 0.40 percent per year in Britain and Germany. The inflation differential is significantly different from zero at the 5 percent level in the United States and at the 10 percent level in Germany. In Japan, the inflation differential is much larger at 2.39 percent per year, significant at the 1 percent level.

To see the effects of different sectoral inflation rates on the real exchange rate, consider the breakdown of the general inflation rate into traded and nontraded components:

$$\Delta p_{kt} = (1 - a) \, \Delta p_{kt}^T + a \, \Delta p_{kt}^{NT} \qquad (6.12)$$

where a is the share of nontraded goods in the economy. The change in

13. Because of simultaneity between the dependent variable and Δs_{kt}, they use an instrumental variable estimator.
14. A more precise comparison between inflation rates in the nontraded and traded goods sectors can be made if value-added deflators from the national income accounts are used. But these data are generally available only on an annual basis. See Marston (1987) and De Gregorio, Giovannini, and Wolf (1993).

Table 6.3. *Inflation rates and changes in real exchange rates for CPIs and PPIs in manufacturing (PPIM), 1973(6)-1992(12).*

| | Average inflation rates | | | |
	U.S.	Britain	Germany	Japan
CPI	5.98	9.00	3.47	4.60
PPIM	5.13	8.62	3.02	2.21
Difference	0.85	0.38	0.45	2.39
(s.e.)[a]	(0.41)	(0.43)	(0.27)	(0.64)
[p-value]	[0.036]	[0.378]	[0.095]	[0.000]

| | Average changes in real exchange rates | | |
	£/$	DM/$	¥/$
CPI			
Average	0.26	-0.37	2.49
(s.e.)[a]	(2.79)	(2.74)	(2.61)
[p-value]	[0.925]	[0.894]	[0.342]
PPIM			
Average	0.74	0.03	0.95
(s.e.)[a]	(2.74)	(2.79)	(2.54)
[p-value]	[0.787]	[0.990]	[0.709]

[a] The numbers in parentheses are heteroskedasticity-consistent standard errors. The p-values in square brackets test whether the differences in inflation rates or average changes in real exchange rates are significantly different from zero.

the real exchange rate between country k and the United States is then given by:[15]

$$\Delta n_{kt} = \Delta p_{kt} - \Delta p_{At} - \Delta s_{kt} = (\Delta p_{kt}^T - \Delta p_{At}^T - \Delta s_{kt})$$
$$+ a\left[(\Delta p_{kt}^{NT} - \Delta p_{kt}^T) - (\Delta p_{At}^{NT} - \Delta p_{At}^T)\right] \tag{6.13}$$

15. The expression would have additional terms if the share of nontraded goods was different in the second country than in the first.

According to this expression, changes in the real exchange rate can occur for two reasons: (1) There can be changes in the relative price of traded goods, or (2) there can be a greater gap in sectoral inflation rates in one country than another. If country k has a relatively higher inflation rate in the nontraded sector, for example, then country k's currency must appreciate in real terms if defined in terms of a general price index even if the prices of its traded goods remain equal to those in the United States.

The conventional explanation for higher inflation in the nontraded sector is found in the productivity growth hypothesis formulated by Balassa (1964) and Samuelson (1964). This hypothesis states that the secular rise in the relative prices of nontraded to traded goods is due to higher productivity growth in the traded sector. The Balassa-Samuelson model is developed in a static framework where savings and investment decisions are left unspecified. Obstfeld (1993b), however, has recently developed an intertemporal version of the Balassa-Samuelson model where productivity growth differentials lead to deterministic trends in the real exchange rate. He shows that the real exchange rate follows a stationary process as long as any stochastic shocks to productivity growth are mean-reverting.

The Balassa-Samuelson model has recently come under attack by Rogoff (1992), who argues that the model rests on restrictive assumptions about factor mobility: that factors are mobile between sectors and financial capital is internationally mobile. As Rogoff shows, if factors are immobile between sectors and the country's capital markets are closed to international borrowing and lending, then demand variables such as government spending also affect relative sectoral prices. (Factor immobility means that demand shocks in one sector necessarily lead to relative price changes between sectors.) What is more surprising is that, if internal factor immobility is combined with international mobility of capital, then productivity growth ceases to influence relative sectoral prices at all. In that case, relative sectoral prices follow a random walk, but for very different reasons than in Roll's model. Rogoff argues that factors are relatively immobile in the short run; so at best the Balassa-Samuelson model is likely to apply only in the *long run*.

Whether the productivity growth model holds only in the long run or not, there seems to be a general pattern of higher inflation in the nontraded sector in the long run. De Gregorio, Giovannini, and Wolf (1993) study 14 OECD countries over the 1970–85 period and find that all but one have higher inflation in the nontraded sector (the exception being Canada with an inflation differential of −0.03 percent). If inflation rates differ between sectors, that means firms from different sectors of the economy face different real interest rates.

How do differences in sectoral inflation rates affect the values of the real exchange rate that apply to the various sectors? The answer lies in the lower half of Table 6.3. In the case of comparisons between Britain or Germany and the United States, there is a relatively small effect because sectoral inflation gaps are very similar in the three countries. Only in the case of Japan is the sectoral inflation gap dramatic enough to make a major difference to real exchange rates. If the CPI is used to measure real exchange rates, the yen appreciated in real terms by 2.49 percent per annum over the period 1973–92.[16] If the PPI in manufacturing is used instead, then the yen appreciated by only 0.95 percent per annum. Of course, firms in the manufacturing sector are most exposed to international competition; so the fact that the average appreciation is so much smaller in that sector makes a significant difference to trade performance. The relatively large gap between inflation rates in Japan is attributed to the relatively large gap in productivity growth rates by sector in Japan.[17]

There is also evidence that gaps between changes in real exchange rates extend to individual sectors of manufacturing. Figure 6.3 reproduces the results of a study of real exchange rates by sector of manufacturing (Marston, 1991). Producer price indexes for the U.S. and Japan are used to form sectoral real exchange rates over the period from 1975 to 1987.[18] The diagram compares average (log) changes in the real exchange rates by sector with those of manufacturing as a whole.[19] The 1.6 percent figure for textiles, for example, indicates that the real exchange rate for the textile sector rose at an annual rate 1.6 percent faster than in manufacturing as a whole.

It is evident from Figure 6.3 that average changes in real exchange rates vary widely across sectors of manufacturing. In the electrical machinery sector, at the other extreme from textiles, the real exchange rate increased 2.7 percent per annum *less* than in manufacturing as a whole. One explanation for this pattern lies in productivity growth differentials. Presumably Japanese (and American) productivity growth takes place at a much more

16. Although this appreciation is economically quite significant, it is not statistically significant, no doubt because of the volatility of the nominal exchange rate series.
17. See the evidence in Hsieh (1982) and Marston (1987).
18. The price data for subsectors of Japanese and U.S. manufacturing are taken from the OECD, *Indicators of Industrial Activity,* and U.S. Department of Commerce, *Business Conditions Digest* (for the U.S. motor vehicle series).
19. The figures are calculated as the average of the log changes over the January 1975 to December 1987 period and are expressed in percent per annum. As in the case of the economy-wide real exchange rates, a rise in the rate represents a rise in the relative price of Japanese goods.

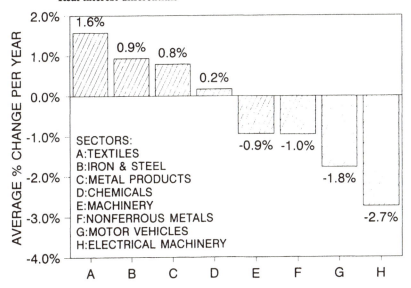

Figure 6.3. Sectoral real exchange rates (Japanese/U.S.): change in sectoral rate relative to manufacturing, 1975–1987.

rapid pace in electrical machinery than in textiles.[20] If the gap is larger in Japan than the United States, then there will be a relative decline in Japanese prices for electrical machinery over time. In comparing the United States and Japan, therefore, it is important to distinguish between firms from various sectors of the economy. The real appreciation of the yen tends to be greatest in the nontraded sector and smallest in the most dynamic sectors of manufacturing.

So changes in real exchange rates differ systematically across sectors of these economies. The evidence reported in Table 6.3 has one other implication that is at least as important as that concerning sectoral inflation rates. With the exception of the CPI-based real exchange rate for the yen, all of the real exchange rates have remarkably small average changes over the last 20 years. The average changes for the £/$ and DM/$ real exchange rates are less than 1 percent per annum, and substantially less in all but one case. (The average change in the FF/$ real exchange rate, not reported in Table 6.3, is −0.09 percent per annum). All of these changes in real exchange rates are insignificantly different from zero.

20. Using annual data from the national income accounts, Marston (1987) shows that there is a high correlation between average changes in productivity growth by sector of manufacturing and average changes in real exchange rates.

The evidence thus suggests that, except for the yen, deviations from PPP are on average close to zero in the long run. This evidence is consistent with the random walk theory of real exchange rates since, if the real exchange rate follows a random walk, the unconditional (as well as conditional) expected value of the change in the exchange rate is equal to zero. But it is also consistent with mean-reverting real exchange rates. So this property of real exchange rates does not help us to distinguish between different versions of PPP. But it is an important finding because of its implications for average real interest rates. For it is the average change in real exchange rates that helps to determine the average real interest differential.

II.   Estimates of real interest differentials for short-term interest rates

Having examined nominal interest differentials in Chapters 4 and 5 and real exchange rate changes in the last section, I now turn to real interest differentials. And as in the case of nominal interest differentials, I investigate a parity condition linking interest rates from different countries.

A.   Real interest parity

Real interest parity, or the equality of real interest rates, has been investigated in almost as many studies as uncovered interest parity.[21] Yet, unlike UIP, there is no sound theoretical rationale behind real interest parity, since there is no set of agents willing and able to take advantage of deviations from real interest parity. To show this is the case, I first define several real interest rates facing firms in the American and foreign markets.

Consider an American firm that can borrow either in its own market or in country k's market. If the cost of borrowing in currency k is expressed in dollars, then the firm faces two alternative real interest rates:

$$E_t \, r_{At} = i_{At} - \pi_{At} \tag{6.14a}$$

$$E_t \, r_{At}^* = (i_{kt} - \Delta x_{kt}) - \pi_{At} \tag{6.14b}$$

The real interest costs of borrowing at home (r_{At}) and abroad (r_{At}^*) are *expected* or ex ante costs; so they are preceded by an expectations sign. Both real interest costs are deflated by the same expected inflation rate used to deflate any financing by this firm.[22] It is obvious that these two real interest

---

21. A number of these studies will be cited when empirical work is discussed.
22. If the firm were a multinational with major sales abroad, it might make sense to deflate by a weighted average of foreign and American inflation rates, but the same deflator should be used for both American and foreign financing.

rates collapse to one if (nominal) uncovered interest parity holds, since the expected nominal costs of borrowing in the two markets are the same.

A firm from country k faces a separate set of real interest rates. The real interest costs of financing in k's market and in the American market are given by:

$$E_t\, r_{kt} = i_{kt} - \pi_{kt} \tag{6.15a}$$

$$E_t\, r_{kt}^* = (i_{At} + \Delta x_{kt}) - \pi_{kt} \tag{6.15b}$$

Both interest costs are expressed in currency k before being deflated by the expected inflation rate in currency k. As in the American case, these costs are distinct unless UIP holds.

Using the real interest rates defined above, real interest parity (RIP) can be written as:

$$E_t\, r_{At} = E_t\, r_{kt} \tag{6.16}$$

That is, the real cost of financing for the American firm borrowing in its own market is equal to the real cost of financing for country k's firm borrowing in k's market. In a frequently cited study of ex ante PPP, Adler and Lehman (1983) argue that real interest parity is ensured by "financial arbitrage" in bonds.[23] However, since there is no single borrower (or investor) who compares these two real interest rates, there is no direct arbitrage that ensures that Equation (6.16) holds. An American firm, for example, may compare $E_t r_{At}$ with $E_t r_{At}^*$, but will not compare either real interest rate with $E_t r_{kt}$. Real interest parity might be brought about indirectly by trade flows under the same conditions that equalize other factor prices,[24] but it is doubtful that the researchers who have tested real interest parity had such an indirect mechanism in mind.

Real interest parity *will* hold under two conditions, which are made apparent by decomposing the differential between the real interest rates as follows:[25]

$$E_t\, r_{kt} - E_t\, r_{At} = [i_{kt} - (i_{At} + \Delta x_{kt})] - [\pi_{kt} - (\pi_{At} + \Delta x_{kt})] \tag{6.17}$$

The first term in parentheses is the uncovered (nominal) interest differential, while the second term is the expected deviation from PPP. So real interest parity must hold if (1) UIP holds and (2) ex ante PPP holds. Real interest parity involves "financial arbitrage," but of nominal, not real, re-

23. Adler and Lehmann allow for a constant differential between the real interest rates. They use real interest parity as an indirect way to derive the expectations form of PPP, in contrast to Roll (1979) who appeals directly to commodity arbitrage.
24. I am grateful to James Lothian for this point. In most trade models, the real returns on equity (or "capital"), rather than the real returns on bonds, are analyzed.
25. Several studies emphasize the link between the two underlying parity conditions and real interest parity including Cumby and Obstfeld (1984), Mishkin (1984), and Frankel (1986).

turns.[26] The second condition involving ex ante PPP, however, is a condition involving goods markets, not financial markets.

The sharp distinction between real interest rates facing domestic and foreign firms becomes blurred if both sets of firms are multinationals with worldwide sales (and even worldwide production). With increasingly integrated financial markets, it is the prices faced by firms which distinguish their real costs of financing from those of other firms. Most firms in the G-5 countries, however, sell more to their own markets than do foreign firms. So domestic prices matter more to the domestic firm than to foreign firms. As long as that is the case, real interest differentials will continue to depend on the relative prices of domestic and foreign goods (and hence on expected deviations from PPP) rather than on financial conditions alone.

A similar point can be made about the real returns faced by investors who consume both foreign and domestic goods. Consider an extreme case. Suppose that both American and foreign investors consume the *same* basket of goods (with a equal to the share of American goods in the basket). Then the real returns faced by each set of investors on their own assets are defined by deflating the nominal interest rate in their country by their expected inflation rate.

$$i_{At} - \{a\, \pi_{At} + (1-a)(\pi_{kt} - \Delta x_{kt})\} \tag{6.18a}$$
$$i_{kt} - \{a\, (\pi_{At} + \Delta x_{kt}) + (1-a)\pi_{kt}\} \tag{6.18b}$$

Both American and foreign investors deflate their nominal returns by a common expected inflation rate, even though this inflation rate is expressed in each investor's own currency. It can be shown that these two real returns are equal as long as *UIP* holds. So in this extreme case relative prices (and deviations from ex ante PPP) do not matter. In actual practice, however, domestic investors consume a higher proportion of domestic goods than do foreign investors.[27] So relative prices *do matter* to real returns on investment just as they matter to the real costs of financing.

B.   Tests of real interest parity

Real interest parity is an ex ante concept involving expected rather than actual inflation. Since expected inflation rates are unobservable, so also are (expected or ex ante) real interest rates. What we can observe are ex post real interest rates defined by using actual inflation rates. Figures 6.4 and 6.5 illustrate how volatile actual real interest rates can be. Figure 6.4

26. Strictly speaking, the term "arbitrage" should be confined to riskless operations rather than to the risky positions required to ensure that UIP holds.
27. With pricing to market, moreover, domestic investors often face different prices for the same goods than faced by foreign investors.

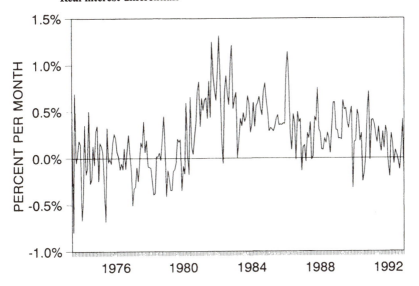

Figure 6.4. Real interest rate for dollar: 1-month Eurodollar rate and U.S. CPI.

presents the Eurodollar interest rate deflated by the inflation rate of the U.S. CPI, while Figure 6.5 presents the Euromark rate deflated by the German CPI inflation rate. It is interesting to note that both real interest rates become persistently positive in the early 1980s when inflation rates were receding from their earlier peaks. Throughout the sample period, however, the real interest rate series remain very volatile.

Actual real interest rates differ from expected real rates by forecast errors in predicting inflation rates. If the forecast error in predicting the inflation differential is denoted as μ_{kt}, then observed (or ex post) real interest differentials can be written as follows:[28]

$$r_{kt} - r_{At} = E_t r_{kt} - E_t r_{At} - \mu_{kt} \tag{6.19}$$

If real interest parity holds and if inflation forecast errors are random, then the observed real interest differential should be random as well. In this case, we can test real interest parity by determining whether real interest differentials are systematically related to variables in the current information set. If that information set is denoted by Z_{kt}, the test involves a regression of the real interest differential on Z_{kt}:

$$r_{kt} - r_{At} = \Phi_k Z_{kt} + u_{kt} \tag{6.20}$$

---

28. μ_{kt} is defined as $(\Delta p_{kt} - \Delta p_{At}) - (\pi_{kt} - \pi_{At})$.

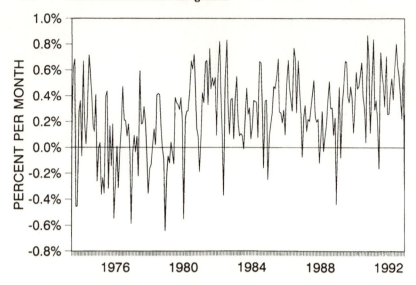

Figure 6.5. Real interest rate for mark: 1-month Euromark rate and German CPI.

This test is analogous to tests of UIP and PPP in Chapters 4 and 6, respectively.[29]

Table 6.4 reports tests of real interest parity for the one-month Eurocurrency rates used earlier. Real interest rates are defined using both consumer prices and producer prices in manufacturing. The information variables represent a combination of those used to test UIP and PPP: the simple interest differential $(i_{kt} - i_{At})$, the share yield in each country, and the inflation differential over the past 12 months. There are 13 information variables in all (four interest differentials, five share yields, and four inflation differentials). The χ^2 test reported is to determine if the coefficients in an equation are equal to zero. (As in previous tests, the constant is not included among the coefficients to be tested.)

The results are definitive. The χ^2 statistics are all statistically significant at the 1 percent level with the exception of the CPI-based interest differential for Japan, which is statistically significant at the 5 percent level. So there is strong evidence that real interest differentials for one-month Eurocurrency rates are systematically related to variables in the current information set.

29. Previous tests of real interest parity of a similar form include Mishkin (1984), Mark (1985), Kester and Luehrman (1989), and Dutton (1993).

Table 6.4. *Tests for predictable components of real interest differentials: Eurocurrency one-month interest rates, 1973(6)-1992(12).*

Currencies	CPI $\chi^2(13)$ [p-value]	PPI in manufacturing $\chi^2(10)$ [p-value]
£/$	62.23 [0.000]	101.5 [0.000]
FF/$	180.8 [0.000]	
DM/$	128.9 [0.000]	107.3 [0.000]
¥/$	22.59 [0.047]	74.56 [0.000]

Notes: The χ^2-statistic tests the joint hypothesis that the coefficients of the information variables are equal to zero.

The evidence is even stronger in the case of national loan rates. Table 6.5 reports tests of real interest parity for three-month bank loan rates and three-month Eurocurrency rates. The national loan rates and Eurocurrency rates, which are available only through December 1991, are the same series discussed in Chapters 2 and 3. Table 6.5 presents χ^2 statistics testing whether coefficients of the information variables are jointly significant.[30] For both CIP-based and PPI-based tests, the χ^2 statistics are statistically significant at the 1 percent level or lower. Thus the systematic behavior found in one-month rates is clearly evident in three-month rates.

30. Because the monthly observations of the three-month rates overlap, a generalized method of moments (GMM) estimator is used that adjusts for serial correlation as well as heteroskedasticity.

Table 6.5. *Tests for predictable components of real interest differentials: three-month bank loan and Eurocurrency rates, 1973(6)-1991(12).*

	Loan rates		Eurocurrency rates	
	CPI $\chi^2(13)$ *[p-value]*	*PPI in manufacturing* $\chi^2(10)$ *[p-value]*	*CPI* $\chi^2(13)$ *[p-value]*	*PPI in manufacturing* $\chi^2(10)$ *[p-value]*
£/$	100.4 [0.000]	250.2 [0.000]	82.09 [0.000]	149.4 [0.000]
FF/$	446.2 [0.000]		180.6 [0.000]	
DM/$	178.6 [0.000]	185.6 [0.000]	125.5 [0.000]	124.9 [0.000]
¥/$	80.81 [0.000]	93.64 [0.000]	106.8 [0.000]	76.64 [0.000]

Notes: Estimation is by GMM with correction for heteroskedasticity and serial correlation (due to overlapping observations). The χ^2-statistic tests the joint hypothesis that the coefficients of the inflation variables are equal to zero.

C.   *Interpretation of departures from the three parity conditions*

As explained earlier in this section, real interest parity is best interpreted as a joint hypothesis involving UIP and PPP. So it is useful to think of departures from real interest parity as departures from these two underlying parity relationships. Recall from Chapter 4 that uncovered interest differentials can be attributed to risk premiums or to forecast errors in predicting the exchange rate. If ρ_{kt} is the risk premium and ε_{kt} is the forecast error, $\Delta s_{kt} - \Delta x_{kt}$, then the observed uncovered interest differential is given by:

$$i_{kt} - i_{At} - \Delta s_{kt} = \rho_{kt} - \varepsilon_{kt} \tag{6.21}$$

In a similar way, deviations from PPP can be attributed to expected deviations from PPP, θ_{kt}, or to forecast errors in predicting either exchange rates or inflation differentials:

$$\Delta p_{kt} - \Delta p_{At} - \Delta s_{kt} = \theta_{kt} + \mu_{kt} - \varepsilon_{kt} \tag{6.22}$$

Under the expectations theory of PPP, θ_{kt} would be equal to zero and the forecast errors, μ_{kt} and ε_{kt}, would be random variables with an expected value of zero.

Given Equations (6.21) and (6.22), real interest differentials can be decomposed as follows:

$$r_{kt} - r_{At} = \rho_{kt} - \theta_{kt} - \mu_{kt} \tag{6.23}$$

According to this expression, real interest differentials arise because of risk premiums in the foreign exchange market, expected deviations from PPP, or forecast errors in predicting inflation. Equation (6.23) shows that exchange rate forecast errors have no effect on the real interest differential. As Mishkin (1984) and others have emphasized, this explains why real interest differentials are so much less volatile than nominal interest differentials or deviations from PPP. Figure 6.6 illustrates this point by comparing uncovered (nominal) interest differentials with real interest differentials for the mark relative to the dollar. The nominal series is several times more volatile than the real series. There is a second important point that emerges from comparing Equations (6.21–6.23). There is a common factor, the foreign exchange risk premium (ρ_{kt}), that causes departures from both uncovered interest parity and real interest parity, but does not affect the PPP equation.

These two observations suggest a way of interpreting equations explaining departures from the three parity conditions. Consider the three-equation system relating each differential to the same set of information variables, Z_{kt}.

$$i_{kt} - i_{At} - \Delta s_{kt} = \gamma_k Z_{kt} + u'_{kt} \tag{6.24a}$$

$$\Delta p_{kt} - \Delta p_{At} - \Delta s_{kt} = \lambda_k Z_{kt} + u''_{kt} \tag{6.24b}$$

$$r_{kt} - r_{At} = \phi_k Z_{kt} + u_{kt} \tag{6.24c}$$

If the respective coefficients (γ_k, λ_k, and ϕ_k) are significantly different from zero, the fitted values from these regressions represent the systematic component of any departures from the three parity conditions. But those systematic components can be interpreted in terms of the risk premium and forecast errors in Equations (6.21–6.23).

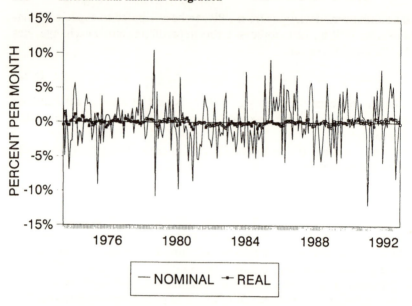

Figure 6.6. Nominal and real interest differentials: 1-month Eurodollar and Euromark rates and CPIs.

Consider two alternative cases:

Case 1: $\gamma_k \neq 0$, $\phi_k \neq 0$, but $\lambda_k = 0$. That is, there are systematic departures from uncovered interest parity and real interest parity, but not from purchasing power parity. In this case, the evidence of systematic departures from UIP and RIP is consistent with there being a foreign exchange risk premium, ρ_{kt}, causing departures from both parity conditions. It is possible to test for a common factor affecting Equations (6.24a) and (6.24c) by testing the cross equation restriction, $\gamma_k = \phi_k$. Since the dependent variable in Equation (6.24b) is linearly related to those in (6.24a) and (6.24c),[31] however, this restriction is equivalent to the test of $\lambda_k = 0$ in Equation (6.24b).

Case 2: $\gamma_k \neq 0$, $\lambda_k \neq 0$, but $\phi_k = 0$. In this case, the evidence of systematic departures from UIP and PPP is consistent with an exchange market forecast error, ε_{kt}, causing (systematic) departures from both parity conditions. The common factor in Equations (6.24a) and (6.24b) can be tested by the cross-equation restrictions, $\gamma_k = \lambda_k$. But this restriction is equivalent to the test of $\phi_k = 0$ in Equation (6.24c).

31. The PPP deviation is equal to the UIP deviation less the RIP deviation.

Table 6.6. *Tests for predictable components in UIP, PPP, and RIP deviations for one-month Eurocurrency rates and consumer price indexes, 1973(6)-1992(12).*

	UIP	PPP	RIP
£/$	28.56 [0.000]	22.91 [0.000]	28.41 [0.000]
FF/$	12.19 [0.016]	7.12 [0.130]	131.0 [0.000]
DM/$	21.02 [0.000]	17.18 [0.002]	76.33 [0.000]
¥/$	4.51 [0.341]	2.98 [0.562]	15.01 [0.004]

Notes: The table reports the results of a χ^2 (4) test and its p-value for the restriction $\gamma_k = 0$, $\lambda_k = 0$, and $\phi_k = 0$, respectively. (As in previous tests, the constant is omitted from each of these tests.) The set of current information variables common to all three regressions consists of the interest differential, share yields in both countries, and inflation differentials over the past 12 months.

If instead of these cases, there is evidence of systematic departures from *all three* parity conditions, then this is consistent with the coexistence of *both* foreign exchange risk premiums *and* systematic forecast errors in the foreign exchange market. It should be noted, however, that the same pattern is also consistent with there being no systematic forecast errors, since ex ante deviations from PPP (θ_{kt}), together with risk premiums (ρ_{kt}), are sufficient to account for deviations from all three parity conditions.

What does the evidence actually suggest? In previous tests for one-month Eurocurrency rates and one-month inflation rates reported in Chapters 4 and 6, all three differentials have been shown to be systematically related to variables in the current information set. Table 6.6 reports an analogous set of tests, but this time with all three equations (6.24a–6.24c) using a common set of information variables: interest differentials, share yields, and inflation differentials over the previous three months. The χ^2 statistics in the table test the joint significance of the information variables in each equation: $\gamma_k = 0$ in the UIP equation, $\lambda_k = 0$ in the PPP equation, and $\phi_k = 0$ in the RIP equation. For every exchange rate except

Table 6.7. *Correlation between UIP, PPP, and RIP deviations: actual and fitted values, 1973(6)-1992(12).*

Correlations between:	UIP and PPP deviations	UIP and RIP deviations	PPP and RIP deviations
£/$			
Actual	0.980	0.002	-0.197
Fitted	0.974	0.488	0.279
FF/$			
Actual	0.993	0.125	0.006
Fitted	0.984	0.911	0.824
DM/$			
Actual	0.994	0.066	-0.039
Fitted	0.988	0.571	0.436
¥/$			
Actual	0.980	0.043	-0.159
Fitted	0.964	0.754	0.554

Notes: The fitted values are those from the regressions reported in Table 6.6.

the ¥/$ rate, deviations from UIP and PPP are systematically related to current information variables (although the *p*-value for $\lambda_k = 0$ in the FF/$ equation is only 0.130). For all four exchange rates, deviations from RIP are systematically related to these variables.

Table 6.7 provides additional evidence concerning the relative importance of different factors in causing departures from the three parity conditions. Recall that one factor, the exchange market forecast error (ε_{kt}), causes deviations from UIP and PPP but not deviations from RIP. The table reports correlations between each pair of deviations using both actual deviations and the fitted values from the regressions of Table 6.6.

In the case of the *actual* values, the correlations between UIP and PPP deviations are very close to unity because of the predominant importance of exchange market forecast errors (ε_{kt}), while the correlations between deviations from either parity condition and RIP deviations are close to zero (and negative in some cases). These results should not be surprising since the correlations reflect random as well as systematic forecast errors (and random errors in forecasting exchange rates are so large).

In the case of the *fitted* values from the regressions reported in Table 6.6, the differences are not as dramatic. But it is still true that the correlations between the UIP and PPP deviations are close to one and much larger (except in one case) than those between either set of deviations and deviations from RIP.[32] Since the fitted values represent the systematic components of the deviations, this evidence is consistent with there being a systematic forecast error in the foreign exchange market driving both deviations from UIP and deviations from PPP.[33] On the other hand, there are large correlations between the fitted values of the UIP and RIP deviations, which is consistent with there being a risk premium separating both nominal and real returns. Once again, the empirical evidence cannot rule out either systematic forecast errors or risk premiums.

D.   Patterns of real interest differentials

Having examined the systematic movements of real interest differentials, it is now useful to ask how large are these differentials on average. Over the 20 years of floating exchange rates, have there been large differentials between the real interest rates of the G-5 countries? Can such differentials be traced to their underlying determinants in nominal interest differentials and PPP deviations? And finally, are these differentials larger for real interest rates defined for national loans rather than Eurocurrency deposits and loans?

Table 6.8 provides some answers to the first two questions. In the last column it reports *unconditional* estimates of the average real interest differentials formed from one-month Eurocurrency rates and producer price indexes in manufacturing. (For the French case, the real interest differentials must be computed using consumer price indexes.) The average real interest differential ranges from -0.21 percent for Germany to 1.22 percent for France. All except France's are insignificantly different from zero. So even though these real interest differentials vary systematically over time, they are *on average* close to zero.

Table 6.8 also reports the average deviations from UIP and PPP that underly the real interest differentials. As reported earlier, all of these average deviations are rather small. It should not be surprising that average

32. In the case of the ¥/$ equations, the coefficients in two of the three equations are not statistically significant; so not much reliance should be placed on the correlations between these fitted values.

33. Once again, however, we cannot rule out another explanation of the results: that correlations between risk premiums and ex ante PPP deviations, ρ_{kt} and θ_{kt}, account for the high correlations, although it may be difficult to rationalize such high correlations between ρ_{kt} and θ_{kt}.

Table 6.8. *Unconditional estimates of deviations from UIP, PPP, and RIP for one-month Eurocurrency rates and producer price indexes in manufacturing, 1973(6)-1992(12).*

	UIP deviations	PPP deviations	RIP deviations
£/$			
Average differential	0.48	0.74	-0.26
(s.e.)	(2.73)	(2.74)	(0.54)
[p-value]	[0.862]	[0.787]	[0.629]
FF/$ [a]			
Average differential	1.13	-0.09	1.22
(s.e.)	(2.67)	(2.65)	(0.32)
[p-value]	[0.673]	[0.973]	[0.000]
DM/$			
Average differential	-0.18	0.03	-0.21
(s.e.)	(2.75)	(2.79)	(0.46)
[p-value]	[0.948]	[0.990]	[0.647]
¥/$			
Average differential	1.76	0.95	0.81
(s.e.)	(2.58)	(2.54)	(0.64)
[p-value]	[0.497]	[0.709]	[0.211]

[a] The PPP and RIP deviations for the FF/$ rate are defined using consumer price indexes.

real interest differentials are close to zero if the underlying determinants of these differentials are themselves close to zero. The largest differentials, the UIP and PPP deviations for Japan, offset one another so that the average real interest differential is smaller than its components.

If average real interest differentials are small for the unregulated Eurocurrency markets, then it is natural to ask whether the same is true of the national loan markets. Table 6.9 reports average real interest differentials defined using three-month national loan rates. The table provides a range of estimates of average differentials using both loan rates and three-month Eurocurrency rates (to match the maturity of the loan rates). The first and second columns of the table give estimates of average differentials for

Table 6.9. *Range of estimates of real interest differentials: three-month interest rates, 1973(6)-1991(12).*

	Loan rates		Eurocurrency rates
	Based on CPI	Based on PPI in manufacturing	Based on PPI in manufacturing
£/$			
Average differential	-1.31	-1.65	-0.64
(s.e.)	(0.61)	(0.69)	(0.67)
[*p*-value]	[0.034]	[0.018]	[0.342]
FF/$[a]			
Average differential	-0.35		0.98
(s.e.)	(0.42)		(0.34)
[*p*-value]	[0.399]		[0.005]
DM/$			
Average differential	0.74	0.24	-0.65
(s.e.)	(0.40)	(0.60)	(0.54)
[*p*-value]	[0.069]	[0.691]	[0.230]
¥/$			
Average differential	-3.14	-1.52	0.81
(s.e.)	(0.52)	(0.94)	(0.98)
[*p*-value]	[0.000]	[0.109]	[0.408]

[a] In the case of the French franc, the real interest differential for the Eurocurrency rates is defined using the CPI rather than the PPI in manufacturing.

loans using the two alternative price indexes. The third column then gives the average differential for Eurocurrency deposits using the PPI for manufacturing.

For three of the four exchange rates, all except the ¥/$, the three measures of real interest differentials give similar results. In these cases, the average real interest differentials using national loan rates are not that different from the average differentials using Eurocurrency rates. Average differentials between national loan and Eurocurrency rates for Britain, France, or Germany are largely cancelled out by similar differentials between U.S. loan rates and Eurodollar rates. And average differentials between consumer price indexes and producer price indexes in one currency are largely cancelled out by similar differentials in the other currency.

In the Japanese case, interest differentials vary widely depending on how they are measured. The average real interest differential between Japanese and U.S. loan rates is over 3 percent per annum using the consumer price index. This measure of the real interest differential (or similar measures based on bank loan rates and other broad-based price indexes) is most often cited in studies of relative financing costs between the two countries.[34] Notice that the differential is negative, meaning that Japanese real interest rates are below U.S. real interest rates by over 3 percent. If real interest rates are defined using manufacturing prices (as in column 2), then the average real interest differential is cut in half to −1.52 percent per annum. The differential then turns a positive 0.81 percent rather than negative when Eurocurrency rates are substituted for loan rates. In that case *U.S.* rather than Japanese real interest rates are lower.

What accounts for this large discrepancy between real interest differentials measured with loan rates and with Eurocurrency rates? First, as explained in Chapter 2, Japanese and American loan rates are systematically biased in such a way that the measured differential, with Japanese real interest rates 3.14 percent below U.S. rates, *overstates* the true differential. Japanese loan rates understate the true cost of borrowing, which includes the cost of holding compensating balances. U.S. rates overstate the true cost of borrowing since firms regularly borrow below the U.S. prime loan rate. Second, Japanese consumer price inflation exceeds the inflation rate in manufacturing. Measuring real financing costs using manufactured prices results in a higher Japanese real interest rate. This effect alone lowers the real interest advantage for Japan from 3.14 to 1.52 percent in Table 6.9. So in the case of comparisons between Japan and the United States, the choice of interest rate and price series makes a major difference.[35] If real interest rates are measured with Eurocurrency rates and manufacturing prices, the differential for Japan relative to the United States is as small as for other industrialized countries.

---

34. Studies of relative financing costs between the United States and Japan include Friend and Tokutsu (1987), Hatsopoulos and Brooks (1986), and Bernheim and Shoven (1987). Frankel (1991) provides a useful survey. In contrast to the other studies, Kester and Luehrman (1989) find relatively small real interest differentials by comparing U.S. Treasury bills and gensaki rates as well as Eurodollar and Euroyen rates.

35. This would also be true of comparisons between Japan and other countries.

III.   Real interest differentials for bonds

If average real interest differentials are generally small between short-term instruments like national bank loans or Eurocurrency deposits (or loans), then it is natural to ask if the same is true of real interest differentials between bonds. As explained in Chapter 2, firms in many industrial countries rely much more on national and Eurocurrency bank loans than on bonds for financing, the major exceptions being larger firms in the United States and Britain where the corporate bond market is well developed. But as Chapter 2 showed, there is a clear trend toward greater reliance on direct bond finance in all of the major industrial countries.

A.   Alternative definitions of real interest rates for bonds

The real interest rate for a medium- or long-term bond is more difficult to define than for a short-term instrument. If the bond has a maturity of n periods, one definition of the real interest rate would be the expected real cost of financing over n periods. The nominal cost of financing can be measured by the *yield to maturity* of the n period bond, $_ni_t$.[36] So the real cost can be obtained by deflating by some measure of expected inflation $_n\pi_t$:

$$E_t\left(_nr_t'\right) = {_ni_t} - {_n\pi_t} \tag{6.25}$$

This is the definition of the real interest rate found in the literature comparing the cost of capital internationally.[37] Since what is being measured is the cost of financing over n periods, the expected inflation rate should match the horizon of $_ni_t$. That is, $_n\pi_t$ should be interpreted as the inflation rate expected over the life of the bond. Unless the bond is a pure discount bond, moreover, the inflation rate has to be defined so as to match the intermediate as well as terminal cash flows on the bond. As a result, this version of the real interest rate is difficult to implement empirically.[38]

---

36. To simplify the notation, the subscript k for country k is omitted from the expressions in this section. All interest rates and returns are expressed in percent per period, although in the tables they are expressed in percent per annum.

37. Most of these studies calculate a weighted average of the real rate on bank loans and the real rate on bonds where the latter is defined as in Equation (6.25). See, for example, Friend and Tokutsu (1987), Hatsopoulos and Brooks (1986), and McCauley and Zimmer (1989).

38. An alternative interpretation of Equation (6.25) is that $_nr_t'$ is being measured over a shorter interval than the maturity of the bond, but then some strong assumptions have to be made about the relationship between the yield to maturity of the bond and expected yields over shorter intervals.

An investor evaluating this bond would normally prefer to examine returns over a shorter horizon than the maturity of the bond. In fact, the investor may be interested in returns over a holding period corresponding to the maturity of short-term assets like Eurocurrencies. The nominal return over such a period is given by the *holding period yield,* $_nH_t$, defined as the capital gain plus coupon payment received on the bond between t and $t + 1$:

$$_nH_t = \left(\frac{B_{t+1}}{B_t} - 1\right) + \frac{C}{B_t} \tag{6.26}$$

where B_t is the price of the bond and C is the coupon. The second definition of the real interest rate is formed by deflating the holding period yield (in logs) by the same one-period expected inflation rate used to deflate Eurocurrency deposits:[39]

$$E_t\left(_nr_t\right) = E_t\left(_nh_t\right) - \pi_t \tag{6.27}$$

where $_nh_t = \ln\left(1 + {}_nH_t\right)$. This second measure of the real interest rate is linked to the first measure, since the price paid for the bond (and hence the yield to maturity) is related to expected holding period returns. But the yield to maturity reflects expected holding period returns from the current period until the maturity of the bond.

Of the two measures of real interest rates, there is no doubt that the measure based on holding period yields is simpler in concept and easier to implement empirically. But to provide some comparisons with the literature on the cost of capital, I will present estimates of average real interest rates based on yields to maturity in addition to those based on holding period yields. For both measures, I will use yields on government bonds rather than corporate bonds. As explained in Chapter 2, in most countries the government bond market is much larger and more liquid than the corporate market. For that reason, internationally diversified portfolios are said to hold much larger proportions of government bonds than corporate bonds. To measure real returns for investors, therefore, it is preferable to use government bonds. To measure the real cost of financing for firms, however, it would be preferable to use corporate bond yields. But government bond data are more readily available and are of higher quality than corporate bond data.

For data on yields to maturity, Morgan Guaranty Trust's *World Financial Markets* provides yields on medium-term government bonds back through the early 1970s. These series will be examined for the period starting in June 1973 (the same as the Eurocurrency data) and ending in March

39. This is the measure used by Huizinga and Mishkin (1984), who examine real returns on a variety of longer-term U.S. bonds.

1992. To convert nominal yields into real interest rates, I need a measure of expected inflation over the life of a bond. Although I experimented with various time series forecasting models of inflation, the series I chose fit as well as the others and has the advantage of simplicity: a three-year moving average of past inflation rates with linearly declining weights.[40] This series is designed to capture the slow adjustment of longer-term inflationary expectations.

For the second measure of the real interest rate, Morgan Guaranty Trust recently developed a series for holding period yields based directly on bond market prices. This series, which is based on prices for a broad range of intermediate-term government bonds accessible to international investors, extends back to December 1985.[41] For the period prior to 1985, I have constructed a holding period series from Morgan's yield to maturity data using a linear approximation due to Shiller (1979). The linear approximation is for an n-period bond with yield to maturity (in levels) of $_nI^*$ and duration $_nD$.[42] The duration of a bond is a coupon-adjusted time to maturity (to reflect the fact that coupons shorten the effective maturity of the bond). If c is the coupon rate (expressed as a fraction of the principal), then the duration of this bond is given by:

$$_nD = \frac{[gc + 2\,g^2\,c + \ldots + n\,g^n\,c + n\,g^n]}{[gc + g^2\,c + \ldots + g^n\,c + g^n]} \quad (6.28)$$

where $g = 1/[1 + {}_nI^*]$. For a bond selling at par, the coupon rate is equal to $_nI^*$. In that case, the duration is given by $_nD = (1 - g^n)/(1 - g)$. The holding period yield from t to $t + 1$, $_nH_t$, can then be expressed as a function of current yields to maturity, $_nI_t$, by linearizing Equation (6.26) around $_nI^*$ to obtain:

$$_nH_t \cong (_nD)\,_nI_t - (_nD - 1)_{n-1}I_{t+1} \quad (6.29)$$

So the holding period yield in period t is related to the yield to maturity of an n period bond at time t relative to the yield to maturity of an $n-1$ period bond at $t+1$. Figure 6.7 compares the derived series for U.S. bonds with the corresponding Morgan series based directly on bond price data. Over the period when both series are available, December 1985 to Febru-

---

40. It would be preferable to use actual inflation forecasts if they were available. Frankel (1991) provides estimates of real interest rates for 1989 and 1990 using survey estimates of the inflation rate over the next ten years (to match the maturity of the bonds being analyzed).

41. The bonds are described in Morgan Guaranty Trust (1989). They are generally shorter in maturity than the earlier yield to maturity series published by Morgan, with the biggest differences occurring in the case of U.S. and British bonds.

42. This particular formulation using durations is from Shiller, Campbell, and Schoenholtz (1983).

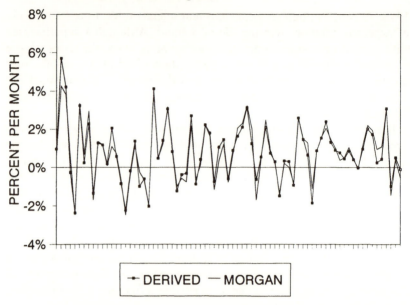

Figure 6.7. Comparison between derived and Morgan holding period
yields for U.S. bonds, 1985(12)–1992(2).

ary 1992, the correlation coefficient between the derived and Morgan series is 0.96.[43] The combined holding period series extends from June 1973
to December 1992.

Over the long run, average holding period yields should be nearly equal
to average yields to maturity. This is indeed the case for the full sample
period over which holding period yields and yields to maturity are both
available, 1973(6)–1992(3). Table 6.10 reports average holding period
yields and average yields to maturity for the G-5 countries. The differentials between the two series range from 0.01 percent for Britain to −0.71
percent for France.

Changes in inflation rates are soon reflected in both series as interest
rates adjust to inflation rates. But since holding period yields reflect realized capital gains and losses that occur when interest rates change, they
are more sensitive to the changes in inflation. In the late 1970s, rising
inflation pushed up interest rates in most of the industrial countries. Figure 6.8 shows the movement of yields to maturity on three of the national
bonds over the 20-year period. Yields in the U.S. and French markets
begin and end the sample period below 9 percent, but in the late 1970s

43. The correlation between the corresponding series for Britain is 0.92, for France 0.89, for
    Germany 0.93, and for Japan 0.88.

Table 6.10. *Comparison of average holding period yields and average yields to maturity on government bonds, 1973(6)-92(3).*

	U.S.	Britain	France	Germany	Japan
Full sample					
1973(6)-92(3)					
$_nh_t$	8.97	11.44	10.56	8.15	7.18
$_ni_t$	9.48	11.43	11.27	7.88	7.10
Difference	-0.51	0.01	-0.71	0.27	0.08
1973(6)-80(12)					
$_nh_t$	5.05	10.06	7.01	8.62	6.91
$_ni_t$	8.59	12.77	10.92	8.04	8.10
Difference	-3.54	-2.71	-3.91	0.58	-1.19
1981(1)-92(3)					
$_nh_t$	11.62	12.36	12.95	7.83	7.36
$_ni_t$	10.08	10.52	11.52	7.77	6.42
Difference	1.54	1.84	1.43	0.06	0.94

Notes: Yields to maturity are from Morgan Guaranty Trust, *World Financial Markets*. Holding period yields are from Morgan Guaranty Trust from 1985(12)-1992(3) and are calculated from yields to maturity for the earlier period.

and early 1980s they rise to over 15 percent in response to higher inflation in both countries. Japanese yields also fluctuate widely, but on average are much lower than yields in the United States and France because of lower inflation in Japan. During the period of rising inflation in the late 1970s, average holding period yields fell far short of average yields to maturity. Table 6.10 breaks the 20-year sample into two parts, the decade of the 1970s and later. In the earlier period, holding period yields in the countries that suffered most from inflation, Britain, France, and the United States, were at least 2½ percent below yields to maturity. This discrepancy between the two series led to very different experiences for firms and investors. Firms that borrowed in the bond markets were fortunate enough to lock in coupons at the relatively low rates prevailing in the mid-1970s. Investors in bonds, in contrast, were unfortunate enough to lock in those same coupons at a time when unanticipated increases in inflation were occurring. But beginning in 1982, the fortunes of the two sets of agents

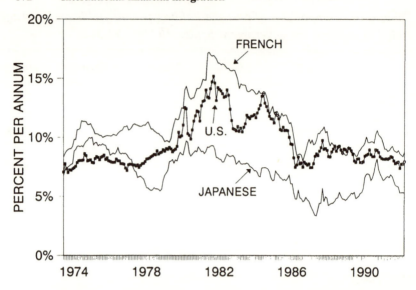

Figure 6.8. Yields to maturity on U.S., Japanese and French government bonds, 1973(6)–1992(3).

were reversed as the general level of interest rates came down.[44] Because holding period yields are so sensitive to short-run variations in bond market conditions, comparisons between real interest rates will be confined to the sample period as a whole.

B.   Estimates of real interest differentials for bonds

Table 6.11 compares the two measures of real interest differentials for bonds. The left side of the table reports average real interest differentials based on one-month holding period yields and actual inflation rates over the month. The right side reports average real interest differentials based on yields to maturity and a weighted average of past inflation rates. Recall that in the case of yields to maturity, past inflation rates are used as a proxy for the inflation rates expected over the life of the bond. The two measures give similar results, although the real interest differentials based on holding period yields are generally more positive (indicating higher real interest rates in the non-U.S. countries). In all cases the two measures are within 1 percent of one another (using the same price indexes in each instance). All those based on yields to maturity are statistically different

---

44. Many corporate bonds, however, are callable, and in times of declining yields there is an incentive to retire the bonds prior to scheduled maturity.

Table 6.11. *Average real interest differentials on government bonds, holding period yields and yields to maturity, 1973(6)-1992(3).*

	Holding period yields Actual inflation		Yields to maturity Weighted average of past inflation	
	CPI	PPI in manufacturing	CPI	PPI in manufacturing
£/$				
Differential	-0.84	-1.14	-1.44	-1.21
(s.e.)	(2.42)	(2.41)	(0.13)	(0.24)
[p-value]	[0.728]	[0.637]	[0.000]	[0.000]
FF/$				
Differential	0.21		0.29	
(s.e.)	(1.71)		(0.12)	
[p-value]	[0.901]		[0.012]	
DM/$				
Differential	1.83	1.32	0.97	0.85
(s.e.)	(1.55)	(1.67)	(0.15)	(0.24)
[p-value]	[0.238]	[0.432]	[0.000]	[0.000]
¥/$				
Differential	-0.49	1.10	-1.38	0.49
(s.e.)	(1.66)	(1.81)	(0.15)	(0.15)
[p-value]	[0.767]	[0.544]	[0.000]	[0.002]

Notes: The holding period yields are deflated by actual inflation over the same one-month holding period. The yields to maturity are deflated by a three-year weighted average of past inflation rates with linearly declining weights.

from zero (at the 1 percent level), while none of those based on holding period yields is. The standard errors of the latter are much larger because holding period yields are so much more volatile than yields to maturity and because the one-month inflation rates used in the holding period measure are more volatile than the three-year weighted averages used in the yield to maturity measure. But as in the case of short-term interest rates, the average real interest differentials for bonds are relatively small however

Table 6.12. *Tests for predictable components of real interest differentials: holding period yields on government bonds, 1973(6)- 1992(12).*

Currencies	CPI $\chi^2(13)$ [p-value]	PPI in manufacturing $\chi^2(10)$ [p-value]
£/$	51.85 [0.000]	23.49 [0.009]
FF/$	43.79 [0.000]	
DM/$	76.85 [0.000]	34.59 [0.000]
¥/$	59.09 [0.000]	26.56 [0.003]

Notes: The χ^2-statistic tests the joint hypothesis that the coefficients of the information variables are equal to zero.

they are measured, ranging from -1.44 percent for Britain to 1.83 percent for Germany.

Table 6.12 presents evidence about whether real interest differentials based on holding period yields are systematically related to variables currently known to investors.[45] The variables in the current information set consist of the nominal interest differential between country k and the United States (using yields to maturity), the share yields in those two countries, and the inflation differential over the past 12 months. The evidence is quite conclusive: real interest differentials for all four countries are systematically related to those variables. The p-values for the χ^2 tests are below 1 percent in all cases. So, despite the fact that average real

45. As defined here, the real interest differentials based on yields to maturity reflect only current and past information; so they are necessarily related to currently known variables. The real interest differentials based on holding period yields, in contrast, reflect returns over the following month.

differentials for holding period yields are not statistically different from zero, there is a statistically significant time variation in the real differentials. These results should not be surprising given the evidence presented earlier that real short-term interest differentials are systematically related to an analogous set of variables.

Returning to the evidence concerning real interest differentials in Table 6.11, we see that the choice between price indexes makes little difference except in the case of Japan. The shift from CPIs to manufacturing prices changes the real interest differential for Japan from negative to positive. So as in the case of short-term rates, real interest rates for manufacturing are lower in the U.S. than in Japan. Table 6.11 shows a real interest disadvantage for the United States, but vis-à-vis Britain, not Japan (or Germany).

Why then have observers claimed that Japanese firms have the advantage of lower real interest rates? One reason is that too much attention has been focused on the 1970s when Japanese rates were relatively low. Figure 6.9 shows the time series for Japanese and U.S. rates based on yields to maturity and the CPI. During the mid-1970s, Japanese rates were evidently much lower than U.S. rates. In fact, over the period 1973(6)–1980(12), this measure of Japanese real rates was on average 1.95 percent lower. But, more important, Japanese real rates were thought to be lower because the real interest rates were typically defined for broad-based price indexes. If the manufacturing price index is used instead to reflect the inflationary experience of internationally competitive manufacturing firms, then the real interest advantage for Japan is not apparent. Consider Figure 6.10 where real interest rates based on the PPI for manufacturing are presented. Over the 1973(6)–1980(12) period, the average differential was +1.71 percent, indicating lower real interest rates in the United States rather than Japan. So the key issue is which real interest rate, the rate facing manufacturing firms or firms throughout the rest of the economy, is being measured.

In no other set of countries does the distinction between real interest rates facing manufacturing firms and other firms make such a difference. Even the average real interest differentials between Japan and the United States, however, have to be regarded as small by any economic standard. So average real interest differentials for bonds are as small as for the Eurocurrency rates considered earlier in the chapter.

IV. Some conclusions regarding real interest differentials

The evidence in this chapter allows us to draw a few conclusions about real interest rate behavior:

Figure 6.9. U.S. and Japanese real interest rates: yields to maturity and CPI indexes, 1973(6)–1992(3).

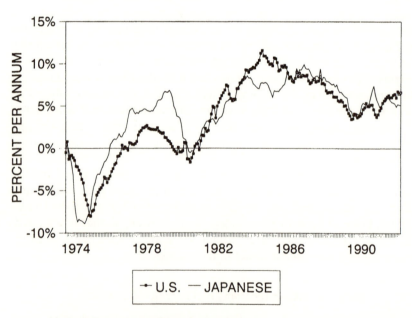

Figure 6.10. U.S. and Japanese real interest rates, 1973(6)–1992(3): yields to maturity and PPI in manufacturing.

1. Despite widespread misconception, real interest differentials do not offer profit opportunity for any individual investor or borrower since no single agent compares real interest rates across countries. So real interest rate parity must rely on the two underlying parity conditions: uncovered interest parity and purchasing power parity.

2. Average (ex post) real interest differentials can be decomposed into (nominal) uncovered interest differentials and deviations from PPP. Chapter 4 showed that uncovered interest differentials are small on average over the last 20 years, and this chapter showed that deviations from PPP are also small. So it should not be surprising that average real interest differentials are also quite small on average.

3. Real interest differentials are systematically related to variables currently known to investors. This is true of real interest differentials based on short-term Eurocurrency rates or bank loan rates as well as long-term bond yields. So real interest parity is soundly rejected despite the fact that *on average* real interest differentials are close to zero.

4. Deviations from UIP and PPP are highly correlated whether these deviations are measured by actual uncovered interest rate and inflation differentials or by fitted values formed by regressing these differentials on variables in the current information set. This evidence is consistent with there being a common factor, exchange rate forecast errors, driving both differentials.

5. Despite the fact that real interest differentials are small on average, differentials between the United States and Japan are very sensitive to the choice of price index. If the short-term differential is based on prices in manufacturing, the average differential is 1.5 percent per annum smaller than the differential based on consumer prices. It also makes a major difference (over 2 percent per annum) whether real interest differentials are measured using national bank loan rates or Eurocurrency rates. Those differentials based on Eurocurrency rates are less than 1 percent per annum, and it is the United States that benefits from the lower rates.

Real interest rates matter a lot for investment and borrowing decisions. But there is no clear pattern of lower real rates in one country or another. In Chapter 7, I relate these findings about real interest rates to the larger issue of financial integration between countries.

Progress toward international financial integration

Financial markets in the 1990s offer opportunities to firms and investors that were difficult to imagine in the 1960s. In place of the tightly controlled national markets where bank financing predominated, we now have markets spanning national boundaries open to competition from other countries, other currencies, and other financial instruments.

I. Progress toward integrating markets in the same currency

In the major industrial countries, national regulations and conventions that limited competition in national markets have been or will soon be removed, or they will be rendered irrelevant by the development of alternative financial instruments. Controls on international capital flows have been abolished almost completely, thus opening the national markets in these countries to international competition. Financial integration *within* currency areas has progressed to the point where there are only negligible differentials between interest rates on national money market instruments and Eurocurrency rates in the same currency.

A. *Deregulating national markets*

In assessing the progress made in deregulating national markets, it is well to remember how tightly controlled interest rates were 20 or 30 years ago. Deposit rates were then regulated in most countries, and CD markets were unknown or, as in the case of the United States, subject to interest rate ceilings. Firms looking for short-term financing had to rely on national bank loans at interest rates that in most cases were governed by official regulations or market conventions. Some longer-term financing was available in bond markets, but except in the United States, the corporate bond markets remained largely dormant until the 1980s.

Deregulation has proceeded at a different pace in each country. But by the mid-1980s, markets for CDs were established in all five countries with the deregulation of deposit rates occurring earlier in several countries. Commercial paper was introduced in all countries by the mid-1980s except in Germany where the market was not introduced until 1991 but where floating rate notes appeared in 1985. With competition from other markets, bank loans have became increasingly competitive. In Japan, for example, the loan rate is now closely tied to money market rates, while in the United States banks rely much less on the sluggish prime rate as a pricing standard, instead offering loans at rates competitive with commercial paper. In all five countries, there is increasing reliance on bond financing and on swaps. These instruments offer medium-term, fixed-rate financing to firms who would previously have had to rely on short-term or medium-term bank loans.

While acknowledging these substantial changes, it is important to recognize the limits to deregulation. Although securitization has begun in all markets, and although direct rather than indirect financing is the coming trend, most firms still rely primarily on bank loans for financing. There is no doubt that firms are increasingly issuing bonds as an alternative to bank financing. And the markets for interest rate and currency swaps are growing rapidly. But in several countries, the trend toward bond financing is in its early stages. And in all countries except the United States, bank loans provide over 80 percent of outside financing.

B.   Liberalizing capital flows

In a world where funds can move freely between Tokyo, Frankfurt, Paris, London, and New York, it is difficult to remember how important capital controls once were. In the late 1960s, U.S. controls on outflows of funds led to 4 percent differentials between Eurodollar rates in London and CD rates in New York. In the early 1970s, German controls on inflows of funds permitted interbank rates in Frankfurt to remain over 6 percent above rates on Euromarks in London. Nor were the 1980s free of controls. French controls on outflows of funds led to gaps of over 8 percent between interbank rates in Paris and Eurofranc rates in London. These gaps in interest rates testify to the effectiveness of the controls. Those who claim that capital controls are always ineffective in preventing capital flows may be right in the sense that controls can be evaded, at a price, however they are fashioned. But the controls studied here were effective enough to open large differentials between national money market rates and Eurocurrency rates in London.

Once controls were removed, beginning with Germany and the United States in the early 1970s, interest differentials vanished. The French were the last to remove controls, beginning that process in 1986 and completing it three years later. Now, in principle at least, all capital flows between the G-5 countries and markets abroad should be free of controls. Table 7.1 compares average three-month interest rates in the national and Eurocur-

Table 7.1. *Recent interest differentials in the same currency: national minus Eurocurrency rates, 1986(1)-1991(12).*

Currency	Average national interest rate	Average Eurocurrency interest rate	Difference
Dollar	7.36	7.45	-0.09
Pound sterling	11.93	11.88	0.05
French franc[a]	8.90	8.94	-0.04
Deutschemark	6.34	6.26	0.08
Yen	5.69	5.64	0.05

National money market rates: (all three-month maturities)
United States: Certificate of deposit rate
Britain: Interbank rate
France: Interbank rate
Germany: Interbank rate
Japan: Certificate of deposit rate

Eurocurrency rates: three-month rate in London.

[a] Interest rates for the franc are calculated beginning in April 1986 after the French government began to remove its capital controls.

rency markets over the recent five-year period, January 1986 to December 1991, when no controls were binding.[1] The national interest rates are either interbank rates or CD rates. The interest differentials between the two sets of markets are remarkably small, all being less than 0.10 percent. Indeed, the differentials between national and Eurocurrency rates are small enough so that we can think of there being one money market, spanning national boundaries, in each of the currencies. Thus there is a yen money market offering nearly identical rates in Tokyo and London, a franc

1. Average interest rates for the franc are calculated beginning in April 1986 because the French government began removing its controls only in early 1986. See the discussion in Chapter 3.

money market offering nearly identical rates in Paris and London, and similar worldwide markets in the other G-5 currencies.

The unification of national and international markets by currency does not extend to all instruments. Each national market has its own peculiar array of financial instruments that differ from the money market instruments in Table 7.1 as well as from the Eurocurrency deposits and loans and from national instruments elsewhere. But most remaining differentials are attributable to the fact that deregulation has yet to apply throughout national financial markets, especially to instruments available to small depositors and investors.

II.   Differentials between markets in different currencies

The G-5 countries all retain their separate currencies, although the three European countries have plans, now postponed, to join other EEC countries in adopting a single common currency. As long as national instruments are denominated in separate currencies, costs of financing will differ between currencies, although these differentials are much larger ex post than ex ante. And with real exchange rates varying over time, the real costs of financing will also differ between firms from different countries.

To compare financing costs for different firms, it is useful to ask three questions: (1) Are the expected costs of financing (or the returns from investing) in any individual market the same regardless of who is borrowing (or investing)? (2) Are the expected costs of financing in *different* markets the same regardless of currency? (3) Are the expected *real* costs of financing for one country's firms financing in their own market the same as those of another country's firms financing in their own market? The first question has been addressed earlier in this chapter. For example, if markets are deregulated and capital controls removed, there should be no difference between what a Japanese firm pays for financing in New York and what an American firm pays, as long as each firm calculates costs in the same currency. The second and third questions involve markets in different currencies; so the comparison is much harder to make.

A.   *Differentials in nominal financing costs*

The breakdown of the Bretton Woods system of fixed exchange rates has led to much larger volatility of exchange rates. Standard deviations of the changes in dollar exchange rates, one measure of such volatility, are three or more times larger since 1973 than they were in the 1960s. With increased volatility of exchange rates has come larger variations in financing costs across currencies. These financing costs can be measured by using

Eurocurrency interest rates so as to avoid the distortions found in national markets (especially in the 1970s). Eurodollar loan rates can be compared with the costs of borrowing in other Eurocurrencies, expressing that cost in dollars by taking into account currency gains or losses. In that case variations in financing costs are simply due to the currency denominations of the loans rather than to any controls or regulations. Similarly, Eurodollar deposit rates can be compared with the dollar returns on other Eurocurrency deposits (interest rate plus any currency gains or losses). One critical question is whether or not these variations in financing costs or variations in returns are due to more than random forecast errors.

Researchers have devoted considerable effort to determining whether *ex ante* as well as *ex post* costs of financing (or returns from investing) differ across currencies. The evidence suggests that ex ante uncovered interest differentials are *on average* quite small, in some cases as small as covered interest differentials. Nonetheless, there are statistically significant departures from uncovered interest parity over time. The key question that this study has been unable to resolve is whether these differentials are due to time-varying risk premiums or systematic forecast errors. The study has rejected the hypothesis that a single latent variable model can explain such ex ante returns. But it could still be that there are risk premiums driving these differentials that cannot be represented by the latent variable model. On the other hand, the ex ante differentials could equally well be explained by systematic forecast errors, perhaps due to peso-type phenomena. Tests using actual forecasts of future exchange rates found supporting evidence for both explanations.

Whatever the cause, differences in financing costs across currencies pose problems for firms operating internationally. Ex post differences in financing costs are often large and are always volatile. Ex ante interest differentials, estimated in this study using variables currently known to investors, are almost as large. These differentials are sometimes over 10 percent per annum and they swing from positive to negative from one year to the next. Firms with operating exposures in several currencies must contend with sharp changes in their cash flows due to these exchange rate changes. Receivables and payables as well as debt and interest payments are all sensitive to exchange rate fluctuations.

Thus, there is a definite answer to the question of whether financing costs in different markets are the same regardless of currency: Financing costs over any term except the long run vary widely by currency whether measured ex ante or ex post. Eurocurrency markets may be functioning free of distortions or controls, but returns across currencies are volatile nonetheless.

B.   Differences in real financing costs

Even if there were no differentials in the nominal costs of financing in one currency relative to another, there could be differentials in the *real* costs of financing. That is, Japanese firms might pay more for financing in Japan than U.S. firms pay in the United States even though nominal returns on Japanese and U.S. assets, expressed in a common currency, were equal. Real interest rates might differ because there might be expected changes in real exchange rates. Real interest differentials depend not only on expected nominal interest differentials, but also on expected deviations from purchasing power parity.

In assessing real interest differentials, we must again distinguish between (long-run) *average* differentials and differentials in any given period. Contrary to many claims, average real interest differentials are very similar across countries. Even in the case of Japan and the United States, whose financing costs are often compared, there is no evidence that real interest rates are consistently higher in one country than the other. In any such comparison, researchers must be careful to choose interest rates that accurately measure financing costs, and to choose price indexes that are appropriate for the firms under study. Evidence based on Eurocurrency rates as well as national bond rates suggests that average differentials are generally less than 2 percent per annum, and in many cases are much smaller.

Despite the fact that average real interest differentials are small, there is strong evidence that real interest parity fails to hold in the short run. Whether one looks at Eurocurrency rates or national loan rates or bond yields, real interest differentials are systematically related to variables currently known to investors. As in the case of nominal interest differentials, it is not clear whether these differentials are due to risk premiums or to systematic forecast errors. But there is suggestive evidence that systematic forecast errors play a major role. Deviations from uncovered interest parity and purchasing power parity are highly correlated even when these deviations are measured using *ex ante* estimates formed from the fitted values of regressions. Since risk premiums enter only the nominal interest rate regressions, while exchange rate forecast errors affect both regressions, the high correlation between the two sets of estimates suggests the importance of the latter.

How important are these variations in real interest differentials? The differentials seem to persist for several years at a time and are large enough to be economically significant. It is also evident that these real interest differentials would be much smaller if nominal exchange rate changes were smaller. So once again we find that the currency factor is separating markets, not the regulations and controls that were so important in earlier decades.

C.   *Financing costs within the European Monetary System*

If the volatility of exchange rates leads to differentials in financing costs between markets and between firms, what is the solution? At one extreme we have the United States (or Belgium and Luxemburg) as one model of a currency area in which exchange rate problems are avoided altogether because there is a unified currency. In such a currency area, there can be no differentials in interest rates due to currency factors (although there may be differences in the interest rates paid by Massachusetts and Pennsylvania due to default risk). At the other extreme we have the present system of flexible exchange rates where exchange rates can fluctuate widely whether measured in nominal or real terms. In between these extremes lies the European Monetary System, a currency area where until recently exchange rates were fixed within narrow bands but where the bands were potentially adjustable. A key question confronting policy makers is whether a credible system of fixed rates can be established without introducing a single national currency?

Firms within the EMS should have been shielded from the worst effects of fluctuating exchange rates. This study, however, has shown that the EMS has had only mixed success to date. It is true that exchange rate volatility has been reduced for currencies within the EMS. The standard deviations of changes in the FF/DM and lira/DM exchange rates are one-half as large in the EMS period than earlier. But uncovered interest differentials persist, at least for some currencies. While the average uncovered differential between the guilder and mark is one-third its size under flexible rates, the differential between the franc and the mark is actually larger in the EMS. That differential averages almost 2 percent per annum in the 1979–92 period. The differential between the lira and mark is even larger.

Why have uncovered interest differentials persisted in the EMS? One reason is that the EMS bands for the franc and lira have lacked credibility among market participants. Interest differentials between the franc and mark have been too large to be consistent with credible bands, as have interest differentials between the lira and mark. Investors in the bond market have evidently demanded devaluation premiums in anticipation of expected realignments. Evidence from regressions, moreover, suggests that the EMS bands themselves have failed to serve as a stabilizing force. A rise in either the FF/DM or lira/DM rate towards its upper EMS band *increases* expectations of devaluation, rather than stabilizing those expectations.

If the G-5 countries want to reduce the effects of exchange rate volatility, they should heed the lessons of the EMS. Fixed but adjustable exchange rates leave countries vulnerable to speculative crises and devaluations. These crises will occur even with capital controls, but countries without capital controls are even more vulnerable. The experiences of countries in the EMS suggest that perhaps only a common currency, not just fixed exchange rates, will succeed in equalizing financing costs across European countries. The speculative crisis of September 1992 certainly provides evidence in favor of that point of view. It is true that the Dutch have managed to avoid the speculative crises suffered by France and Italy. But it is unlikely that the French and Italians will achieve the same close coordination of policies with Germany that has been the key to success for Holland – unless they join a single currency system.

In any case, the G-5 countries as a whole are unlikely to adopt a single currency. If flexible exchange rates are here to stay for the Group of Five countries, whether or not exchange rates become fixed between the European members, what can firms do to cope with flexibility? The answer must not lie in a return to capital controls, as some have advocated, nor in a return to regulation of financial markets and instruments. Instead we need continued deregulation, which will make the newer financial instruments available to a wider array of firms. We also need continued innovation in the financial markets. Firms with widespread global operations need new and more creative hedging instruments to cope with exchange risk. Consider how remarkable are the interest rate and currency swaps introduced only a little more than a decade ago. They have provided firms with opportunities for fixed-interest financing in a variety of currencies that would have been simply unavailable in the 1970s and earlier. Consider also how well futures and forward contracts have served for short-term hedging. Ten years ago these markets were restricted in two of the G-5 countries, Japan and France, as well as in many countries outside the G-5. Even today markets for these instruments are either nonexistent or are restricted in many nonindustrial countries. But where these markets are available, existing short-term contracts are easily hedged. Currency options provide an additional method of short-term hedging. Consider also the development of other debt instruments such as Eurobonds, floating rate notes, and commercial paper (new to some of the G-5 countries). These debt instruments, together with interest rate and currency swaps, offer to firms that have international operations new ways to structure financing to help to neutralize the effects of longer-term foreign exchange risk. In general, such exposure management cannot eliminate all exchange risks, but it can certainly reduce such risks. Without the deregulation and liberalization of the past 20 years, even this would not be possible.

References

Abuaf, Niso, and Philippe Jorion. 1990. "Purchasing Power Parity in the Long Run." *Journal of Finance* 45 (March): 157–74.

Adler, Michael, and Bernard Dumas. 1983. "International Portfolio Choice and Corporation Finance: A Synthesis." *Journal of Finance* 38 (June): 925–84.

Adler, Michael, and Bruce Lehmann. 1983. "Deviations from Purchasing Power Parity in the Long Run." *Journal of Finance* 38 (December): 1471–87.

Aliber, Robert Z. 1973. "The Interest Rate Parity Theorem: A Reinterpretation." *Journal of Political Economy* 81 (November/December): 1451–59.

Alworth, J. S., and C. E. V. Borio. 1993. *Commercial Paper Markets: A Survey.* BIS Economic Papers No. 37 (April). Basle: Bank for International Settlements.

Artis, M. J., and Mark P. Taylor. 1989. "Abolishing Exchange Control: the U.K. Experience." CEPR Discussion Paper No. 294 (April).

Balassa, Bela. 1964. "The Purchasing Power Parity Doctrine: A Reappraisal." *Journal of Political Economy* 72 (December): 584–96.

Baltensperger, Ernst, and Jean Dermine. 1987. "Banking Deregulation in Europe." *Economic Policy* 4 (April): 63–109.

Bank for International Settlements. 1986. "Currency and Interest Rate Swaps." *Recent Innovations in International Banking,* Chapter 2. Basle: Bank for International Settlements.

Bank for International Settlements. 1991. *61st Annual Report,* 10th June. Basle: Bank for International Settlements.

Bank of Japan. 1988. *Recent Developments in the Long-Term Bond Market,* Special Paper No. 170 (December). Tokyo: Bank of Japan.

Bank of Japan. 1991. *Recent Developments in Lending Rates: Changing Behavior of Banks under Interest Rate Liberalization,* Special Paper No. 206 (September). Tokyo: Bank of Japan.

Bekaert, Geert, and Robert J. Hodrick. 1992. "Characterizing Predictable Components in Excess Returns on Equity and Foreign Exchange Markets." *Journal of Finance* 47 (June): 467–509.

Bernheim, B. Douglas, and John B. Shoven. 1987. "Taxation and the Cost of Capital: An International Comparison." In *The Consumption Tax: A Better Alternative?* ed. Charles E. Walker and Mark A. Bloomfield. Cambridge: Ballinger Publishing.

Bertola, Giuseppe, and Ricardo J. Caballero. 1992. "Target Zones and Realignments." *American Economic Review* 82 (June): 520–36.

Bertola, Giuseppe, and Lars E. O. Svensson. 1993. "Stochastic Devaluation Risk and the Empirical Fit of Target Zone Models." *Review of Economic Studies,* forthcoming.

Bilson, John. 1981. "The Speculative Efficiency Hypothesis." *Journal of Business* 54 (July): 435–52.

Bodnar, Gordon M. 1993. "The Impact of Capital Liberalization on the Financial Markets in the European Monetary System." *Journal of International Financial Markets, Institutions, and Money,* forthcoming.

186

Branson, William H. 1993. "Comment on Eichengreen and Wyplosz." *Brookings Papers on Economic Activity* No. 1: 125–29.

Campbell, John Y., and Richard H. Clarida. 1987. "The Term Structure of Euromarket Interest Rates: An Empirical Investigation." *Journal of Monetary Economics* 19 (January): 25–44.

Campbell, John Y., and Y. Hamao. 1992. "Predictable Stock Returns in the United States and Japan: A Study of Long-Term Capital Market Integration." *Journal of Finance* 47 (March): 43–69.

Cassel, Gustav. 1921. *The World's Monetary Problems.* London: Constable.

Chen, Zhaohui, and Alberto Giovannini. 1993. "The Determinants of Realignment Expectations Under the EMS: Some Empirical Regularities." NBER Working Paper No. 4291 (March).

Claassen, Emil, and Charles Wyplosz. 1982. "Capital Controls: Some Principles and the French Experience." *Annales de l'INSEE* Nos. 47–48: 237–67.

Clinton, Kevin. 1988. "Transactions Costs and Covered Interest Arbitrage: Theory and Evidence." *Journal of Political Economy* 96 (April): 358–70.

Collins, Susan M. 1992. "The Expected Timing of EMS Realignments: 1979–83." NBER Working Paper No. 4068 (May).

Cook, Timothy Q. 1986. "Treasury Bills." In *Instruments of the Money Market,* ed. Timothy Q. Cook and Timothy D. Rowe, pp. 81–93. Richmond, Va.: Federal Reserve Bank of Richmond.

Cumby, Robert E. 1988. "Is it Risk? Explaining Deviations from Uncovered interest Parity." *Journal of Monetary Economics* 22 (September): 279–99.

Cumby, Robert E., and John Huizinga. 1992. "Investigating the Correlation of Unobserved Expectations: Expected Returns in Equity and Foreign Exchange Markets and Other Examples." *Journal of Monetary Economics* 30 (November): 217–53.

Cumby, Robert, and Maurice Obstfeld. 1984. "International Interest Rate and Price Level Linkages under Flexible Exchange Rates: A Review of Recent Evidence." In *Exchange Rate Theory and Practice,* ed. John Bilson and Richard Marston, pp. 121–51. Chicago: University of Chicago Press.

de Boissieu, Christian. 1990. "The French Banking Sector in the Light of European Financial Integration." In *European Banking in the 1990s,* ed. Jean Dermine, pp. 181–226. Oxford: Basil Blackwell.

De Grauwe, Paul. 1992. *The Economics of Monetary Integration.* Oxford: Oxford University Press.

De Gregorio, José, Alberto Giovannini, and Holger C. Wolf. 1993. "Sectoral Inflation: Empirical Regularities from Regions and Countries." *European Economic Review,* forthcoming. (Presented at the NBER Summer Institute in International Macroeconomics, July 1993.)

Deutsche Bundesbank. 1985. "Freedom of Germany's Capital Transactions with Foreign Countries." *Monthly Report* 37 (July): 13–23.

Dickey, D. A., and W. A. Fuller. 1979. "Distribution of the Estimators for Autoregressive Time-Series with a Unit Root." *Journal of the American Statistical Association* 74: 427–31.

Diebold, Francis X., Steven Husted, and Mark Rush. 1991. "Real Exchange Rates under the Gold Standard." *Journal of Political Economy* 99 (December): 1252–71.

Dooley, Michael P., and Peter Isard. 1980. "Capital Controls, Political Risk, and Deviations from Interest-Rate Parity." *Journal of Political Economy* 88 (April): 370–84.

Dumas, Bernard. 1992. "Dynamic Equilibrium and the Real Exchange Rate in a Spatially Separated World." *Review of Financial Studies* 5 (No. 2): 153–80.

Dumas, Bernard. 1992. "Partial-Equilibrium vs. General-Equilibrium Models of International Capital Market Equilibrium." In *Handbook of International Macroeconomics,* ed. Rick van der Ploeg, forthcoming.

Dutton, Marilyn Miller. 1993. "Real Interest Parity: New Measures and Tests." *Journal of International Money and Finance* 12 (February): 62–77.

Eichengreen, Barry, and Charles Wyplosz. 1993. "The Unstable EMS." *Brookings Papers on Economic Activity* 1: 51–124.

Engel, Charles M. 1984. "Testing for the Absence of Expected Real Profits from Forward Market Speculation." *Journal of International Economics* 17 (November): 299–308.

Engel, Charles M., and James D. Hamilton. 1990. "Long Swings in the Dollar: Are They in the Data and Do Markets Know It?" *American Economic Review* 80 (September): 689–713.

Fama, Eugene F. 1970. "Efficient Capital Markets: A Review of Theory and Empirical Work." *Journal of Finance* 25 (May): 383–417.

Fama, Eugene F. 1984. "Forward and Spot Exchange Rates." *Journal of Monetary Economics* 14 (November): 697–703.

Fama, Eugene F., and Kenneth R. French. 1988. "Dividend Yields and Expected Stock Returns." *Journal of Financial Economics* 21 (September): 3–26.

Fama, Eugene F., and G. William Schwert. 1977. "Asset Returns and Inflation." *Journal of Financial Economics* 5 (November): 115–146.

Feldman, Robert Alan. 1986. *Japanese Financial Markets: Deficits, Dilemmas, and Deregulation.* Cambridge: MIT Press.

Fijii, Tomoko. 1992. *A Primer on Yen Fixed-Income Markets.* Japanese Economic and Market Analysis Series. Tokyo: Salomon Brothers.

Flood, Robert, Andrew Rose, and Donald Mathiesen. 1991. "Is the EMS the Perfect Fix? An Empirical Examination of Exchange Rate Target Zones." In *Carnegie-Rochester Conference Series on Public Policy No. 19,* ed. Alan H. Meltzer and Charles Plosser, pp. 7–65. Amsterdam: North-Holland.

Frankel, Jeffrey. 1984. *The Yen-Dollar Agreement: Liberalizing Japanese Capital Markets,* Policy Analyses in International Economics No. 9. Washington: Institute for International Economics.

Frankel, Jeffrey A. 1986. "International Capital Mobility and Crowding-Out in the U.S. Economy: Imperfect Integration of Financial Markets or of Goods Markets?" In *How Open Is the U.S. Economy?* ed. R. W. Hafer, pp. 37–67. Lexington, Mass.: Lexington Books.

Frankel, Jeffrey A. 1991. "The Japanese Cost of Finance: A Survey." *Financial Management* 20 (Spring): 95–127.

Frankel, Jeffrey A., and Kenneth A. Froot. 1987. "Using Survey Data to Test Standard Propositions Regarding Exchange Rate Expectations." *American Economic Review* 77 (March): 133–53.

Frankel, Jeffrey, and Alan MacArthur. 1988. "Political vs. Currency Premia in International Real Interest Rate Differentials: A Study of Forward Rates for 24 Countries." *European Economic Review* 32 (June): 1083–1114.

Fratianni, Michele, and Jurgen von Hagen. 1990. "German Dominance in the EMS: The Empirical Evidence." *Open Economies Review* 1: 67–87.

French, Kenneth R., and James M. Poterba. 1991. "Investor Diversification and International Equity Markets." *American Economic Review* 81 (May): 222–6.

Frenkel, Jacob A. 1978. "Purchasing Power Parity: Doctrinal Perspective and Evidence from the 1920s." *Journal of International Economics* 8 (May): 169–91.

Frenkel, Jacob, and Richard Levich. 1975. "Covered Interest Arbitrage: Unexploited Profits?" *Journal of Political Economy* 83 (April): 325–38.

Frenkel, Jacob A., and Assaf Razin. 1980. "Stochastic Prices and Tests of Efficiency of Foreign Exchange Markets." *Economics Letters* 6: 165–70.

Friend, Irwin, and Ichiro Tokutsu. 1987. "The Cost of Capital to Corporations in Japan and the U.S.A." *Journal of Banking and Finance* 11 (June): 313–27.

Froot, Kenneth A., and Jeffrey A. Frankel. 1989. "Forward Discount Bias: Is It an Exchange Risk Premium?" *Quarterly Journal of Economics* 104 (February): 139–61.

Froot, Kenneth A., and Kenneth Rogoff. 1991. "The EMS, the EMU, and the Transition to a Common Currency." *NBER Macroeconomics Annual 1991* 6: 269–317.

Froot, Kenneth A., and Richard H. Thaler. 1990. "Anomalies: Foreign Exchange." *Journal of Economic Perspectives* 4 (Summer): 179–92.

Giavazzi, Francesco, and Alberto Giovannini. 1989. *Limiting Exchange Rate Flexibility: The European Monetary System.* Cambridge: The MIT Press.

Giavazzi, Francesco, and Marco Pagano. 1988. "The Advantage of Tying One's Hands." *European Economic Review* 32 (June): 1055–82.

Gibbons, Michael, and Wayne Ferson. 1985. "Testing Asset Pricing Models with Changing Expectations and an Unobservable Market Portfolio." *Journal of Financial Economics* 14 (June): 217–36.

Giovannini, Alberto. 1990. "European Monetary Reform: Progress and Prospects." *Brookings Papers on Economic Activity* 2: 217–91.

Giovannini, Alberto, and Phillipe Jorion. 1987. "Interest Rates and Risk Premia in the Stock Market and in the Foreign Exchange Market." *Journal of International Money and Finance* 6 (March): 107–23.

Glen, Jack D. 1992. "Real Exchange Rates in the Short, Medium, and Long Run." *Journal of International Economics* 33 (August): 147–66.

Goldstein, Morris, David Folkerts-Landau, Peter Garber, Liliana Rojas-Suarez, and Michael Spencer. 1993. *International Capital Markets: Part 1. Exchange Rate Management and International Capital Flows.* Washington, D.C.: International Monetary Fund.

Grabbe, Orlin. 1991. *International Financial Markets.* New York: Elsevier.

Grauer, F., Robert Litzenberger, and Richard Stehle. 1976. "Sharing Rules and Equilibrium in an International Capital Market Under Uncertainty." *Journal of Financial Economics* 3 (June): 233–56.

Grønvik, Gunnvald. 1986. "The Forward Foreign Exchange Market: Is the Growth of Bank Lending a Result of a Large Demand for Kronor on the Forward Market? Or the Reverse?" (in Norwegian). *Sosialøkonomen* No. 6: 19–29.

Gros, Daniel. 1988. "Dual Exchange Rates in the Presence of Incomplete Market Separation: Long-Run Effectiveness and Policy Implications." *International Monetary Fund Staff Papers* 35 (September): 437–60.

Guitián, Manuel, Massimo Russo, and Giuseppe Tullio. 1988. *Policy Coordination in the European Monetary System.* Occasional Paper No. 61. Washington: International Monetary Fund.

Hakkio, Craig. 1986. "Does the Exchange Rate Follow a Random Walk? A Monte Carlo Study of Four Tests for a Random Walk." *Journal of International Money and Finance* 5 (June): 221–29.

Hamada, Koichi, K. Iwata, and Y. Ishiyama. 1977. "On the Disequilibrium of the Commercial Loan Market in Japan." *The Economic Review* 28.

Hansen, Lars, and Robert Hodrick. 1983. "Risk Averse Speculation in the Forward Foreign Exchange Market: An Econometric Analysis of Linear Models." In *Exchange Rates and International Macroeconomics,* ed. Jacob A. Frenkel, pp. 113–52. Chicago: University of Chicago Press.

Hatsopoulos, George N., and Stephen H. Brooks. 1986. "The Gap in the Cost of Capital:

Causes, Effects, and Remedies." In *Technology and Economic Policy*, ed. Ralph Landau and Dale W. Jorgenson, pp. 221–80. Cambridge: Ballinger Publishing Co.

Harvey, Campbell, 1991. "The World Price of Covariance Risk." *Journal of Finance* 46 (March): 111–57.

Hodgman, Donald R. 1974. *National Monetary Policies and International Monetary Cooperation.* Boston: Little, Brown and Company.

Hodrick, Robert. 1987. *The Empirical Evidence on the Efficiency of Forward and Futures Foreign Exchange Markets.* New York: Harwood Academic Publishers.

Hodrick, Robert, and S. Srivastava. 1984. "An Investigation of Risk and Return in Forward Foreign Exchange." *Journal of International Money and Finance* 3 (April): 5–29.

Hsieh, David A. 1982. "The Determination of the Real Exchange Rate: the Productivity Approach." *Journal of International Economics* 12 (May): 355–62.

Hsieh, David A. 1988. "The Statistical Properties of Daily Foreign Exchange Rates: 1974–1983," *Journal of International Economics* 24 (February): 129–45.

Huizinga, John, and Frederic S. Mishkin. 1984. "Inflation and Real Interest Rates on Assets with Different Risk Characteristics." *Journal of Finance* 39 (July): 699–712.

International Monetary Fund. 1975. *Twenty-Sixth Annual Report on Exchange Restrictions.* Washington, D.C.: International Monetary Fund.

Isard, Peter. 1977. "How Far Can We Push the 'Law of One Price'?" *American Economic Review* 67 (December): 942–8.

Isberg, Bjorn. 1993. "Tests of Uncovered Interest Parity," University of Stockholm, unpublished paper.

Ito, Takatoshi. 1986. "Capital Controls and Covered Interest Parity Between the Yen and the Dollar." *Economic Studies Quarterly* 37 (September): 223–40.

Ito, Takatoshi, and Kazuo Ueda. 1981. "Tests of the Equilibrium Hypothesis in Disequilibrium Econometrics: An International Comparison of Credit Rationing." *International Economic Review* 22 (October): 691–708.

Japan Fair Trade Commission. 1991. *Survey of Compensating Balances.* Tokyo: Japan Fair Trade Commission.

Japan Securities Research Institute. 1992. *Securities Market in Japan, 1992.* Tokyo: Japan Securities Research Institute.

Keim, Donald B., and Robert F. Stambaugh. 1986. "Predicting Returns in the Stock and Bond Markets." *Journal of Financial Economics* 17 (December): 357–90.

Kenen, Peter B. 1976. *Capital Mobility and Financial Integration: A Survey.* Princeton Studies in International Finance No. 39. Princeton: International Finance Section.

Kenen, Peter B. 1992. *EMU After Maastricht.* Washington, D.C.: Group Of Thirty.

Kester, W. Carl, and Timothy A. Luehrman. 1989. "Real Interest Rates and The Cost of Capital: A Comparison of the United States and Japan." *Japan and the World Economy* 1 (July): 279–301.

Knetter, Michael M. 1989. "Price Discrimination by U.S. and German Exporters." *American Economic Review* 79 (March): 198–210.

Kravis, Irving B., Z. Kenessey, Alan W. Heston, and Robert Summers. 1975. *A System of International Comparisons of Gross Product and Purchasing Power.* Baltimore: Johns Hopkins University Press.

Kreicher, Lawrence L. 1982. "Eurodollar Arbitrage." *Federal Reserve Bank of New York Quarterly Review* (Summer): 10–22.

Krugman, Paul R. 1987. "Trigger Strategies and Price Dynamics in Equity and Foreign Exchange Markets." NBER Working Paper No. 2459.

Krugman, Paul R. 1991. "Target Zones and Exchange Rate Dynamics." *Quarterly Journal of Economics* 106 (August): 669–82.

Levich, Richard M. 1985. "Empirical Studies of Exchange Rates: Price Behavior, Rate Determination, and Market Efficiency." In *Handbook of International Economics,* ed. R. W. Jones and P. B. Kenen, Vol. II, pp. 979–1040. Elsevier Science Publishers B.V.

Lewis, Karen K. 1989. "Changing Beliefs and Systematic Rational Forecast Errors with Evidence from Foreign Exchange." *American Economic Review* 79 (September): 621–36.

Lewis, Karen K. 1990. "The Behavior of Eurocurrency Returns Across Different Holding Periods and Monetary Regimes." *Journal of Finance* 45 (September): 1211–36.

Lewis, Karen K. 1994. "International Financial Markets." In *Handbook of International Economics,* ed. Gene Grossman and Kenneth Rogoff. Amsterdam: North-Holland.

Ljung, C. M., and G. E. P. Box. 1978. "On a Measure of Lack of Fit in Time Series Models." *Biometrika:* 297–303.

Lothian, James R., and Mark P. Taylor. 1992. "Real Exchange Rate Behavior: The Recent Float from the Perspective of the Past Two Centuries," Fordham University, unpublished paper.

Lyons, Richard K. 1993. "Tests of Microstructural Hypotheses in the Foreign Exchange Market," paper presented at the NBER Summer Institute.

MacKinnon, James G. 1990. "Critical Values for Cointegration Tests," USCD Economics Discussion Paper 90-4.

Mark, Nelson C. 1985. "Some Evidence on the International Equality of Real Interest Rates." *Journal of International Money and Finance* 4 (June): 189–208.

Marston, Richard C. 1976. "Interest Arbitrage in the Euro-currency Markets." *European Economic Review* 20 (January): 1–13.

Marston, Richard C. 1985. "Stabilization Policies in Open Economies." In *Handbook of International Economics,* ed. Ronald W. Jones and Peter B. Kenen, Vol. II, pp. 859–916. Amsterdam: North Holland.

Marston, Richard C. 1987. "Real Exchange Rates and Productivity Growth in the United States and Japan." In *Real-Financial Linkages among Open Economies,* ed. Sven W. Arndt and J. David Richardson, pp. 71–96. Cambridge: MIT Press.

Marston, Richard C. 1990. "Pricing to Market in Japanese Manufacturing." *Journal of International Economics* 29 (November): 217–36.

Marston, Richard C. 1991. "Price Behavior in Japanese and U.S. Manufacturing." In *Trade with Japan: Has the Door Opened Wider?* ed. Paul Krugman, pp. 121–46. Chicago: University of Chicago Press for the NBER.

Marston, Richard C. 1992. "Interest Differentials under Bretton Woods and the Post-Bretton Woods Float: the Effects of Capital Controls and Exchange Risk." In *A Retrospective on the Bretton Woods System: Lessons for International Monetary Reform,* ed. Michael D. Bordo and Barry Eichengreen, pp. 515–38. Chicago: University of Chicago Press for the National Bureau of Economic Research.

Marston, Richard C. 1993. "Determinants of Short-Term Real Interest Differentials between Japan and the United States." *Monetary and Economic Studies* 11 (July): 33–61.

Mason, Richard. 1987. *The Yen Bond Markets.* Tokyo: Credit Suisse First Boston.

McCauley, Robert N., and Steven A. Zimmer. 1989. "Explaining International Differences in the Cost of Capital." *Federal Reserve Bank of New York Quarterly Review* 14 (Summer): 7–28.

McCulloch, J. Houston. 1975. "Operational Aspects of the Siegel Paradox: Comment." *Quarterly Journal of Economics* 89 (February): 170–5.

Meese, Richard, and Kenneth Rogoff. 1988. "Was it Real? The Exchange Rate-Interest Rate Differential Relation over the Modern Floating-Rate Period." *Journal of Finance* 43 (September): 933–48.

Mishkin, Frederic S. 1981. "The Real Interest Rate: An Empirical Investigation." In *The*

Costs and Consequences of Inflation, ed. Karl Brunner and Allan H. Meltzer, Carnegie-Rochester Conference Series on Public Policy, pp. 151–200. Amsterdam: North-Holland Publishing Company.

Mishkin, Frederic S. 1984. "Are Real Interest Rates Equal Across Countries? An Empirical Investigation of International Parity Conditions." *Journal of Finance* 39 (December): 1345–57.

Morgan Guaranty Trust. 1989. "The J. P. Morgan Government Bond Index." *World Financial Markets* (November 22): 5–13.

Mullineux, Andrew. 1987. *International Banking and Financial Systems: A Comparison.* London: Graham & Trotman.

Mussa, Michael. 1979. "Empirical Regularities in the Behavior of Exchange Rates and Theories of the Foreign Exchange Market." In *Policies for Employment, Prices, and Exchange Rates,* ed. Karl Brunner and Allan H. Meltzer, Carnegie-Rochester Conference Series on Public Policy, pp. 9–57. Amsterdam: North Holland Publishing Co.

Obstfeld, Maurice. 1986. "Capital Mobility in the World Economy: Theory and Measurement." In *The National Bureau Method, International Capital Mobility, and Other Essays,* ed. Karl Brunner and Alan H. Meltzer, Carnegie-Rochester Conference Series on Public Policy, pp. 55–103. Amsterdam: North-Holland Publishing Company.

Obstfeld, Maurice. 1993a. "International Capital Mobility in the 1990s." Paper prepared for a conference celebrating the fiftieth anniversary of the Princeton Essays in International Finance (April).

Obstfeld, Maurice. 1993b. "Modelling Trending Real Exchange Rates." Center for International and Development Economics Research Working Paper No. C93-011, University of California at Berkeley (February).

Organization for Economic Cooperation and Development. 1988. *Economic Survey: United States.* Paris: OECD.

Otani, Ichiro, and Siddharth Tiwari. 1981. "Capital Controls and Interest Rate Parity: the Japanese Experience, 1978–81." *IMF Staff Papers* 28 (December): 793–815.

Popper, Helen. 1993. "Long-term Covered Interest Parity: Evidence from Currency Swaps." *Journal of International Money and Finance* 12 (August): 439–48.

Porter, Michael G. 1971. "A Theoretical and Empirical Framework for Analyzing the Term Structure of Exchange Rate Expectations." *IMF Staff Papers* 18 (November): 613–45.

Richardson, J. David. 1978. "Some Empirical Evidence on Commodity Arbitrage and the Law of One Price." *Journal of International Economics* 8 (May): 341–51.

Rogalski, Richard J., and Joseph D. Vinso. 1978. "Empirical Properties of Foreign Exchange Rates." *Journal of International Business Studies* 9 (Fall): 69–79.

Rogoff, Kenneth. 1979. "Essays on Expectations and Exchange Rate Volatility." Ph.D. Dissertation, Massachusetts Institute of Technology.

Rogoff, Kenneth. 1992. "Traded Goods Consumption Smoothing and the Random Walk Behavior of the Real Exchange Rate." NBER Working Paper No. 4119 (July).

Roll, Richard. 1979. "Violations of Purchasing Power Parity and Their Implications for Efficient International Commodity Markets." In *International Finance and Trade,* ed. Marshall Sarnat and G. P. Szego, pp. 133–76. Cambridge, Mass.: Ballinger Publishing Co.

Rose, Andrew K., and Lars E. O. Svensson. 1991. "Expected and Predicted Realignments: The FF/DM Exchange Rate During the EMS." NBER Working Paper No. 3685 (April).

Rose, Andrew K., and Lars E. O. Svensson. 1993. "European Exchange Rate Credibility Before the Fall." NBER Working Paper No. 4495 (October).

Rowe, Timothy D. 1986. "Commercial Paper." In *Instruments of the Money Market,* ed. Timothy Q. Cook and Timothy D. Rowe, 111–25. Richmond: Federal Reserve Bank of Richmond.

Samuelson, Paul A. 1964. "Theoretical Notes on Trade Problems." *Review of Economics and Statistics* 46 (May): 145–54.

Sercu, Piet. 1980. "A Generalization of the International Asset Pricing Model." *Revue de l'Association Francaise de Finance* 1: 91–135.

Shiller, Robert J. 1979. "The Volatility of Long-Term Interest Rates and Expectations Models of the Term Structure." *Journal of Political Economy* 87 (December): 1190–219.

Shiller, Robert J., John Y. Campbell, and Kermit L. Schoenholtz. 1983. "Forward Rates and Future Policy: Interpreting the Term Structure of Interest Rates." *Brookings Papers on Economic Activity* 1: 173–217.

Siegel, Jeremy. 1972. "Risk, Interest and Forward Exchange." *Quarterly Journal of Economics* 86 (May): 303–09.

Solnik, Bruno. 1974. "An Equilibrium Model of the International Capital Market." *Journal of Economic Theory* 8 (May): 500–24.

Solnik, Bruno. 1991. *International Investments,* 2nd ed. New York: Addison-Wesley Publishing Company.

Stulz, Renee. 1981. "A Model of International Asset Pricing." *Journal of Financial Economics* 9 (December): 383–406.

Suzuki, Yoshio, ed. 1987. *The Japanese Financial System.* Oxford: Clarendon Press.

Svensson, Lars E. O. 1991a. "The Simplest Test of Target Zone Credibility." *IMF Staff Papers* 38 (September): 655–65.

Svensson, Lars E. O. 1991b. "The Term Structure of Interest Rates in a Target Zone: Theory and Swedish Data." *Journal of Monetary Economics* 28 (August): 87–116.

Svensson, Lars E. O. 1992. "The Foreign Exchange Risk Premium in a Target Zone with Devaluation Risk." *Journal of International Economics* 33 (August): 21–40.

Svensson, Lars E. O. 1993. "Assessing Target Zone Credibility: Mean Reversion and Devaluation Expectations in the ERM, 1979–92." *European Economic Review* 37 (May): 763–93.

Svensson, Lars E. O. 1993. "The Simplest Test of Inflation Target Credibility." NBER Working Paper No. 4604 (December).

Swary, Itzhak, and Barry Topf. 1992. *Global Financial Deregulation: Commercial Banking at the Crossroads.* Oxford: Blackwell Publishers.

Takeda, Masahiko, and Philip Turner. 1992. "The Liberalisation of Japan's Financial Markets: Some Major Themes." *BIS Economic Papers,* no. 34 (November). Basle: Bank for International Settlements.

Tesar, Linda L., and Ingrid M. Werner. 1992. "Home Bias and the Globalization of Securities Markets." NBER Working Paper No. 4218 (November).

Ungerer, Horst, Owen Evans, Thomas Mayer, and Philip Young. 1986. *The European Monetary System: Recent Developments,* Occasional Paper No. 48 (December). Washington: International Monetary Fund.

Westerfield, Janice M. 1977. "An Examination of Foreign Exchange Risk under Fixed and Floating Rate Regimes." *Journal of International Economics* 7 (May): 181–200.

White, Halbert. 1980. "A Heteroskedasticity-Consistent Covariance Matrix and a Direct Test for Heteroskedasticity." *Econometrica* 48 (April): 721–46.

Willemse, Rob J. M. 1986. "Large Certificates of Deposit." In *Instruments of the Money Market,* ed. Timothy Cook and Timothy D. Rowe, pp. 36–52. Richmond: Federal Reserve Bank of Richmond.

Wolfson, Martin H., and Mary M. McLaughlin. 1989. "Recent Developments in the Profitability and Lending Practices of Commercial Banks." *Federal Reserve Bulletin* 75 (July): 461–73.

Wyplosz, Charles. 1988. "Capital Flow Liberalization and the EMS: A French Perspective." *European Economy* 36 (May): 85–103.

Index